S0-AIL-605

FLORIDA STATE
UNIVERSITY LIBRARIES

OCT 29 1996

TALLAHASSEE, FLORIDA

Social History, Popular Culture, and Politics in Germany
Geoff Eley, Series Editor

*A History of Foreign Labor in Germany, 1880–1980: Seasonal Workers/
Forced Laborers/Guest Workers*
    Ulrich Herbert, translated by William Templer

*Reshaping the German Right: Radical Nationalism and Political Change
after Bismarck*
    Geoff Eley

*The Politics of the Body in Weimar Germany: Women's Reproductive
Rights and Duties*
    Cornelie Usborne

The Stigma of Names: Antisemitism in Germany Daily Life, 1812–1933
    Dietz Bering

*Forbidden Laughter: Popular Humor and the Limits of Repression in
Nineteenth-Century Prussia*
    Mary Lee Townsend

From Bundesrepublik *to* Deutschland: *German Politics after Unification*
    Michael G. Huelshoff, Andrei S. Markovits, and Simon Reich,
    editors

*The People Speak! Anti-Semitism and Emancipation in
Nineteenth-Century Bavaria*
    James F. Harris

*The Origins of the Authoritarian Welfare State in Prussia:
Conservatives, Bureaucracy, and the Social Question, 1815–70*
    Hermann Beck

*Technological Democracy: Bureaucracy and Citizenry in the
German Energy Debate*
    Carol J. Hager

Society, Culture, and the State in Germany, 1870–1930
    Geoff Eley, editor

Paradoxes of Peace: German Peace Movement since 1945
    Alice H. Cooper

Jews, Germans, Memory: Reconstructions of Jewish Life in Germany
    Y. Michal Bodemann, editor

Jews, Germans, Memory

Reconstructions of Jewish Life in Germany

Y. Michal Bodemann, Editor

Ann Arbor

THE UNIVERSITY OF MICHIGAN PRESS

DS
135
G332
J49
1996

Copyright © by the University of Michigan 1996
All rights reserved
Published in the United States of America by
The University of Michigan Press
Manufactured in the United States of America
♾ Printed on acid-free paper

1999   1998   1997   1996   4   3   2   1

A CIP catalog record for this book is available from the British Library.

No part of this publication may be reproduced, stored in a
retrieval system, or transmitted in any form or by any means,
electronic, mechanical, or otherwise without the written
permission of the publisher.

Library of Congress Cataloging-in-Publication Data

Jews, Germans, memory : reconstructions of Jewish life in Germany / Y.
   Michal Bodemann, editor
      p.   cm.—(Social history, popular culture, and politics in
   Germany)
   Includes bibliographical references and index.
   ISBN 0-472-10584-1 (hardcover : alk. paper)
      1. Jews—Germany—History—1945–   2. Holocaust survivors—
   Germany—History. 3. Germany—Ethnic relations. I. Bodemann,
   Y. Michal, 1944–   . II. Series.
   DS135.G332J49   1996
   943'.004924—dc20   95-49368
                                                                      CIP

For Natascha, Naomi, and Nurit, with love.

Acknowledgments

The idea for this volume goes back to a conference, "How Can Jews Live in Germany Today?," held at the University of Toronto from 15 to 18 November 1989. I would like to thank the Goethe Institut Toronto and the Social Science and Humanities Research Council of Canada (SSHRCC) for their financial support in relation to this conference and subsequent research. Special thanks to Dr. Lotte Köhler, Munich, for her spontaneous and most generous personal donation to put this project into motion, and to Robin Ostow, with whom I shared so many ideas and discussions over all these years.

Contents

The Situation of the Jews in Today's Germany

Micha Brumlik

1

Whoever takes up the question of the status and identity of Jews in Germany today, in 1990, will not be able to avoid considering the impact and consequences of the process of German unification. However, we have research findings only on the Federal Republic of Germany and, at best, sparse data concerning the small number of Jews in the German Democratic Republic (GDR), so that we can confidently speak only about Jews in the Federal Republic. The future chapter of a new Jewish community will, of necessity, be written only later on. Conversely, a glance at the history of the Jews both in the Federal Republic (Richarz 1988) and in the GDR assumes the character of a review of a historical epoch that is now nearing its end.

With these considerations in mind, I would like to develop my topic based upon the following five theses:

1. Jews living in the Federal Republic of Germany consider themselves as Jews in Germany and not as German Jews.
2. The subjective and objective conditions for the establishment of a Jewish community were nowhere so unfavorable as in postwar Germany—with the possible exception of Arab and Islamic dictatorships.
3. Until 1985, Jews in the Federal Republic of Germany were not able to develop a reasonable sense of self-consciousness or a self-image because their leadership was grounded in the fatal

Originally published as the 1990 Paul Lecture, Jewish Studies Program, Indiana University, Bloomington, Indiana.

tradition of "Schutzjudentum," or "protected Jewry," and Jews willingly acceded to its symbolic use.

4. Jews in the GDR found themselves in a similar, symbolically exploitable dependence on the dominant regime, although, by comparison with the Federal Republic, in a still deeper, inward dependence upon that regime.

5. The future of Jews now living in the Federal Republic and the GDR is uncertain. A situation that one could unpleasantly describe as an inner ghetto—characterized by excessive demands by the non-Jewish environment and internal weaknesses of the Jewish community, coupled with the increasingly open appearance of anti-Semitism—results in a continuing paradox, a state of abnormal normality between Jews and Germans. In addition, the expected immigration of East European Jews, primarily of Russian Jews, might alter the situation of Jews in Germany in an unforeseeable manner.

2

One immediately discovers an anomaly in viewing the demographic development of Jews living in the Federal Republic of Germany. For the past thirty-five to forty years this community has not changed in numbers from its early base of approximately thirty thousand officially registered members. (The community's actual size may include an additional twenty thousand or more unregistered persons.) How is this possible given a higher than average death rate? The following is a short historical overview on this point.

Of approximately half a million Jews living in the prewar German Reich, until 1933, about fifteen thousand still were alive and living in Germany at war's end in 1945. These people survived by hiding (cf. König 1967; Maor 1961; Richarz 1982; Benz 1988), or were spared as "privileged persons," or as "star bearers," or as "half-Jews" who were simply not caught up in the extermination apparatus.

Moreover, between 1945 and 1948 about two hundred thousand Jews were in internment camps on the territory of the western occupation forces. Pursuant to international usage these persons were designated as "DPs." These displaced persons ended up in the Western Zone owing to a variety of causes. For one, they were freed by the Allies during the last months of the war from concentration camps, such as Bergen-Belsen or Dachau, located in the Reich's interior. We know that the SS, faced with the advance of the approaching Red Army, evacuated a portion of the camps in Poland forcing the remaining prisoners into the Reich's interior under conditions of shocking agony, where they very often died of hunger or disease. Other Jews in Eastern Europe, primarily in Poland, were freed by the Red Army and attempted in 1945 and 1946 to reach their former homes. Naturally, these people were forced to flee to the West, given the political conditions in postwar Poland. One of the main reasons for this exodus was the fact that returning Jews often enough were received with disdain, hatred, and sometimes outbursts of violent anti-Semitism among the Polish population. During the Polish civil war between nationalists and communists there took place, for example, an event of horrifying proportions. In Kielce in July 1946 a bloody massacre was carried out by anti-Semites against Jews returning from the Soviet Union. Approximately fifty persons were murdered then (Hillel 1985). However, this act was not the only one of its kind. These and other events were taken up by Zionist emissaries and used to increase political pressure, primarily on the U.S. administration of the internment camps and hence on the U.S. government. The purpose was to bring the United States to finally approve establishment of a Jewish State in Palestine (Zertal 1989). In internment camps located in the Western Zone, particularly in the American and British zones and, to a lesser extent, in the French Zone, a somewhat autonomous Jewish camp administration arose—often in conflict with the military governments—in which the DPs not only established historical commissions for research of Nazi crimes but also formed political parties, professional organizations, and a system of general education (Bauer 1970; Peck 1988; Jacobmeyer 1988; Wetzel 1989).

The self-definition of these nearly quarter million persons is expressed in the name that they conferred upon themselves: "She'erit ha-Peletah," which means both "the surviving remnant" and "the saving remnant." This term comes from the Bible (Haggai 1, 12) and denotes that group of persons who survived the Babylonian exile and returned to Jerusalem. The survivors' political leaders were similarly convinced that Judaism would not have a future in Europe, and particularly not in Germany, and that future Jewish life could only be maintained in Israel or in the United States (Gringauz 1948).

The psychological condition among survivors was characterized, on the one hand, by a tremendous will to live—the birth rate in internment camps was at that time the highest among all of Jewry—and, on the other, by mental distraction, authoritarianism, and immense emotional tension (Pinson 1947; Kugelmann 1989). The founding of an Israeli state meant the end of a last final flowering of a Jewish-Yiddish culture in Germany. Although several internment camps had been disbanded—the last in Bavaria in 1956—the camps dramatically emptied in 1948. Most people immigrated to the United States or, primarily, to Israel.

Of the 250,000 internees, only a small fraction of 15,000 remained in

Germany. This number included those who physically or psychologically were simply not able to migrate onward. In addition, there were a few, who, despite the best of intentions, were not able to see themselves coping with a life of hardships in Israel. It was these Jews and a few German Jews who had been in hiding or those Jews who returned directly after the war who founded the first Jewish communities (Maor 1961; Wetzel 1989; Bodemann 1988). Initially these were not thought of as permanent establishments but rather as temporary institutions, which should guarantee those Jews asserting reparation claims against Germany a minimum of Jewish religious services and facilities. With the exception of a few returning leftist-oriented Jews or conscious German nationalist Jews (Schoeps 1989), no one could imagine or in any case even wish that a Jewish community would again arise on German territory.

The process of establishing communities, achieved primarily through the entry of DPs into religious congregations formed by German Jews, did not run its course without problems. Cultural contrasts, political antitheses, and the lack of a common language impeded the formation of coherent communities. A small minority of extremely assimilated German Jews, who in no way had been especially close to the Jewish community prior to the war, represented the cadres of the first postwar communities. They were often opposed by a majority of East European Jews, who in their own way had often likewise assimilated (in Poland, Hungary, etc.) yet who did not naturally belong to German culture. In other words, the basis of the Jewish community in postwar Germany consisted of East European—primarily Polish—Jews and not German Jews. Thus, one may state that the Jewish community residing today in the Federal Republic of Germany, which is largely made up of the offspring of DPs, represents a community of Jews *in* Germany and not a community of *German Jews*. At least not German Jews in the sense conveyed by the poets Heinrich Heine and Else Lasker-Schüler, the philosophers Moses Mendelssohn and Martin Buber, the writer Jakob Wassermann, and the painter Max Liebermann when they speak of "German" Jews. Instead, Jewry in the Federal Republic of Germany developed upon the initial base of a remnant community of DPs augmented by subsequent episodes of immigration and reimmigration. The first instance of immigration or reimmigration occurred when those German Jews who, by 1938 at the latest, had migrated to Palestine—owing more to Nazi coercion than their own political will—returned to the German Federal Republic in the early 1950s, induced by reparation settlements. As we shall see, waves of immigration occurred commensurate with political rejection and developments in communist East and Central Europe.

A first group of Rumanian Jews came to the Federal Republic of Germany in the early 1950s in the wake of the Israeli-Rumanian emigration treaty. In 1956, Hungarian Jews fled to Germany fearing an anti-Semitic right-wing backlash from the Hungarian uprising. Liberal Czecho-slovakian Jews emigrated to the Federal Republic following the failure of Prague Spring in 1968. Anti-Semitic violence in communist Poland in 1968 moved many Polish Jews to seek asylum in Germany. Since the outset of the 1960s, there has been—with intermittent interruptions—a continually growing immigration from the Soviet Union. This immigra-tion increased in the first months of 1990 due to revived anti-Semitism provoked by the Pamjat movement. I have not mentioned in the forego-ing the immigration for pragmatic reasons of Israelis who come to the Federal Republic for commercial or educational purposes and then re-main. Also worthy of mention is the reimmigration of older German Jews, who, having attained pension age, wish to spend their retirement years in the Federal Republic amid Germany's material security.

These several instances of immigration explain the fact that the number of officially registered Jews, namely thirty thousand persons, has not changed for more than thirty-five years, despite a rise in the average lifespan of older persons within the Jewish population and a relatively low birth rate. It may be gathered from this short demo-graphic overview that the Jewish population living in the Federal Re-public of Germany today constitutes a multifariously differentiated and heterogeneous community which, for reasons yet to be considered, was nevertheless outwardly represented by "German" Jews well into the 1980s.

3

In 1492, when the Catholic regents Ferdinand and Isabella resolved to drive the Jews out of Spain, a country in which Jews had evolved a long and rich tradition, Jewish religious leaders imposed a ban on this coun-try. For nearly four hundred years Jews actually avoided Spain. Of course, religious bans no longer have any obligatory power in the twenti-eth century. Yet at the same time a kind of ban on German territory is embedded in the consciousness and psyche of Jews today. Germany, the land of the murderers, was a country in which Jews, at least in the 1950s and 1960s, were always forced to reckon that the neighbors, streetcar conductors, or bakers could have been former concentration camp henchmen or simple soldiers who had participated in deportations or mass shootings. Moreover, until recently a number of high office bearers (including former ministers, chancellors, and federal presidents) had once been Nazi party members. One recalls as well that there were waves of anti-Semitism in postwar Germany, primarily in the 1950s, which were definitely more vehement than any present anti-Semitic statements (Wetzel 1989; Jacobmeyer 1988). These and the conditions to be described below have made it difficult for Jews to gain a foothold inwardly and outwardly in Germany.

To begin with, Jews manifestly lived in Germany as undesired guests. With the exception of a few mayors, there is no indication whatsoever that prominent German politicians, left wing or right wing, wanted to bring back former German citizens who had been forcibly expelled because they were Jews. This failure illustrates the fact that, intentionally or not, the new German republic has accepted in principle the national socialist policy of expelling Jews. Those Jews who lived in the Federal Republic of Germany lived there mostly unwillingly. Moreover, they lived with a sense of conscious guilt and were torn by inner conflict. For about forty years now there has existed a copious psychiatric and psychoanalytical literature concerning the question of coming to grips with the experience of the concentration camps (Eissler 1963–64); Niederland 1980; Grubrich-Simitis 1979). This literature primarily grapples with the psychic and psychosomatic processing of extreme trauma and has alluded to such expected phenomena as severe illness, insomnia, and nightmares, in addition to the so-called Survival Guilt Syndrome. This syndrome, which is often expressed as self-reproach, is understood to mean the survivors' feelings of having unjustly witnessed the deaths of spouses, parents, or children. Persons suffering from this syndrome confront themselves frequently with the question of why they themselves, of all people, were to earn the right to life even as loved family members perished. Indeed, people in other countries besides Germany suffer from this syndrome, be they in Israel, the United States, or Canada. The burden associated with this trauma is the same; however, in the perpetrators' country it is much greater, if solely for the reason that the perpetrators have remained omnipresent. Hence the status of Jews in postwar Germany has been distinguished by the very fact of living in Germany. The inner conflict of Jews in Germany was commensurate with a considerable measure of conscious guilt and self-contempt. For most Jews in the western world and in Israel it was regarded to be morally impossible to live in Germany under these conditions. Here are two examples by way of illustration. First, in 1950 the Jewish Agency issued an appeal to all Jews living in Germany to leave the country (Bodemann 1988, 58). Second, an embarrassing debate took place in Cologne in the 1950s as to whether the children of employees at the Israeli mission should attend the same kindergarten attended by the children of DPs. From these and similar events there ensued a strong feeling of self-contempt, indeed even a sense of self-hatred, over and above the Survival Guilt Syndrome. A further, more critical element appeared among those German

Jews who had left Israel at the beginning of the 1950s to return to Germany. In Zionist thinking, immigration to Israel is commonly defined as a form of spiritual as well as physical advancement, or *aliyah*, while emigration is deemed a form of moral decline or *yeridah*. It was thought to be particularly abominable, even downright contemptuous, to leave the state of Israel and settle in Germany. This experience of "moral decline" most heavily burdened an entire generation of the children of German Jews who had reimmigrated (Speier 1988).

In addition to the psychological ban, to "being undesired," to conscious guilt, self-contempt, and the contempt of outsiders, any autonomous formation of an identity as German Jews seemed impossible.

National socialism had destroyed all essential components of prewar Jewish identity, i.e., the religious, literary, and artistic culture of German Judaism as well as the secular Yiddish culture of Polish Jews, which was often associated with socialism. Many survivors had additionally lost their faith in God. It was no longer possible for many to understand and accept the idea that God would have permitted the Holocaust. Out of a once rich Jewish culture directly after the war Israel and Zionism seemed to be almost all that remained. One may say that both of these elements actually constituted a psychological anchor for most Jews, whose self-consciousness had not survived the experience of the *shoah* and who now saw a kind of salvation from national socialism in a strong Jewish state, protected by its own army. For most, the country and state of Israel constituted the sole content and theme of Jewish identity—at least during the formative phase of the communities and well into the 1970s. This emphasis on Israel additionally contributed to the so-called packed-bag mentality among members of the first and second generations throughout the 1960s. There developed a schizoid attitude that expressed itself in unfulfilled emigration fantasies, on the one hand, and, on the other, in de facto residence in Germany and the shame of living there (Oppenheimer 1967; Kuschner 1977; Grünberg 1983; Brumlik 1988b; Kugelmann 1988). The association of such a schizoid posture with existence in Germany, and undoubtedly traumatic delayed effects of concentration camp imprisonment, passed on to the second generation (Grubrich-Simitis 1979), encumbered the postwar generation, which was slowly assuming leadership within the Jewish communities, with a moral, intellectual, and spiritual burden that finds its equal nowhere else in the Jewish world. Nevertheless, the fact that success was achieved in setting up reasonably functioning communities—which even today contribute considerably to the cultural life of the cities in which they are located (primarily Berlin, Frankfurt, and Munich)—is evidence of the fact that, despite trauma and grief, human beings nevertheless possess formative and creative powers that extend beyond merely surmounting extreme situations and afflictions.

4

For some years now a discussion has taken place among Jews in the Federal Republic of Germany regarding how the policy chosen by the first Federal German governments—namely Adenauer's—vis-à-vis Israel is to be evaluated. The issues concerning the so-called restitution payments play a primary role in this discussion. We know from historical research that the first German governments did not in any way whatsoever pay voluntarily and of their own accord. Rather, concessions had to be laboriously wrung from them by Jewish organizations (Hilberg 1982, 782ff.). Conversely, hardly any direct evidence can be found regarding the often-pleaded thesis that the Allies had placed massive pressure on the Federal Republic to make reparation payments (Wolffsohn 1988). Many facts show that the Adenauer government saw itself confronted with pressure exercised by Jewish organizations, although the government greatly overestimated the extent of this pressure and the overrated influence of "world Judaism" whose wishes it had to comply with if the Federal Republic wanted to return to the circle of civilized nations. The granting of payments to individual victims often had a deeply humiliating, humbling, and retraumatizing effect, as proven in the overwhelming majority of cases (Eissler 1963–64; Pross 1988).

There was a heavy price to be paid by the Jews for this "magnanimity" on the part of the German government, namely the acceptance, without major protest, of Adenauer's course of reconciliation with Nazi sympathizers and accomplices. After all, Adenauer did appoint Hans Globke, who had provided commentary on the Nuremberg Racial Laws, as his state secretary. It may not be excluded that Jews in Germany remained silent about this scandal in consideration of ongoing German-Israeli negotiations regarding reparation payments.

Y. M. Bodemann (1988) has attempted to draw a distinction among three phases with respect to political representation of Jews in the Federal Republic of Germany. In the first open and militant phase, between 1945 and 1948, DP representatives in camps as well as the founders of the first cultural communities openly took issue with emerging German institutions as well as with Allied military authorities. As this phase with its "charismatic leaders" drew to a close with the disbanding of the camps, Jewish representation assumed the character, according to Bodemann, of a "bureaucratic patronage" in the second phase. During this phase a series of primarily German-Jewish function-aries settled reparation matters in close agreement with Federal German authorities and without democratic rights of codetermination at the grass roots level of the Jewish communities and, in so doing, repro-duced the immobility and authoritarianism of the Adenauer era within the Jewish community. According to Bodemann, this phase of "bureau-cratic patronage" gave way at the beginning of the 1960s to a "phase of atrophy," that is, a deflation of Jewish life, under the leadership of certain individuals. This phase found fitting expression in the person of Werner Nachmann, who as chairman of the Central Council main-tained the closest of relations with the Federal Republic's conservative establishment, on the one hand, and, on the other, tolerated no resis-tance whatsoever to his self-glorifying exercise of power. Moreover, as we now know, he systematically embezzled interest income from repara-tion payments for concentration camp victims. Since Nachmann's sui-cide in 1988, one can observe a certain change of generations in the Jewish communities' leadership, a growing liberalism within the larger communities, and, increasingly, the acceptance of pluralism within Jew-ish life. Although press, public relations work, and political representa-tion still predominantly fit the pattern of earlier conservative, noncriti-cal, blind support for Israel and essentially undemocratic ways, the fact cannot be overlooked that tendencies are emerging in Jewish culture, the press, and among the public that are independent of the estab-lished, tax-regulated communities. In addition to the official *Allge-meine Jüdische Wochenzeitung*, a number of independent Jewish maga-zines such as *Nudnik*, *Tacheles*, *Semit*, a critical quarterly magazine, and *Babylon*, an intellectually demanding semiannual magazine, have been able to establish themselves. Publications such as the *Frankfurter Jüdische Nachrichten*, published twice or three times per year, are no-ticeably more critical and open than the official press. The founding of the Hochschule für Jüdische Studien in Heidelberg over ten years ago, the new Salomon Ludwig Steinheim Institute in Duisburg, and the establishment of communal Jewish museums in Frankfurt and West Berlin are evidence that a very active—although still weak—infrastruc-ture for Jewish intellectual life now exists.

Furthermore, a Jewish Federal German literature has begun to emerge. It includes thus far works of unpretentious autobiographical reflection (Broder and Lang 1979; Fleischmann 1980), short novels (Seligmann 1989), piercing short stories (Biller 1990), and ironic psycho-logical studies of high literary merit (Dische 1990). Some of this work is partially based on American Jewish prototypes. Although diverse in form, the themes are primarily the same and deal with overcoming trauma, the experience of sexual and erotic tension with the non-Jewish environment, and the question of what it means to live as a Jew in Germany today after the Holocaust.

The fact that this kind of literature has emerged and that it additionally meets with a certain interested response within the established German-Jewish community is an indication of a growing cultural pluralism, which, under favorable conditions, may also be followed by political pluralism.

5

The situation in the soon-to-be former German Democratic Republic is very different. The Jewish community in the GDR encompasses hardly more than four hundred officially registered members. However, we know that approximately three thousand more fully assimilated Jewish communists live there. These are people who wanted to build a better Germany in the GDR following the Second World War. Significant names from the Weimar Republic's leftist intellectual scene were found among reimmigrants: Arnold Zweig, Anna Seghers, Walter Felsenstein, head of the Komischen Oper and protagonist of the realist music theater, as well as Helene Weigel, Brecht's most important actress. Berlin's division at the outset of the 1950s also resulted in a splitting of the community so that only about two hundred members remained in East Berlin. Although no bloody anti-Semitic Stalinist purge took place in the GDR, there were indeed campaigns against so-called West emigrants, which were accompanied by anti-Semitic undertones. Although the GDR showed respect for the individual Jewish victims of national socialism in a material and religious manner, it cannot be overlooked that the "anti-Zionism" of the East German Communist government was clearly of an anti-Semitic nature (Eschwege 1988).

Moreover, it must be kept in mind that prior to eight years ago East German historical scholarship was kept spellbound in its purely mechanical application and economic understanding of Marxism and hence hardly made any contributions to research on the Nazi mass annihilation of Jews. Similarly, the small amount of literature dedicated to anti-Semitism as a constituent feature of national socialism (Pätzold 1983) has had extraordinary difficulty in recognizing the independent nature of Jew-hatred as a phenomenon in its own right (Pätzold and Runge 1988). With the demise of the SED (Socialist Unity party) state, the modest beginnings of a Marxist consideration of the Holocaust in the GDR have, after a short time, already reached their end.

New polls and interviews divulge the fact that Jews in the GDR suffer from considerable identity conflicts (Ostow 1988). In this connection it is not so much the question of the self-image of the small group of avowed congregation members that is of interest but rather the "genealogy movement" among former Communists or their children, who have taken up the search for their Jewish roots out of a strengthened opposition to the Communist SED regime. The short stories of Barbara Honigmann illustrate this state of mind precisely. Interestingly enough, the SED has definitely promoted this new establishment of Jewish identity in recent years in the interests of reaching a better settlement with the West. Before the fall of the Berlin Wall the East German government had stated its willingness to limit anti-Zionist propaganda and to pay reparations to victimized Jews. This positive turn toward the Jews is by no means a result of the 1989 revolution. Rather it was a conscious political strategy, introduced by the SED, to gain worldwide recognition. This strategy found expression in the reconstruction of the former synagogue in Oranienburgerstraße as well as in plans to better preserve the famous Weißensee Jewish cemetery and the new formation of the prewar orthodox Adass Jissroel congregation. Naturally the establishment of groups in which children of Jewish Communists discuss their self-identity have not resulted in the expected bolstering of small congregations that are overaged and dying out. Interest has been very minimal in Judaism as a culture and in Judaism as a religion among these groups. Hence on the whole the Jewish community in the GDR is a "shrinking minority" (Mertens 1988). It cannot be predicted how this community will develop within the framework of a unified Germany.

6

It has become an accepted custom of political culture in the Federal Republic of Germany to echo a "fatal" philosemitism. The fact that this philosemitism publicly no longer exists certainly became evident at the time of the obscene ritual at Bitburg (Brumlik 1990). Also, the "historians' debate" and the debates regarding the possible establishment of a memorial for all the dead of the Second World War—hence for Wehrmacht soldiers as well as concentration camp victims—indicate once again that a forced reconciliation and compulsive normalization have been intended by the West German government and circles close to it since the mid-1980s. These attempts have resulted in a new self-consciousness among Jews in the Federal Republic of Germany. These Jews have formed themselves into a self-conscious minority since the protests against Bitburg and the campaigns against the public performance of Rainer Werner Fassbinder's play *"Die Stadt, der Müll und der*

Tod" (Brumlik 1988a) as well as the lost battle over the remains of the former Frankfurt ghetto (Best 1988).

Yet the future of a self-conscious Jewry within Germany is also uncertain. On the one hand, it is rather clear—from a demographic viewpoint—that smaller communities are nearing their end due to overaging and that Jewish life will continue to exist primarily in the larger communities, for example, Berlin, Frankfurt, Munich, Hamburg, and communities in the Rhineland. The demographic balance is represented quite differently in these larger cities. In Frankfurt, over 45 percent of all registered members were born after 1945. On the other hand, the Jewish community in the Federal Republic is forced to grapple with the highest rate—nearly 65 percent—of mixed marriages among Jewish communities worldwide (Jüdischer Pressedienst 1987).

Moreover, the known dynamics of the Jewish community in postwar Germany still exist: future survival will depend at least in part on continuing immigration from Eastern Europe. Henceforth, immigration from the Soviet Union could guarantee a consistent maintenance if not further growth of the Jewish population. In any event, Soviet immigrants will soon constitute more than half of all registered Jews in West Berlin. The question of the future of individuals poses larger difficulties. Jewish young people today feel strongly unnerved by a qualitative, if not by a quantitative, increase in anti-Semitic statements. Yet these same young persons have begun increasingly to view Germany as a kind of home (Davidowicz 1989).

A continuing and even growing interest among Germans in getting to know Jews and in learning more about Judaism is to be noted in recent years. This interest cannot be adequately met owing to the small number of organized Jewish communities. Moreover, given the nature of things, the Jews run the risk of being turned into something resembling a museum of Judaism, a people to be visited as if out of antiquarian interest. By contrast a new anti-Semitism is to be noted not only despite Auschwitz but rather because of Auschwitz. This is an anti-Semitism that sees in Jews a living memorial for the greatest disgrace of German history (Funke 1988). It is questionable whether the small community of Jews in the Federal Republic is in a position to carry this double burden of being both a valued and hated monument of German history.

In the future, we are going to be forced to reckon with the emergence of a new community of Jews in Germany with whose characteristics we are not yet familiar. This community will emerge as a consequence of the increasingly difficult situation in Israel and a sprouting anti-Semitism in France and even in the United States, which are altering the usual pattern of emigration of Jews from Germany and also because of the influx of Soviet Jews into the Federal Republic, which is bound to create a new situation.

At this point, only one fact remains certain: An easy reconciliation over graves, such as that attempted at Bitburg, will not occur. Forty or fifty years is very little time in the historical memory of the Jews, especially when viewed against the backdrop of the *shoah*. Whether a unified Germany is willing to sincerely attempt to make a new beginning with the Jews living there will become clearer once we see if the temptation can be resisted to elevate November 9—the day of German disgrace and of Jewish suffering—to a national holiday, this despite everyone's elation over the fall of the Berlin Wall.

Postscriptum, March 1994

At the present time, it is becoming apparent that the position of the Jews in the reunited Germany is changing dramatically. First, the demographic dimensions of the Jewish community have increased. Due to emigration from the former Soviet Union, we now have to figure a minimum of forty-five thousand individuals, a number that is still rising. We should not overlook here the numerous difficulties. On one hand, in many Russian Jewish families there are non-Jewish spouses and children, and their identity is very nonreligious. For both these reasons, the Jewish communities are faced with great problems: on one hand, they have to determine who may rightfully become a member of a community; on the other, they have to make sure that the application for membership is indeed well founded and sincere—and not merely designed to gain access to the community's social assistance. In the larger communities it is also apparent that the Russian Jews who live there and who are more or less integrated still do not participate actively in community life. Among the youth, however, we find that integration is making great progress—especially with those children whose families have come from the Russian periphery—the Baltic republics and the Bukowina.

Beyond these demographic changes, which will not come to a conclusion for a long time, there is also a profound change taking place in the identity of Jews in Germany. After the death of Heinz Galinski in 1992, Ignatz Bubis, chair also of the Frankfurt community, was elected president of the Central Council of Jews in Germany. Bubis has taken numerous steps to move away from a position of perpetual admonishing toward an attitude of "critical normality." He involves himself in public demonstrations against xenophobia or right-wing extremism and appears unusually frequently on German television. He is also amenable, however, to symbolisms that express a termination of the German history of the

Second World War and of nazism: in November 1993, he took part in the dedication of the much fought over national Monument Unter den Linden in Berlin, even though this monument honors not only the victims of the Holocaust but in the same breath other victims of the Second World War and even victims of the Stalinist persecutions in the former GDR. His participation there did not meet the full support of the Jewish community: the representatives of the Jewish community of Berlin, for example, stayed away from this ceremony.

In light of such diverse transformations, and especially in view of the xenophobic, anti-Semitic, and racist pogroms of 1992 and 1993 that occurred in the context of the abolition of the asylum law in the German constitution, the Jewish community has to find a new identity. At the present time, three models seem available.

The first is the classical, prewar model of the "German Citizen of Jewish Faith," which certainly has its supporters with such intellectual representatives of German Jewry as politics professor Michael Wolffsohn in Munich. The second model is that of the "Jews in Germany," which prevailed for more than forty years and is the model of large sections of the former DPs and of the Holocaust survivors. The third model, finally, is the attempt to view the small Jewish minority as a "special ethnic group" in the framework of a multicultural society. Such a multicultural society would have its place in a German state that would have to stop defining its citizens ethnically—that is, in terms of their German origins. But the political system of Germany is still far from this development.

We observe, then, ferment and change in all synagogues and communities. To the degree to which the communities grow and rejuvenate, the previous hegemony of orthodox Jewry is coming to an end in the synagogues; and with the end of the Israeli-Palestinian conflict, the previous exclusive orientation toward Israel is being replaced by new reflections on one's own position. With the increasing debate about European unity after the Maastricht Treaty, many Jews in Germany ask themselves whether the idea of a European Jewish renewal might not be an attractive prospect instead.

References

Arndt, Th. A., et al., eds. 1988. *Juden in der DDR: Geschichte-Probleme-Perspektive*. Leiden.

Bauer, Y. 1970. *Flight and Rescue: Brichah*. New York.

Benz, W. 1988. Überleben im Untergrund. In *Die Juden in Deutschland, 1933–1945*, ed. W. Benz, 660–700, Munich.

Best, M., ed. 1988. *Der Frankfurter Börneplatz: Zur Archäologie eines politischen Konflikts.* Frankfurt am Main.

Biller, M. 1990. *Wenn ich einmal reich und tot bin.* Munich.

Bodemann, Y. M. 1988. Staat und Ethnizität: Der Aufbau der jüdischen Gemeinden im Kalten Krieg. In Brumlik 1988b, 49–69.

Broder, H., and M. Lang, eds. 1979. *Fremd im eigenen Land.* Frankfurt am Main.

Brumlik, M. 1988a. Entsorgungsversuche im Frankfurter Müll. In Funke 1988b, 35–59.

Brumlik, M., et al., eds. 1988b. *Jüdisches Leben in Deutschland seit 1945.* Frankfurt am Main.

Brumlik, M. 1988c. Zur Identität der zweiten Generation deutscher Juden nach der Shoah in der Bundesrepublik. In Brumlik 1988b, 172–76.

Brumlik, M. 1990. Das Öffnen der Schleusen—Bitburg und die Rehabilitation des Nationalismus in der Bundesrepublik. In *Die Skandale der Republik*, ed. E. Jacoby, 261–73. Hamburg.

Davidowicz, T. 1989. Zur Identität der dritten Generation nach dem Krieg in Deutschland lebender Juden. Heidelberg. Manuscript.

Dische, I. 1989. *Fromme Lügen.* Frankfurt am Main.

Eschwege, H. 1988. Die jüdische Bevölkerung der Jahre nach der Kapitulation Hitlerdeutschlands auf dem Gebiet der DDR bis zum Jahre 1953. In Arndt 1988, 63–100.

Eissler, K. 1963–64. Die Ermordung von wievielen seiner Kinder muß ein Mensch symptomfrei ertragen können, um eine normale Konstitution zu haben. *Psyche* 17:241–91.

Fleischmann, L. 1980. *Dies ist nicht mein Land.* Hamburg.

Funke, H. 1988a. Bergen-Belsen, Bitburg, Hambach: Bericht über eine negative Katharsis. In Funke 1988b, 20–34.

Funke, H., ed. 1988b. *Von der Gnade der geschenkten Nation.* Berlin.

Gringauz, S. 1947. Our New German Policy and the DPs. *Commentary* 5:508–14.

Gringauz, S. 1989. Das Jahr der großen Enttäuschungen. Reprinted in *Babylon* 5:73–81.

Grubrich-Simitis, I. 1979. Extremtraumatisierung als kumulatives Trauma: Psychoanalytische Studien über seelische Nachwirkungen der Konzentrationslagerhaft bei Überlebenden und ihren Kindern. *Psyche* 33:991–1023.

Grünberg, K. 1983. Folgen nationalsozialistischer Verfolgung bei Kindern von überlebenden Juden in der BRD. Diploma essay, Philipps University, Department of Psychology, Marburg.

Hilberg, R. 1982. *Die Vernichtung der europäischen Juden.* Berlin.

Hillel, M. 1985. *Le Massacre des survivants.* Paris.

Honigmann, B. 1987. *Roman von einem Kinde.* Frankfurt am Main.

Jacobmeyer, W. 1988. Die Lager der jüdischen Displaced Persons in den deutschen Westzonen als Ort jüdischer Selbstvergewisserung. In Brumlik 1988b, 31–48.

Jüdischer Pressedienst. 1987. *Informationen des Zentralrats der Juden in Deutschland Nr. 7/8.* Düsseldorf.

König, J. 1967. *Den Netzen entronnen.* Göttingen.

Kugelmann, C. 1988. Zur Identität osteuropäischer Juden in der Bundesrepublik. In Brumlik 1988b, 177–81.

Kugelmann, C. 1989. Identität und Ideologie der Displaced Persons. *Babylon* 5:65–72.

Kuschner, D. 1977. *Die jüdische Minderheit in der Bundesrepublik Deutschland.* Ph.D. diss., Cologne.

Maor, H. 1961. *Über den Wiederaufbau der jüdischen Gemeinden in Deutschland seit 1945.* Ph.D. diss., Mainz.

Mertens, L. 1988. Schwindende Minorität: Das Judentum in der DDR. In Arndt 1988, 125–59.

Niederland, W. 1980. *Folgen der Verfolgung: Das Überlebenden-Syndrom.* Frankfurt am Main.

Oppenheimer, W. W. 1967. *Jüdische Jugend in Deutschland.* Munich.

Ostow, R. 1988. *Jüdisches Leben in der DDR.* Frankfurt am Main.

Pätzold, K., ed. 1983. *Verfolgung-Vertreibung-Vernichtung.* Leipzig.

Pätzold, K., and I. Runge. 1988. *Pogromnacht 1938.* Berlin.

Peck, A. 1988. Befreit und erneut in Lagern: Jüdische DPs. In *Von der Reichskristallnacht zum Völkermord*, ed. W. H. Pehle, 201–12. Frankfurt am Main.

Pinson, K. 1947. Jewish Life in Liberated Germany: A Study of Jewish DPs. *Jewish Social Studies* 9:101–26.

Pross, C. 1988. *Wiedergutmachung: Der Kleinkrieg gegen die Opfer.* Frankfurt am Main.

Richarz, M. 1982. *Jüdisches Leben in Deutschland: Selbstzeugnisse zur Sozialgeschichte, 1918–1945.* Stuttgart.

Richarz, M. 1988. Juden in der Bundesrepublik Deutschland und in der Deutschen Demokratischen Republik seit 1945. In Brumlik 1988b, 13–30.

Schoeps, J. H., ed. 1990. *Auf der Suche nach einer jüdischen Theologie: Der Briefwechsel zwischen Schalom Ben Chorin und Hans-Joachim Schoeps.* Frankfurt am Main.

Seligmann, R. 1989. *Rubinsteins Versteigerung.* Frankfurt am Main.

Speier, S. 1988. Von der Pubertät zum Erwachsenendasein-Bericht einer Bewußtwerdung. In Brumlik 1988b, 182–93.

Wetzel, J. 1987. *Jüdisches Leben in München, 1945–1951: Durchgangsstation oder Wiederaufbau.* Munich.

Wetzel, J. 1989. "Mir szeinen doh." München und Umgebung als Zuflucht von Uberlebenden des Holocaust, 1945–48. In *Von Stalingrad zur Währungsreform*, ed. M. Broszat et al., 1989, 327–64. Munich.

Wolffsohn, M. 1988. Die deutsch-israelischen Beziehungen. In Brumlik 1988b, 88–107.

Zertal, I. 1989. Verlorene Seelen: Die jüdischen DPs und die israelische Staatsgründung. *Babylon* 5:88–103.

1

Introduction

"How can one stand to live there as a Jew . . .": Paradoxes of Jewish Existence in Germany

Y. Michal Bodemann

1. History through the Duality of Numbers

Many essays on postwar German Jewry begin, appropriately enough, with the history of its numbers; Micha Brumlik's essay at the beginning of this volume has done exactly that for us. Yet, more than it might appear at first glance, a closer examination of the demographic structure and the divergences between the official figures of state-sponsored censuses and the hidden numbers in German Jewry reveals a great deal about its social location in Germany and its internal structure. In June 1933, the Statistische Reichsamt counted 499,682 Glaubensjuden—Jews by faith, that is, Jews registered with Jewish communities—in Germany. This figure represented .76 percent of the total population of Germany, down from its peak of slightly more than 1 percent before 1900, and a decline of 65,000 since the previous census in 1925.[1]

In May 1939, when the next census was taken, after many Jews had fled and after the proclamation of the Nuremberg Laws (1935), the categories and definitions of who was a Jew had changed (Hughes 1955). According to the new racial criteria, which declared individuals with at least three Jewish grandparents to be Jews, there were still 330,539 "Jews" living in Germany, plus an additional 112,582 "Mischlinge," that is, persons with one or two Jewish Grandparents.[2] If we extrapolate these figures back to about 1930, when anti-Semitism and emigration from Germany began to increase, we can assume that approximately

---

1. Statistik des Deutschen Reichs, Band 451, 5 (Berlin, 1936).
2. Statistik des Deutschen Reichs, Band 552, 4 (Berlin, 1944).

100,000 additional persons not members of Jewish communities but Jewish by ancestry in the Nazi definition had been living in Germany then, bringing the total up to about 650,000. If we want to take into consideration some of the impact of Jewish/non-Jewish kin ties, we have to add to this number approximately 350,000 persons of mixed Jewish/non-Jewish background[3] and a near equal number of non-Jews married to Jews or Mischlinge, bringing the total of Jews by descent, by mixed descent, and of non-Jews married to Jews or to Mischlinge up to well over 1 million. The official figures of the German census in 1933 therefore conceal the fact that, demographically speaking, the role and the impact of the Jewish minority in Germany until the end of the Weimar Republic was far greater than is suggested by the standard/official figure of 500,000 Jews.[4] This impact and the visibility of Jewry was greater still if we take into consideration that more than half of the Jewish population had been living in the ten German cities with 500,000 inhabitants or more, where, in terms of the official—conservative—figures of the census, they represented on the average approximately 2.5 percent of the population.[5]

Whether or not, therefore, the German-Jewish symbiosis did or did not exist in the cultural arena may be in doubt;[6] in demographic terms, however, this symbiosis, or, as the *Statistical Yearbook* of 1944 would have it, the "penetration of Jewish blood into the body of the German people [Volkskörper]" (Statistik, Band 552, 4:3) represented without doubt a constitutive element of German society and had left deep imprints.

Six years later, in 1945, this "penetration of Jewish blood" had been successfully stopped in the death factories of the East. Approximately fifteen thousand Jews managed to survive somehow inside Germany itself; of those, a large majority (up to 90 percent) lived in mixed marriages and others survived in hiding or due to bribery or protection by powerful relatives—usually members of the Nazi party or even of the SS.[7]

---

3. This corresponds roughly to the estimates by Herbert Strauss (personal communication, 1988).

4. Contemporary demographers of Jewish diasporas, especially in the North American context, have long abandoned approaches that in population statistics focus exclusively on synagogue membership and discount mixed Jewish/non-Jewish origins (see, e.g., Sidney Goldstein, 1992, "Profile of American Jewry: Insights from the 1990 National Jewish Population Survey," in *American Jewish Yearbook* [New York, American Jewish Committee], 77–176). I subscribe to this position; the conventional approach, on the other hand, ignores the fluidity and the ambiguities of ethnic boundaries.

5. Statistik, 5(1933): 9.

6. See Gershom Scholem, 1976, "Jews and Germans," in *On Jews and Judaism in Crisis: Selected Essays* 13, New York, Schocken Books.

7. Much of this and the following information is collected from various sources in Maor 1961, 1ff.

With the horrors of persecution, the flight, and the annihilation of Jewry from Germany, a revival of Jewish life seemed inconceivable to most,[8] and yet new communities did develop and even began to flourish. While many of the survivors emigrated, others returned, and of the well over 200,000 Eastern European Jewish refugees, housed in DP camps such as Berlin, Föhrenwald, Bergen-Belsen, Landsberg, and Zeilsheim in the western parts of occupied Germany, approximately 12,000 to 15,000 had begun to develop roots in Germany and decided to stay on. In the early 1950s, the total figure for Jews in West Germany can once again be only roughly estimated. This is due, first, to overlapping membership in the Jewish Komitetn of the DPs and in the German-Jewish dominated Gemeinden and, second, because of those other Jews who were not registered at all. With this caveat, we find that in 1950, five years after liberation, 24,431 Jews were registered community members. This figure, which included disproportionate numbers of elderly, declined to 17,427 in 1952 but then began to increase. In 1959, it already listed 23,070 members; in the 1960s the figure rose to around 26,000. Until the early 1980s, the Jewish population remained relatively stable, and only very recently, due to the substantial influx of Soviet Jews, have the numbers begun to rise: the Jewish population in Germany has increased, roughly speaking, by about 50 percent.

According to the statistics compiled by the Central Welfare Office for Jews in Germany (ZWST),[9] there were, in 1990, sixty-six Jewish communities in West Germany. This figure, however, includes communities as small as Celle, with three members, or Goslar, with six; only thirty-three of these communities reported Rosh Hashanah services in 1989, and that number might therefore be a more realistic figure for functioning Jewish communities.

---

8. Hannah Arendt, for example, wrote to her friend Gertrude Jaspers, "But how one can stand to live there [in Germany, YMB] as a Jew, in an environment that does not deem it necessary to even speak about our problem, and that are of course our dead, that I don't know either" (letter of 30 May 1946, in Hannah Arendt and Karl Jaspers, 1985, *Briefwechsel, 1926–1969* [München, Piper Verlag]). Similarly Robert Weltsch: "Is there a future for Jews in Germany? . . . We cannot assume that there are Jews who feel drawn to Germany. It smells of corpses here, of gas chambers and torture cells. But in fact a few thousand Jews still live in Germany. The post war chaos has even turned a part of Germany into a centre for Jews. This is a transitional state as we understand. This leftover of Jewish settlements in Germany shall be liquidated as quickly as possible. Most of the Jews here have unequivocally expressed their will to emigrate to Palestine. Germany is no soil for Jews" (Robert Weltsch, "Judenbetreuung in Bayern," in *Mitteilungsblatt* Nr. 19, Tel Aviv, May 1946, cited in Harry Maor 1961, 34).

9. Detailed reports on these figures appear annually, with reports on the community in general, in the *American Jewish Yearbooks*. For the period from 1987, the reports on West Germany were written by the author, for East Germany, by Robin Ostow.

In January 1986, the ZWST reported a total Jewish membership of 27,538; in January 1990, the figures were virtually unchanged, at 27,711. This is because of the fact that in recent years increases caused by immigration, births, and conversions were roughly equal to the losses through emigration and death; since 1989, however, we have a substantial net increase due almost entirely to immigration from the Soviet Union. This Soviet immigration, viewed with great dismay by the Israeli government and with some ambivalence by the Jewish leadership in West Germany, will bring about the first real change in the structure of the Jewish population in Germany for decades. Between 1987 and 1990, the average age of the community increased from 44.5 to 45.5 years, but figures point to a gradual normalization of the age distribution and a reversal of the tendency of the community to age: those in the age bracket from 0 to 15 have increased in four years from 3,533 to 3,746 persons.

The six largest communities that together constitute about three-quarters of the entire registered Jewish population today are Berlin (9,840), Frankfurt (5,715), Munich (4,168), Hamburg (2,359), Cologne (1,358), and Düsseldorf (1,510);[10] this corresponds roughly to the major pre-1933 centers with the obvious exception of Breslau, of Leipzig, and the addition of Düsseldorf and Munich, whose growth is directly linked to the contingencies of postwar history. Well over half of all registered Jews, then, are concentrated in three cities: Berlin, Frankfurt, and Munich. It is estimated, however, that an additional 20,000 to 30,000 Jews live outside the community; many of those, judging from the complaints of community leaders,[11] do so in order to avoid paying community taxes.[12]

In East Germany, the duality of the official records and unofficial population estimates is even more telling. In 1990, before the changes brought about by the unification process and the Russian-Jewish influx, the Jewish communities of the GDR had a total of 370 Jews. Of those, most lived in East Berlin (204); others lived in Leipzig (45), Dresden (37), Magdeburg (35), and other cities. Yet about ten times that number, estimated from between 2,500 to 4,500, of Jewish or partly Jewish background, had been living in the GDR, and a substantial number of those,

---

10. Figures are those for 1995. Total membership is now at 45,000.

11. For one of numerous examples, see Heinz Galinski's column in *Jüdische Umschau* (Berlin), June 1991. Contrary to the estimates by outside observers, Jewish officials estimate the number of Jews outside the communities to be very small. Galinski, for example, spoke of about a thousand Jews outside the community (Ignatz Bubis, personal communication, Toronto, 6 February 1994).

12. Richarz 1986, 22.

during the last years of the ancien régime, have attempted to return to their Jewish roots or have moved even closer to the official community and sought membership there (Ostow 1989). John Borneman, in this volume, deals in great detail with the multiple reordering of Jewish identity in East and also West Germany.

While the official community is a small remnant of those who first returned from exile and then stayed on in the East after the anti-Jewish purges in the period of the doctors' plot (1953) and the division of the Jewish communities in East and West, it is this larger number of nonregistered persons of Jewish origin who are of particular interest. Most of these are the children or grandchildren of Jewish antifascists who returned to build a "democratic Germany." This group includes such eminent writers as Stefan Heym, who returned from the United States, and Arnold Zweig, who returned from Palestine. In view of the fact that in West Germany the old German Jewry has been almost completely replaced by Jews from the East or from Israel, it could be argued that East German Jewry is the last remnant, in cultural terms, of prewar German Jewry. It will have to be seen whether from this group, with a disproportionately large intellectual middle class and an outstanding literary and scholarly tradition, unification will eventually bring about a revival of some of the spirit and traditions of prewar German Jewry. In some ways, many developments in the East related to the Jews, all the differences between the two states notwithstanding, are astonishingly similar to those in the West; in others, however, they are different. The contributions to this volume by Robin Ostow and John Borneman, as well as my own discussion of crystal night commemorations, discuss these aspects of the Jewish condition in the GDR in greater detail.

2. The Duality of the Beginnings

The history of the reconstruction of the Jewish community in West Germany can be divided into five phases: first, the period of the Sherit Hapletah, that is, temporary structures of collective life by the Eastern Jewish displaced persons, or DPs; second, a largely concurrent period of German-Jewish survivors who lived side by side and partly in rivalry with the Eastern Jews; third, a period of bureaucratic reconsolidation; fourth, of representationism; and fifth, a period of the "functionaries." I will attempt to sketch these phases in the following paragraphs.

The Sherit Hapletah, or "remnant of the saved," was collected in and shaped by the DP camps in the period after the war. This group consisted largely of survivors from the concentration camps and of others who had been in hiding in the forests in the East, had fled to the Soviet Union, or had escaped by other means. Concentration camp inmates were often taken to Germany on forced marches by the Nazis as German troops retreated westward, and the DP camps, from Belsen in the north to Föhrenwald in the south, were, at least until 1947, continuously replenished by refugees from Eastern Europe. The Sherit Hapletah contained a large and diverse variety of people who, in the early months after liberation, were often forced to live side by side with non-Jewish conationals, often active Nazi collaborators in the Ukraine, the Baltic states, Czechoslovakia, Hungary, or Yugoslavia. There surely was a brief time of indecision and reassessment during which many of these individuals had to make up their minds which direction their lives would take. In the weeks and months after the defeat of nazism, before the dimensions of the catastrophe had become fully apparent, there still was a considerable sentiment that Jewish life in Germany should be reestablished.[13] Once they realized, however, that in their hometowns all Jewish life had been wiped out, that they lived in a "prison of antisemitism," as bad if not worse than before the war began,[14] and, most of all, that they had lost

---

13. "At the beginning, in some groups there appears to have been the opinion that one should try to rebuild German Jewry. In essence, these theories have been abandoned" (Gerschom Scholem, "Besuch bei den Juden in Deutschland," *Yedioth*, 22 November 1946).

14. The recognition of anti-Semitism in the postwar period was widespread. For one example among many:

"Wir haben nach der Befreiung gehofft, die Niederlage des Faschismus und die Aufdeckung all seiner Verbrechen gegen die Menschheit würde eine völlige moralische und massenpsychologische Diskreditierung des Antisemitismus bringen. Der Antisemitismus, als mörderisch-räuberisches Ressentiment entlarvt, müßte zum Schand- und Reueempfinden eines jeden Volkes werden. Die Wirklichkeit des Jahres 5706 hat aber ein ganz anderes massenpsychologisches Bild aufgedeckt. Das vom Nationalsozialismus gesäte Gift ist tief in die Seelen der Menschen eingedrungen, In den Jahren der nationalsozialistischen Hetze und Herrschaft wurde mit den Mitteln eines organisierten Riesenstaats und mit Hilfsquellen eines ganzen Kontinents ein Weltriesenbauwerk niederträchtigster Lügen und ein Weltriesenapparat seelischer Zersetzung errichtet, mit dessen Hilfe die Seele der ganzen Menschheit für Jahrhunderte hinaus moralisch verkrüppelt und vergiftet wurde. Der Judenhaß, eingeimpft in das Blut der Völker, lebt in seiner Weiterentwicklung und in seiner Weiterentfaltung fort. . . . Der Hitlerismus ist vernichtet. Aber Hitlers Testament wirkt. Und aus den Ruinen der deutschen Städte, aus ihren Steinen und Monumenten, aus den stillen Landhäusern mit versteckten Mördern steigt das Giftgas des wilden Judenhasses und schleicht über die Erde—still, geheim, mordgeladen und todestragend. (Gringauz 1947, 74)

It is noteworthy that the imagery and the language here is still in the shadow of Nazi propaganda: not the Jewish spirit but anti-Semitism is the poison that has entered the soul of humanity; not Jewish blood but Jew hatred has been injected into the blood of the nations and is expanding throughout the world.

their families and relatives, they became ever more focused on and committed to a new life in Palestine.

Within the Sherit Hapletah, the rejection of Germany and the enthusiasm for a new life in Palestine were strong indeed. Cilly Kugelmann, in this volume, describes in detail how this attitude was furthered by the utter incomprehension in the outside world of what the survivors had gone through, including now the oppressive conditions in the DP camps, with uncomprehending rescuers as well as, of course, the hatred surrounding the survivors in Germany itself. As Earl Harrison, sent by President Truman to Europe to inquire into the conditions in the camps, put it: "we appear to be treating the Jews as the Nazis treated them except that we don't exterminate them. . . . One is led to wonder whether the German people, seeing this, are not supposing that we are following or at least condoning Nazi policy" (quoted in Dinnerstein 1982, 301ff). Within a sea of hostility or indifference, this "remnant of the saved," therefore, became far more than an amorphous and transitory mass of refugees. It saw itself as having a particular national-Jewish mission as the remnant of European Jewry and as a symbol of the common fate of all Jews. This becomes especially apparent in the reminiscences of life in the Belsen DP camp. Norbert Wollheim, for example, vice-chairman of the first and second central committees of Belsen, put it as follows.

A little less than a year after these dark events [i.e., the Exodus affair] on May 15, 1948, the historic act, which was to bring the decisive turn in the history of the Sherit Hapletah took place in Tel-Aviv: the founding of the State of Israel. . . . And in the process of the birth of the new nation, it was the Sherit Hapletah, by its very existence and the unsolved state of its problems, to hold before the world the stern reminder that ultimate freedom can be achieved only through liberation from homelessness. This function the Sheerit Hapleitah has fulfilled with loyalty towards the higher law under which it had originally assembled. (Wollheim 1957, 67–68; see also Kugelmann 1989; Gringauz 1947; and Zertal 1989)

As such, the Sherit Hapletah's role as hindrance or help to Zionist aims (Zertal 1989, 89) was recognized by the Zionist leaders in Palestine, expressed, for example, in Ben-Gurion's visit to the DP camps in Germany in the second half of October 1945.

The ardent Zionism that developed in the camps and the extraordinary blossoming of Jewish culture and debate there clearly was given shape and structure by clandestine emissaries from Palestine, especially the agents of the B'richa who organized the flight from Poland and

Hungary over the Alps to Italy and from there by boat to Palestine. These emissaries also gave the camp inmates a sense of the political and social structures and the type of life awaiting them in Palestine; it is improbable, however, that as Albrich has put it, the B'richa needed to surreptitiously infiltrate the DP organizations in the camps (1987, 47). Nevertheless, the continuing fluctuations in and out of the camps, the problem of idleness—the DPs refused, understandably, to work within the German economy—and especially the emigration of many camp and Komitet leaders to Palestine from late 1947 onward and the decrease in the numbers of DPs led to a great deal of tension, instability, and even chaos in the camps and heightened the tensions with the surrounding German populations (Jacobmeier 1986; Albrich 1987, 178, 183).

The DPs who stayed behind in Germany after 1951 and 1952 were by and large not the most ardent Zionists and rarely of the intellectual or leadership caliber of those who had emerged from within the camps but then left for Palestine. Those left in Germany were no longer the Sherit Hapletah. The entire well-organized structure of the camps fell into decline. Moreover, in the course of time, many DPs had slowly distanced themselves from the camps and had slipped into the cities; they had obviously set root, first through black market activities and then through more legal business ventures, in an environment that they intensely hated, which was still the "land of Amalek," and with their Aliyah "just a matter of time." This group, and what was left of the Yiddish-speaking Komitetn, now merged with the Jewish communities reestablished by the German-Jewish survivors and returnees.

Indeed, the period of the German-Jewish survivors also set in immediately after liberation and was constituted largely by those fifteen thousand Jews who had survived in Germany, supplemented soon after by a group of returnees: Jews who by and large had been at the outer periphery of Judaism, who lived in mixed marriages, and who had regained a Jewish consciousness. As one of these survivors put it,

> Even if the largest part by far of the surviving Jews was composed of partners in mixed marriages, that is, of Jews who had lived mostly at the periphery of Judaism, most were nevertheless prepared to turn the previous union by force into a voluntary union. The years of persecution had left very deep imprints and had made many painfully aware that they were Jewish. Apart from the feeling of gratitude, there was also an almost proud satisfaction vis-à-vis the oppressors, and one wanted to stay within one's own group. (Maor 1961, 5–6)

Despite their distance from the German surroundings, however, they were nevertheless deeply rooted in German society and culture and may, indeed, as one German Jew put it during the early years of nazism, have been yearning for the day when the "rupture between German history and the history of the German Jews" would be overcome (Maor 1961, 5). This yearning for reconciliation may have been exacerbated by the antagonism that developed between Eastern European DPs and the German-Jewish remnant. Below, Michael Brenner describes exactly that antagonism in detail. The antagonism between these two Jewish cultures induced some in the German-Jewish remnant to adopt conciliatory positions vis-à-vis the Germans. There was a clear tendency in the years after the war, on the part especially of the returnees, to declare that the scores were "even" now, or that they had not "stood alone" (Behrend-Rosenfeld 1945). Some Jews were even willing to forgive Germany and resume their lives where they had left off (Weinberg 1945).[15] This was the case particularly frequently among those who had returned from Shanghai to Hamburg and some other German cities, who had an overly rosy picture of Germany,[16] and who played down the role of anti-Semitism in postwar Germany. They stood for a German nationalist and assimilationist position, as represented, for example, in groups such as the Unabhängige Liberale Liste in the Berlin Jewish community council and in similar variants in other major cities. In Berlin, for example, these German-Jewish nationalists were attacked by Heinz Galinski, as in the following open letter to Dr. Erich Simon, deemed to have been an assimilationist and also an advocate of the Reform Judaism.

> 1. The dream of emancipation . . . has turned out to have been an illusion, a seductive chimera and lastly a moral falsehood. We wanted to be Europeans and maintain our Jewishness only insofar as it was reconcilable with this Europeanness. Europe, however, has cruelly expelled us. Today therefore we are only Jews and we are therefore also no longer interested, to make our synagogue service palatable to the German environment. We want to fashion it only according to the traditions of our people . . .

---

15. See, for example, Wilhelm Weinberg (1945), later the Rabbi of Frankfurt, who criticized a Jewish returnee who had written that "we were even now" with the Germans, that there were many dead on both the German and the Jewish side, and that, after all, Jews and Germans spoke the same language.

16. In Hamburg, for example, a group calling itself Die aus Theresienstadt e.V. was basically a pro-German faction that had set itself apart from the Jüdische Gemeinde. They denied that there was anti-Semitism in Germany, and they proclaimed that Jews really wanted to return to Germany (see *Allgemeine Jüdische Wochenzeitung*, 29 October 1948).

Reform in Germany was according to origin and coinage largely anti-zionist. It represented the view that Jews as good German citizens should be attached to Jerusalem neither with their hearts, nor with their heads or with their passports.

To the argument, finally, that "more room should be given to the German mother tongue in the service, Galinski asks,

> Today of all times? . . . Today, when Hebrew has once again be-come the living language of a living people . . . everyone who wishes to keep in step with his religion and people [*Volks-gemeinschaft*][17] has to try to appropriate this language. (Allgemeine Jüdische Wochenzeitung, 17 February 1950)

In the political struggles that ensued, the leadership drawn from these proGerman groups lost out in most communities[18] to what I shall call the mediators—other German-Jewish leaders of an altogether different orientation. In contrast to the former, who were highly assimilated and had lived, albeit under difficult conditions, in Germany or in emigration, these new German-Jewish leaders had typically been sent to concentration camps where they were forced into contact with Ostjuden with whom they learned to communicate and with whom they often developed affective bonds either in the concentration camps or later in the DP camps.[19] Norbert Wollheim put it as follows in his reminiscences.

> But the kind of analysis that is attempted here would be incomplete without the observation that both the creation and preservation of this unity between all Jewish persons in our Zone had its problems and difficulties. After all, it was something of a phenomenon that people from East and West could get together at the Jewish Central

17. "Volksgemeinschaft" was a central concept of Nazism. As we have seen, even after 1945, the jargon of Nazism had crept into the language of Jews and non-Jews alike.

18. This occurred in exemplary fashion in Berlin and Hamburg; in some other, smaller communities such as Stuttgart there developed a rather harmonious division of labor between the highly assimilated Swabian-Jewish honorables (especially lawyers) and the Ostjuden: the Eastern Jews were in charge of the internal, especially religious, life of the communities, whereas the Stuttgart-raised Jews represented the community vis-à-vis German politicians and bureaucrats or before the courts.

19. Several examples fit this category. One is the experience of Norbert Wollheim from Lübeck who played a decisive role in the early postwar years and in the founding of the Zentralrat. Other leaders of this type include Günter Singer, formerly of Breslau, then Erfurt, and from 1953 to his death in 1989 leader of the community in Hamburg; Philipp Auerbach in Munich; and, last but not least, Heinz Galinski in Berlin.

Committee, talking in Yiddish or German, and find common ground for joint coordinated action. Of course, the unique historic circumstances which had brought us together supplied the binding element for our affective cooperation. But this alone does not explain the phenomenon. Because ultimately the solution of this problem was the realisation of the people themselves that insight and understanding would transform themselves into fruitful unity. And therewith, the Belsen Central Committee, where D.P.s and socalled "German Jews" formed an integrated executive, grew beyond its original function as a mere framework for our administrative merger. It was the dynamic search for new Jewish fulfilment, which gave the executive its spiritual strength. A genuine spirit of understanding and comradeship was practised among members of our Central Committee, as well as effective co-operation between Belsen and the smaller Jewish centres of the British Zone . . . (Irgun Sheerit Hapleitah 1957, 56ff.)

Accordingly, their followership, outside the grandes familles of German-Jewish stock or the highly assimilated ones was drawn from a mixed German and Eastern Jewish base, in which, however, the former DPs were the backbone in community elections. It was this coalition, because of its electoral base typically Zionist more in words than in deeds,[20] and on account of this electorate opposed to a revival of Reformjudentum and of course antiassimilationist, that wielded political control in the

---

20. An example among many for this rhetorical Zionism is the following statement by Heinz Galinski, chair of the West Berlin community in 1957.

We who were able to survive the times of horror, are always aware that as Jews we constitute an indivisible community. This recognition also determines our attitude to the State of Israel. Not only because innumerable former German Jews, from our ranks, have created for themselves a new life in Israel; no: mostly because Israel represents the realisation of our almost two thousand year old dream; because it is the Land of our forefathers, the land promised to our people. We therefore stand by Israel and try and help the Yishuv with all possible means to build the Jewish State. . . . As an expression of Jewish solidarity, we were represented at the congresses of the Jewish and Zionist organisations, of the ORT, the Youth Aliyah, and all other important initiatives of political, philanthropic and social nature. (Cited in Maor 1961, 99ff.; my emphasis)

In 1959, the general secretary of the Zentralrat (not a camp survivor) is far more blunt: "The German Jews of today as a collectivity are far too small and too weak to be able to afford a subdivision into Zionists and non-Zionists . . . and I am of the view that Jews in West Germany, if they profess Zionism, belong to Israel" (ibid., 100).

German communities for several decades if not until today;[21] it is a coalition, on the other hand, whose leadership, despite its protests against neonazism and anti-Semitism in West Germany, has maintained, often, but not always, in opportunist fashion, cordial ties to the German political elite and has supported, *grosso modo*, the political aims of West German governments.

3. German Jews and Ostjuden: Duality in the Period of Bureaucratic Reconsolidation (1950–69)

The period of bureaucratic reconsolidation set in with the gradual withdrawal of international Jewish organizations such as the Jewish Agency, the American Joint Distribution Committee (AJDC), Hebrew Immigrant Aid Society (HIAS), the ORT, the American Jewish Committee (AJC), and the Jewish Restitution Successor Organisation (JRSO) and the founding of a number of German-Jewish organizations at the national level—from 1950 onward, most notably, the Zentralrat der Juden in Deutschland—and the reestablishment of the Zentralwohl-fahrtsstelle (Central Welfare Agency). Other organizations founded in the early years include the Zionistische Jugend Deutschlands, the Jüdische Frauenbund (half of whose sections were founded, however, before 1950 (Maor 1961, 145), and the Gesellschaften für Christlich-Jüdische Zusammenarbeit, or WIZO.

During this period, one might argue that Jewish life in Germany runs along two separate tracks, German and the Eastern Jewish, respectively: the former represented by Karl Marx, editor of the *Allgemeine Jüdische Wochenzeitung*, who sought to find justifications for living as a (German) Jew in Germany; the latter represented by the appointment of Hendryk George van Dam, a lawyer, as general secretary of the Zentralrat. Van Dam's task was mostly to negotiate and coordinate Wiedergutmachung with the West German authorities and setting the local Jewish communities on a more solid legal and financial basis. His practical material concerns corresponded, therefore, more directly to the needs of the Ostjuden who, clearly more than their German counterparts, saw themselves as sitting on packed suitcases and without any interest in maintaining a long-term existence in Germany. Indeed, in these early years, the organized representation of Jewry came closest to being a pure interest group of people seeking compensation for damages

---

21. See the open letter by Galinski to Dr. Erich Simon, *Allgemeine Jüdisch Wochenzeitung*, 17 February 1950, cited above.

sustained[22]—a group, as we have seen, however, which had to continuously justify its presence in Germany vis-à-vis especially Israel and the North American Jewish organizations.

In contrast to the situation before 1933, the main emphasis in this group lay on welfare services to its communities and individual members. Maor, for example, analyzed the budgets of the large majority of individual communities for 1957–58 and found that 51.7 percent of their budget was spent on welfare and social work, 24.2 percent on administration, and only 19.7 percent and 4.4 percent on religious and educational functions, respectively (Maor 1961, 134). This appears to be almost a reversal of the budgetary structure of many Jewish communities elsewhere in the world.

While van Dam, particularly in editorials of the *Allgemeine Jüdische Wochenzeitung*, represented the social work apparatus of organized German Jewry, Marx attempted to articulate this community's raison d'étre in Germany. Marx's role was characterized by his political allies as follows.

> In his efforts to build renewed trust into the German people and its government, he has pointed repeatedly not only to the achievements of restitution, but also to the great sacrifices of life and property which had been made by non-Jewish Germans. (Lamm and Lewy 1962, p. 2)

Yet Marx had obvious difficulties trying to give a persuasive answer and to justify Jewish life in Germany.

> Not a few people in the world, Jews and non-Jews, can even nowadays understand how the former pariahs are psychologically able to live in Germany and even participate in the reconstruction of a new German democracy. This is not the moment, today, to deal with this very serious question. However, when one has decided in the positive, one should also have the courage to stick to one's decision and to look freely and openly into the face of the surrounding world. We have good reasons to reject the establishment of a curtain stronger than steel and more impenetrable than ivory, because this curtain is woven of resentments and aversions, instincts and negations. At the very least one can expect that the

---

22. Maor (1961, 153) speaks here, similarly, of an Interessengemeinschaft von Geschädigten "mit stark affektivem Charakter" (an interest group of victims "with a strongly affective character").

members of the Jewish community, in accordance with their tradition, have the courage to affirm their own existence. They should not sway like a reed in the wind in the conflict of emotions and of various unprovable opinions. (Karl Marx, *Allgemeine Jüdische Wochenzeitung*, 20 September 1957)

The moral values of Judaism and the traditions of prewar German Jewry were being advertised to the German public, but there was also some expression of vigilance against the revival of Nazi excesses, rarely at the cost, however, of reconciliation with the new West German state.[23] One might argue, therefore, that van Dam represented the institutional base and Marx the ideological superstructure of this new community, a division of labor that may also be viewed as a division on behalf of the Eastern and German-Jewish groups, respectively, in this ethnically divided community.

How do we explain the radical distinction between the periods before and after the early 1950s? Here we have to take a look at the constellation of forces at the time. In the period of the Sherit Hapletah, Jews in Germany—those in the German Gemeinden and the Eastern Komitetn that formed the nucleus of the later communities—were associated with powerful allies and typically in opposition to German local, zonal, and federal governments. Jews found recourse with and assistance from the international Jewish organizations operating in Germany, with the occupying powers, with antifascist groups such as the Vereinigung der Verfolgten des Nationalsozialismus (VVN), and, lastly, through the large number of DPs. In 1950, with the increased intensity of the Cold War and the strategy to integrate West Germany into the western alliance, this constellation changed. Jews could no longer rely on the Americans to help them against the Germans; Jewish organizations such as the Sochnut left Germany with the emigration of most DPs and declared that Jewish life in Germany already had ended or had to come to an end very soon;[24] and

---

23. This was hinted at by Norbert Wollheim shortly before his departure for the United States. While the "Jewish group in Germany should not be turned into the pariahs of the Jewish people," he could "not defend, however, the ambition-crazed Jews who, on this and the other side of the Elbe, are looking to make a career" (28 March 1950, from a speech delivered in Cologne on 18 March). In his much discussed book, *Die zweite Schuld* ("The Second Guilt"), the German-Jewish author Ralph Giordano castigated the German failure in the 1950s to deal with the consequences of the Shoah and the exculpation of Nazi war criminals. It is important to point out, however, that individuals such as Karl Marx were accomplices in this exculpation. Unfortunately, Giordano, who was clearly aware of the problematic role of Marx and other Jewish leaders (Giordano 1987) failed to address this openly in his book.

24. See the statement by Robert Weltsch quoted in footnote 7.

with the Cold War the antifascist organizations, tagged as Communist fronts, were being destroyed in the West.

At the same time, many postwar Jewish leaders—Yossel Rosensaft, Hans Erich Fabian, Norbert Wollheim, Philipp Auerbach, Benno Ostertag, and many others—had either emigrated or died. One might say that by the early 1950s the community had lost much of its Jewish backbone. Separated from their erstwhile allies, and with a leadership in which reconciliation with Germany was a strong motivating force, the Jewish community, severely isolated and a pariah among world Jewry, virtually threw itself into the arms of its erstwhile adversaries and deadly enemies: the Germans. This move toward the Germans on the part of the Jewish leadership coincided with a rising wave of philosemitism and interest in Israel, as discussed in detail below by Frank Stern.

The demise of Philipp Auerbach, president of the Bavarian Restitution Office, may serve as an illustration of this historical turning point in two respects. The "Auerbach scandal," revolving around financial improprieties concerning DPs who were leaving for Israel, developed at a time when Auerbach had lost precisely the constellation of allies mentioned earlier: the support of the Allies who had now turned their attention to the Germans; of the DPs, most of whom had emigrated; of the VVN, which he had quit after being pressured by the SPD whose member he was—the VVN's social democratic members were forced by the SPD's Unvereinbarkeitsbeschluss (irreconcilability clause) to associate with Communists; and, finally, of the international organizations, most of whom had left Germany. Unquestionably, virulent postwar anti-Semitism also played a major role. Auerbach's demise came about because this "King of the Jews of Bavaria" was not sufficiently opportunistic and not sufficiently compliant in the face of an ever stronger and self-confident West German state. From being an asset to the local government, Auerbach increasingly became a liability, and he found himself no longer untouchable as had been the case in the earlier years.[25]

It is important to see, however, that the leadership of the community, while generated from the inside, is also shaped by a selection process in which the young West German state itself had a major role. By bestowing favors on the more opportunistic and compliant leadership, providing them with funding for Gemeinde projects, giving them public recognition, granting them interviews, and inviting them as community leaders on important international trips, a largely subservient leadership was being created or sustained in these otherwise stable and

---

25. An (albeit rather critical) analysis of Auerbach that deemphasizes the anti-Semitic element is Goschler 1989.

relatively uneventful years while more critical and self-assured voices were pushed into the background.[26]

There began to be new developments only after about 1969 when a new leader, Werner Nachmann, emerged on the scene. If we look at his public pronouncements, we find that the theme of vigilance against neonazism and careful observation of the trials of Nazis moves into the background. Nachmann, in the name of German Jewry, had made peace with Germany. Now Israel becomes a more important theme than in the years of van Dam. Auschwitz is invoked on occasion, it seems, in order to receive funding for synagogues and as an attempt to bolster the significance of the Jewish community—whose insignificance, smallness, and irrelevance to German politics is lamented on some occasions in the *Allgemeine*. The theme of Wachsamkeit, vigilance, is supplanted by Verständigung, understanding, and by the idea that Germans and Jews should live "normally" with each other.[27] This is driven to the point where West German Jewry is proclaimed to be a "loyal part of German society" (Die jüdische Gemeinschaft in der Bundesrepublik ist ein loyaler, trotz ihrer kleinen Zahl zur Mitarbeit bemühter Teil der deutschen Gesellschaft" (Allgemeine Jüdische Wochenzeitung, Rosh Hashana message, 1984).

As stated earlier, until 1969 the Jewish representatives acted as representatives of an interest group much like the Vertriebenenverbände (Association of Refugees from the Eastern Territories) or of the war wounded. Under Nachmann, however, the attempt is made to play an autonomous role in world politics: Nachmann and Galinski have a great deal more to say on international terrorism, Soviet Jews, the Helsinki Charter, and peace and disarmament. How do we explain this change—this move away from a position of vigilance against neonazism, at that time? The late 1960s was also the time of the student movement, and it is the time of an SPD-led coalition government in the Federal Republic. I would argue that—albeit imperfectly and in problematic ways—the student movement did assume a major anti-Nazi watchdog function in West Germany. For the Jewish establishment loyal to the Bonn governments, a united

---

26. One such case is that of Rabbi Robert Raphael Geis whose progressive political views soon became far too uncomfortable for both Jews and Germans and who, already in the 1950s, was increasingly marginalized (Susanne Geis, personal communication, 1989).

27. One of Nachmann's favored, and often cited, slogans was "Wir sollten doch einfach ganz normal miteinander leben" (We should simply live completely normally with each other). From establishing normality, Nachmann proceeded, in the spirit of his mentor Karl Marx, to defending Germany abroad: "I see it as my task to present the correct picture of Germany, of its citizens and parties whenever there are tendencies to portray the 'evil German' " (cited in Neustadt 1987, 102).

struggle with the students would have been too close for comfort. Moreover, some initiatives and gestures on the part of the SPD (such as Willy
Brandt at the Warsaw Ghetto monument) may have taken the wind out of
the sails of the Zentralrat.

4. Atrophied Representationism: The Marginalization of "Memorial Site Jewry"

I describe the post-1969 period as that of *atrophied representationism*. In
these years—as shown, for example, in my analysis of the greetings of
Rosh Hashanah—the Central Council assumes a quasi-pontifical authority, making general moral pronouncements and sweeping evaluations of
world affairs. This is a far cry from its New Years' messages in the 1950s
when the Zentralrat was attempting to draw attention to itself, mostly
on the basis of the "hard and difficult" work in the year that had passed.
It is important to see that the direction the Zentralrat has taken since is
not dependent on the personality of Werner Nachmann or Alexander
Ginsburg alone. We find similar statements from within the local communities, and the pronouncements of someone who stands in glaring contrast to Nachmann, Heinz Galinski, are just as bureaucracy- and
organization-oriented in the 1950s as they are oriented toward world
politics in the 1980s. There is little difference here between various
leaders, then. Whether there is a fundamental change taking place with
Ignatz Bubis as Galinski's successor is still an open question. There is
also no doubt that, despite variations in style and politics, there are no
disagreements about the major concerns and the major themes seen to
be of relevance to the Jewish community. We might say that in the
Nachmann era the Jewish leadership in Germany had reached a
consensus—a consensus with which both the German and the Eastern
Jews could live. It was, moreover, a period when the Jewish community
was most harmoniously integrated, at least on the surface, into the
German political establishment.

On the basis of this sketch of the original parameters of the new
Jewish community in Germany, we might now consider possible models
of the future course of development. There is, first of all, the question of
the new political constellation. Jewish representatives such as Galinski
and Bubis claim that the long-lasting international isolation of German
Jewry has finally been overcome and that, for example, the meeting of
the World Jewish Congress in 1990 was the prestigious recognition of the
new international position of German Jewry.[28] In purely formal terms,

28. See, for example, Galinski's editorial in the community's monthly Bulletin,
Berlin Umschau, May 1990.

this may indeed be true, and the stigma of treason may be fading, but little has changed in terms of the comparative international weight of German Jewry: in quantitative and qualitative respects, the new Jewish community in Germany is rather weak compared not only to British or French Jewry but even to Italian and Dutch Jewry.

Not only in terms of numbers, but also in terms of the quality of the community, especially its cultural achievements—this community has little to offer and no international recognition—it has largely remained as Maor characterized it in 1961, a community of small businesspeople and pensioners very much at the periphery of German economic life (1961, 176ff.). Germany today, and especially the old West Germany, has a minute number of internationally recognized Jewish academics and intellectuals, no autonomous religious culture or rabbis of international stature, and no internally generated and autonomous political-cultural milieu. This is reflected in its leadership as well: Otto Nachmann and his son Werner, a family in the used-textile business, and Galinski, a life-long Jewish functionary who had trained as a sales apprentice before being shipped to Auschwitz. Compared to Jewish leadership in other countries, this leadership is not particularly distinguished by education, by family background, or by wealth, and therefore it lacks independence and the autonomy to work for the community without economic gain.[29] With Bubis, this has changed to some extent: he is economically independent. Like the others, and due to his time in the camps, however, he lacks formal education and comes from an undistinguished family.

In addition, the Jewish leadership in postwar Germany—notoriously distrustful of Jews abroad—is still suspected of being opportunist and is distrusted on other counts as well: these leaders hold on to their positions for an extraordinary length of time and monopolize power, which in the end is not an expression of the strength of the community but rather a sign of the weakness of Jewish life as the various scandals amply demonstrate. While it is true that over the past decades Jews have fulfilled a role in German ceremonial politics, have rarely missed a relevant international reception, and have served as a lubricant in difficult state visits between Israel and West Germany, their role as mediators paints a deceptive picture of their actual role in political life.

The Jewish community and their leadership have successively lost influence in two respects. In the 1950s and 1960s, the community—albeit not rooted in this culture and having little connection to it—had to represent the German-Jewish prewar heritage in the new, western Germany. Slowly, however, this culture was being appropriated by the Ger-

---

29. For a very similar diagnosis, see Maor 1961, 154ff.

mans themselves,[30] not in the least by the student movement—
symbolized, for example, in the role of Horkheimer and Adorno or the
friendship between Rudi Dutschke and Ernst and Karola Bloch. The
current extension of this elective affinity is clearly visible in certain
milieux of the Greens, who, their ambivalences about Jews notwithstanding, have attempted to identify with certain Jewish concerns, traditions,
and institutions. This appropriation of Jewish issues, however, has taken
a great deal of wind out of the sails of the Jewish community by depriv-
ing it of a cultural monopoly.

But, just as the community at large has lost its monopoly over
German-Jewish cultural traditions, the Jewish leadership has lost its role
as mediator in German politics. German-Israeli relations no longer require the intervention of German-Jewish representatives because today
not Germany but Israel is being ostracized internationally. Germany has
gained some control over Israel, especially in its role as advocate of
Israeli concerns in Europe. Moreover—and also because of the public
relations of Jews on behalf of Germany, Germany today is being viewed
internationally no longer as the Germany of 1945 or 1965. As we have
seen in the international reaction to unification, the association of Germany with nazism has largely disappeared, and in this direction as well
the role of German Jews as Germany's international mediators has now
become past history. The important international Jewish organizations
prefer to negotiate directly with the German government and vice
versa—much to the chagrin of German-Jewish leaders. Their role in
foreign diplomacy has therefore become virtually irrelevant, and it is no
accident that the Jewish leadership is complaining increasingly that it is
no longer being consulted.[31] The Zentralrat attempted, for example, to
have included in the new preamble to Germany's Grundgesetz (constitution) a section on Germany's responsibility for Auschwitz. This initiative
was as unsuccessful as its attempt to discourage Kohl from going to
Bitburg or the hesitation of Bonn concerning the immigration of Soviet

---

30. This began quite early. See, for example, the statement by SPD leader Erich
Ollenhauer during Rosh Hashanah 1955.

> We remember with particular gratitude the great contribution which our Jewish
> fellow citizens [Mitbürger] have made with respect to the best traditions of the
> spiritual and political life of Germany. We feel deeply obliged to continue these
> traditions and therefore to eliminate some of the unspeakable shame that has
> covered the name of Germany in our generation . . ." (*Allgemeine Jüdische
> Wochenzeitung*, 16 September 1955)

31. See for example, Micha Guttmann, secretary of the Zentralrat, in a public
statement, 25 October 1990, in Berlin.

Jews to Germany. In the latter instance, as in others, non-Jewish forces have been able to accomplish more than the Jews themselves. Until Bubis's election, the role of German-Jewish officials had therefore increasingly turned into what one critic has termed the Gedenkstätten- und Staatsjudentum (memorial site and state Jewry): a hollow representation not of present-day Jewry in Germany but of a glorious German past closely associated with the Jews.[32]

5. From the Martyr-Founders to the Functionaries: The Future of German-Jewish Leadership

In the 1980s, we have seen, however, not only a change in the outer political constellation of forces; inwardly as well, the relationship of Jews to the German state has undergone significant changes. In the late 1940s, the majority of Jews in Germany considered Germans and the German government as antagonists and as a hostile power, and the long provisional republic that followed made it easy for them to define their existence "on packed suitcases" and therefore similarly provisional— even at a time when that provisional republic of Bonn had long ceased to be temporary in nature and when the packed suitcases had begun gathering dust in the back corner.

With unification, the Germans are once again masters in their own house, in their "completed fatherland," as a columnist of *Die Zeit* put it. In the long run, therefore, the fiction of provisionality cannot be maintained, nor will guilt and responsibility even be discussed as in the past. Sooner or later, it will become difficult for Jews to refuse loyalty to this postprovisional state. This is already becoming apparent in the outlook of Jewish youth of the 1990s. The vast majority of these youth have few if any ties to a community and a leadership that largely lives in the past.[33] Their commitment to Israel is largely formalistic and no longer deeply felt. They have, instead, been thoroughly integrated into German society, and the conception of "Jews in Germany," decreed by Goebbels in the mid-1930s and carried on by the majority of the postwar leadership, is once again

---

32. Mario Offenberg, as reported in *Frankfurter Allgemeine Zeitung*, 14 June 1991.

33. Michel Friedman, a lawyer, real-estate developer, member of Frankfurt's city council for the CDU, and director of cultural affairs of Frankfurt's Jewish community, estimates that Jewish communities reach, at the most, 20 percent of Jewish young people today. The following analysis agrees with many of his views, as presented, for example, in a lecture in Berlin on 25 June 1991. At the age of thirty-five, Friedmann is the youngest member by far of the Zentralrat der Juden. For a report on this lecture, see also "Die jüdischen Gemeinden befinden sich in der Krise," a report on this talk published in *die tageszeitung*, 27 June 1991.

giving way to the pre-Shoah notion of "German Jews"—note, for example, Ignatz Bubis's declarations in this regard, which, however, have not attracted the undivided sympathy of many other Jews in Germany. Nevertheless, as Martin Löw-Beer shows in this volume, based upon his analysis of Jewish youth magazines, there is a discernible tendency among the young to identify themselves as German Jews today. There have also been moves recently to change the name of the Zentralrat der Juden in Deutschland to Zentralrat der Deutschen Juden. Ironically, its directorate rejected this change in name on the grounds that it would exclude the new immigrants from the former Soviet Union.[34]

In this context, the new wave of immigration of Soviet Jews will undoubtedly play a role as well. For these immigrants, with the experience of Stalinism and anti-Semitism at home, Auschwitz is a far more distant experience than for the Jews in the West and especially for those in Germany so far. As immigrants, they will likely grant Germany the full loyalty that those Jews who were socialized politically in the early postwar decades have almost invariably refused to give.[35]

At the very least, we can expect deepening, quasi-ethnic divisions within German Jewry—especially between, first, the Soviet immigrants; second, the old Jewry of partly German-Jewish background, with basically pro-German inclinations; and, third, the descendants of former DPs and their wider cultural sphere, in hostile distance to Germany, isolated from their German surroundings, and with deep attachments to Israel. The division between the latter two groups was most recently articulated in the largely nonpublic Jewish discussions on German unification, on one hand, and the question of immigration of Soviet Jews on the other.[36] These rather confused discussions indicate

34. Ignatz Bubis, personal communication, 6 February 1994. I have dealt with this question in "A Re-emergence of German Jewry?" in Sander Gilman and Karin Remmler, eds., *Jewish Culture and Community in Contemporary Germany* (New York: New York University Press, 1994).

35. Some of these immigrants, in total contrast to German Jews, have even postulated a greater cultural proximity to Germany than to Israel. As one of these immigrants has put it, "In der UdSSR hatten wir immer mehr Angst vor Pogromen, ständig wurden mündlich welche angekündigt, und nach den Ereignissen in Armenien haben wir das auch geglaubt. Wenn ich durch Technik-Prüfungen gefallen bin, hat man mir ins Gesicht gesagt, dass das an meinem Judentum liegt. In Israel wollten wir nie bleiben, die deutsche Kultur ist uns viel näher. Auch die Sprache ist dem Jiddischen ähnlicher (Berlin section of *die tageszeitung*, 15 May 1991).

36. I witnessed some of these discussions in the council meetings (Repräsentantenversammlungen) of Berlin's Jewish community between spring 1990 and summer 1991. Traces thereof can be found in the reports on these monthly meetings published in issues of *Berlin-Umschau*, the Berlin Gemeinde's monthly newsletter.

that the old professed consensus within German Jewry has disappeared and that the new internal antagonisms might depoliticize the community and deprive it of its previous unitary impetus.[37]

In terms of further criss-crossing conflicts, the role of East German Jewry may become important. These Jews are the children and grandchildren of German Jews who returned to East Germany after the war to "build socialism." As part of the former political class of the GDR, these Jews are far more deeply rooted than are their counterparts in the West in the old German-Jewish tradition of the old Bildungsbürgertum. In the future, and quantitatively as well,[38] they will constitute an intellectual Jewish stratum of some significance. They have, however, lost their sociopolitical home, and it is an open question how they will define themselves in the future. Especially in light of the new anti-Semitism from some quarters in East Germany, their national-Jewish, religious, or privatistic isolation from their surroundings seems likely (Robin Ostow addresses this in her contribution below). Here as well, the diminishing sociopolitical role of the Jews in a united Germany would be confirmed.

With the new influx of Jews from the East and their greater visibility we may also find a change in the predominant image of Jews in German society: so far, this image had been composed of exotic orthodox piety— the topos of the Jew without history—and that of the patrician German Jew, a combination of estheticizing, well-educated, and art-collecting businessmen, physicians, and lawyers, of scientists and artists—an image that in Jewish public relations has been carefully cultivated in the past. As managers of gambling halls, as ordinary employees, doctors, or engineers, they will likely lose their fear- and respect-inducing aura; their image might move from sacred to profane and turn Jews as carriers of German high culture and as martyrs into more ordinary immigrants instead.

Parallel to German disenchantment due to the new Jewish immigrants we find a disenchantment resulting from the generational change in the Jewish leadership. The old guard cultivated an image of martyrdom combined with responsibility for a democratic Germany. Heinz Galinski, for example, put it this way.

> After returning from the camps, the survivors began the reconstruction in the midst of these ruins. Their first and most important task

---

37. Another division may be that which has occurred recently with the reestablishment of the Gemeinde Adass Jisroel, a second, separatist, neo-orthodox community in East Berlin.

38. It is estimated that approximately three to four thousand persons of Jewish origin were living in the former GDR. See Richarz 1986.

was to protect the democratic social order with all means possible. (*Allgemeine Jüdisch Wochenzeitung,* 5 February 1988)

We find here the historically highly dubious myth of the Jew who in spite of persecution and suffering makes a second sacrifice by going into the service of his tormentors and to rebuild their land. The martyr thus becomes cofounder of the new, decontaminated Germany, and this myth of selfless, complete patriotism has been used effectively in German political discourse. Few speeches of leading German politicians fail to point to the cooperative attitude of the postwar Jewish leadership. Helmut Kohl, for example, put it this way.

> We are especially grateful to those [Jews] who returned to Germany after the bitter experience they had during the Nazi dictatorship and who helped to build the free and democratic system the Federal Republic of Germany embodies. They are a part of us and our country has much to be grateful to them for. (Speech delivered in October 1985 at the Leo-Baeck Institute conference in Berlin)

> For many centuries the Jews have made decisive contributions to German culture and history. . . . It is a fact of historical import that even after 1945 Jewish compatriots were prepared to assist us in building the Federal Republic of Germany. (Speech delivered in the company of President Reagan in Bergen Belsen, 5 May 1985)

This myth, however, and resulting therefrom the commitment to a political mission, is lacking in the younger Jewish generation—lawyers, businesspeople, and journalists. The topos of the martyr-founder can thus no longer be applied to individuals. It could, at the very best, be applied to Jews as a collectivity, in generalized and much weaker terms, to be sure. Now one might think of a new type of ideological labor for Jews: Jews as the embodiment of multiculturalism or at least of pluralism in Germany. Yet, despite some receptivity especially in the new social movements, this society, which in many ways, including the ways it handles immigration, still remains a Volksgemeinschaft, has great diffi-culties with pluralist conceptions of culture. And Jews would turn into one minority among many and obliterate their unique status since Ausch-witz. The Woche der Brüderlichkeit ("week of brotherliness"), a na-tional annual atonement ritual, which turns everything fraternal into exclusively Jewish concerns, is clear proof of this.

In this new, complete fatherland memory as well is being newly structured and constructed. This does not mean, however, that Auschwitz or the Kristallnacht pogroms would disappear from the repertory of the theater of memory. As I show below in the discussion of Kristallnacht, the fear of Jewish representatives that 9 November 1989—the opening of the Wall—would cover up 9 November 1938 has clearly been proven wrong. In 1990 as well, the pogroms were commemorated far more publicly than, say, in 1960 or 1970. It is true, nevertheless, that, almost imperceptively, this culture of memory moves from the memory of history to the memory of commemoration of history. This secondary commemoration is enacted by Jews and Germans alike and therefore brings the Germans to the point of appropriating the Shoah. This is particularly pronounced in the— unquestionably sincere and noble—speeches of President Richard von Weizsäcker who developed the theme of remembrance by citing the words of the Baal Shem Tov, "Forgetting prolongs the exile, and remembrance is the secret of redemption" (Weizsäcker 1987, 19). In this new commemoration, Auschwitz and Kristallnacht turn into a romanticized horror suffered jointly by Germans and Jews; a commemoration of Jews and the decent new Germany against the evil forces in society. The lines of confrontation, therefore, are being blurred—another indication of a certain depoliticization of the Jewish topos.

Forty years ago, Hannah Arendt wrote, in the German edition of *The Origins of Authoritarianism*,

> The Jewish prejudice in favour of the authority of the State was decisive in only one respect: it decided a priori, irrespective of all other historical circumstances and to a certain degree even independent of special functions, that the Jews would constitute, within the societies of nation states, a group specially devoted to the various governments. (1986, 59)

It is a bitter irony that, at least in the western part of postwar Germany, and the massive blow of the Nazi state against the Jews notwithstanding, a historically unprecedented dependency of the Jewish community on the state, and even trust in this state, has been fostered. Unlike few other groups, the Jews are tied to this state and legitimated by it.

This volume, then, discusses many of these issues in greater depth. Micha Brumlik, long active in Jewish affairs in Frankfurt and coeditor of the journal *Babylon*, which appears in Frankfurt and is devoted to Jewish themes, has already sketched for us the most important features of the Jewish condition in Germany; in many ways, it can be read as a summing up of this volume as a whole.

The first section of this book deals with a variety of aspects of the formative years of the Jewish community in Germany and of German-Jewish relations. These postwar years were decisive for the contemporary shape of German Jewry and its role in German society, and they are therefore given particular attention. Cilly Kugelmann portrays what has long been passed over in silence—the early encounter of the outside world with those who survived the camps and the Nazi death machinery. Both Jews and non-Jews who were facing the survivors, Kugelmann argues, were unable to comprehend what had happened, and they were unable to face the survivors adequately. Their particular experience, in turn, including the lack of comprehension in the surrounding Jewish world, shaped the Sherit Hapletah, its silences and its sense of mission, in very particular ways. Michael Brenner, in turn, finds that for the Jews in Germany there was no real Stunde Null and that the long history of miscomprehensions and antagonisms between German Jews and Eastern Jews continued after 1945, once again in Germany. Frank Stern, finally, portrays the contradictory tendencies of anti-Semitism and philosemitism in the postwar period, which have fundamentally shaped German attitudes toward its Jewish minority and the status of Jewry in postwar (West) Germany.

In the second section, five chapters deal in greater detail with the articulation of Jewish and German identities; both identities are deeply intertwined and must be seen as continuously evolving in concert. Robin Ostow retraces the history of Jews in the GDR and the ways in which unification has fundamentally obliterated the social position and self-definition of this tiny community. How and whether this community will survive at all, whether it will be able to articulate a new separate Jewish identity, remains to be seen. John Borneman reports on his and Jeff Peck's research on Jews who returned from exile; their position in Germany, East and West, is one of several factors that have shaped their memory and their particular definition as Jews. Martin Löw-Beer, in his analysis of local Jewish youth magazines in Germany and Austria, detects an ever-increasing acceptance of Germany and a greater, albeit cautious, willingness to integrate in this society. Jack Zipes, reaching back into a longer literary tradition, portrays "operations" on both groups in a variety of novels, between breaking established stereotypes, on one hand, and the cultivation of such stereotypes on the other. Finally, in this section I address the ways in which both Jews and Germans have commemorated Kristallnacht, the pogroms of November 1938. I argue that, in Germany,

Jews have to a considerable extent been dispossessed of their own memory, that memory has been appropriated by new generations in Germany to shape a new identity of the "good Germany"—but also as a means of bringing together democratic, antiracist forces in German society.

The last section, finally, addresses questions related to the future of the Jewish existence in Germany and in Europe. Andrei Markovits, Dan Diner, and Moishe Postone reiterate each in their own way the question how, with the "return of Germany," with the "re-emergence of the past," and with a new constellation of forces in Europe, the Jewish role in Germany might evolve and how Germany's role vis-à-vis the Jews might develop. In a coalition with other forces in German society, Jews might finally break the imagined homogeneity of the German ethnos on one hand, toward some form of a multicultural society; on the other hand, Germany's return as most powerful nation in Europe may very well thwart any such role of the Jews, especially as, argues Postone, the future of Jewry's allies on the democratic side of the spectrum cannot necessarily be relied upon to survive the new political constellation.

In the period of the Sherit Hapletah, in an atmosphere of virulent anti-Semitism and deep hatred of Jews against Germans, a number of violent attacks of one group against the other took place as well. One such attack was directed against meeting places of the DPs in Munich in February 1948. On request by the U.S. military government, the lord mayor of Munich Karl Scharnagl, had the Munich city council issue a statement condemning these actions and appeal to the population to identify the culprits. The "severely suffering population," Scharnagl declared, could not afford that

> provocatory elements can, unrecognised and in the dark, be up to their tricks. One has to ponder how much the Jews . . . had to suffer and that even today the entire civilised world follows with distrust every utterance that comes from the sphere of the German people on the difficult problem of calming down the Jewish people.[39]

Taken it all together, many Jews did splendidly well, materially and socially, in the Bonn republic, and not much less so in the GDR. They may have done less well in terms of their mental health: these injuries, more or less strong and deep, remain. To both states in different ways, Jews have made astonishingly, if not absurdly, important contributions. However, do the Jews today, after the waning of their martyr-founders,

---

39. Stadtarchiv München, Bürgermeister und Rat, no. 1843.

still have something valuable to offer to Germany? This question, which I answer in the qualified negative, will also decide the future of the Jewish community in the united Germany. It would not be surprising if the social contract between Germans and Jews, a contract that existed since the founding of the Federal Republic, would now also undergo a change. In all likelihood, Jewish existence in Germany will be more muted. The "difficult problem of calming down the Jewish people," at any rate, has been skillfully accomplished—to Germany's advantage.

Bibliography

Albrich, Thomas. 1987. *Exodus durch Österreich: die jüdischen Flüchtlinge 1945–1948.* Insbruck: Haymon Verlag.

Arendt, Hannah. 1986 [1958]. *Elemente und Ursprünge totaler Herrschaft,* München: Piper.

Behrend-Rosenfeld, Else R. 1971. *Ich stand nicht allein.* Frankfurt: Europäische Verlagsanstalt.

Dinnerstein, Leonard. 1982. *America and the Survivors of the Holocaust.* New York: Columbia University Press.

Ginzburg, Carlo. 1990. *Ecstasies: Deciphering the Witches Sabbath.* London: Hutchinson Radius.

Giordano, Ralph. 1987. *Die Zweite Schuld, Oder von der Last, Deutscher zu sein.* Hamburg: Rasch und Röhrig.

Goldmann, Nachum et al. 1957. *Irgun Sheerit Hapleitah Me'haezor Habriti.* London: Narod Press.

Goschler, Constantin. 1989. "Der Fall Philipp Auerbach: Wiedergutmachung in Bayern." In Ludolf Herbst and Constantin Goschler, eds., *Wiedergutmachung in der Bundesrepublik Deutschland.* München: R. Oldenbourg Verlag.

Grimm, Jacob, and Wilhelm Grimm. 1854–1960. *Deutsches Wörterbuch.* 16 vols. Leipzig: S. Hirzel.

Gringauz, Samuel. 1989. Das Jahr der großen Enttäuschungen: 5706 in der Geschichte des jüdischen Volkes. *Babylon* 5 (1989): 65–72. Originally published as "Jewish Destiny as the DP's See It." *Commentary* (1947): 73–81.

Hughes, Everett C. 1971. "The Gleichschaltung of the German Statistical Yearbook." In Hughes, *The Sociological Eye.* Chicago: Aldine.

Jacobmeier, Wolfgang. 1986. "Die Lager der jüdischen Displaced Persons in den deutschen Westzonen 1946/47 als Ort jüdischer Selbstvergewisserung." In Brumlik, Micha et al., 1986, *Jüdisches Leben in Deutschland seit 1945.* Frankfurt/M: Jüdischer Verlag Bei Athenäum.

Kohl, Helmut. n.d. "Chancellor Kohl on the German-Jewish Question in Connection With the Role of the Leo Baeck Institute." Ed. Rolf Vogel. Meckenheim: Warlich Druck.

Kugelmann, Cilly. 1989. Identität und Ideologie der Displaced Persons: Zwei historische Texte aus den DP-Lagern. *Babylon* 5: 65–72.

Lamm, Hans, and Hermann Lewy. 1962. Brücken Schlagen. Aufsätze und Reden aus den Jahren 1946 bis 1962 von Karl Marx, Düsseldorf: Kalima Druck.

Maor, Harry. 1961. Der Wiederaufbau der jüdischen Gemeinden in Deutschland (unpublished dissertation) Mainz.

Neustadt, Amnon. 1987. *Israels Zweite Generation: Auschwitz als Vermächtnis.* Berlin: J. H. W. Dietz Verlag.

Ostow, Robin. 1989. *Jews in Contemporary East Germany: The Children of Moses in the Land of Marx.* Basinstoke: Macmillan.

Richarz, Monika. 1986. "Juden in der Bundesrepublik Deutschland und in der Deutschen Demokratischen Republik seit 1945." In Brumlik, Micha et al., 1986, *Jüdisches Leben in Deutschland seit 1945.* Frankfurt/M: Jüdischer Verlag bei Athenäum.

Scholem, Gershom. 1976. *On Jews and Judaism in Crisis: Selected Essays.* New York: Schocken Books 13.

Spamer, Adolf. 1935. *Die Deutsche Volkskunde.* Leipzig: Bibliographisches Institut.

Vogel, Rolf., ed. *Chancellor Helmut Kohl on the German-Jewish Question in Connection with the Role of the Leo Baeck Institute.* Meckenheim, Warlich Druck.

Weinberg, Wilhelm. 1945. " 'Wir sind quitt'! Sind wir wirklich quitt?" *Der Neue Weg* (November–December).

Weizsäcker, Richard von. 1987. *Von Deutschland aus: Reden des Bundespräsidenten.* München: Deutscher Taschenbuch Verlag.

Wollheim, Norbert. 1957. "Belsen: Symbol of Jewish Rebirth." In Irgun she'erit ha-peletah meha-ezor ha-briti, ed. Belzen: Irgun she'erit ha-peletah meha-ezor ha-briti.

Zertal, Idith. 1989. "Verlorene Seelen: Die jüdischen DP's und die israelische Staatsgründung. *Babylon* 5: 88–103.

The Formative Years:
The Sherit Hapletah and the
Contradictions of the New
Jewish Existence in Germany

East European and German Jews in Postwar Germany, 1945–50

Michael Brenner

In contrast to the case in Spain after the expulsion of 1492, a resettlement of Jews in Germany after the Holocaust was never officially prohibited by Jewish authorities. It seems, however, that indignation at the prospect of Jewish settlement in postwar Germany, as expressed by many Jewish leaders and organizations, made any objective treatment of postwar Jewish life in Germany difficult. Not until the 1980s did historiography begin to deal systematically with Jewish life in Germany during the immediate postwar era.[1] Let me mention five reasons, concerning only the settlement of East European Jews, why the short period of active Jewish life in Germany between 1945 and 1950 merits more attention than it has previously received.

First, we are talking about a quite considerable Jewish population in relation to the numbers that prevailed in pre-Nazi Germany. In December 1949, there were almost two hundred thousand East European Jews under the official status of displaced persons (DPs) in Germany, the vast majority of whom lived in the south.[2] To put these numbers into proportion, one has to realize that in Bavaria and other parts of southern Germany there have never been as many Jews as there were one year after the destruction of European Jewry. Ironically, some places that the Nazis never had to make *judenrein* because Jews had never lived there

---

1. Only in the mid-1990s were the first comprehensive accounts of Jewish life in Germany between 1945 and 1950 published. See Michael Brenner, *Nach dem Holocaust: Jüdisches Leben in Deutschland, 1945–1950* (Munich, 1995), and Angelika Königseder and Juliane Wetzel, *Lebensmut im Wartesaal: Die jüdischen DPs (Displaced Persons) im Nachkriegsdeutschland* (Frankfurt am Main, 1994).

2. Yehuda Bauer (*Out of the Ashes: The Impact of American Jews on Post-Holocaust European Jewry* [Oxford and New York, 1989], 271) mentions the different estimations, which range from 165,000 to 190,000.

were eventually populated by several hundreds, if not thousands, of Jews.

Second, if we consider the quality of Jewish life, we can determine that this episode was a unique chapter of Jewish history in modern Germany. Most East European Jews had preserved not only their own cultural heritage but also their own (Yiddish) language. Thus, the Jewish DPs were not only of numerical importance in places where Jews had never lived before, but they also were more visible as a separate group than German Jews had ever been since Emancipation.

Third, there is a political reason. Most Jews living in Germany during the first postwar years envisioned Palestine as their ultimate home. These survivors of the concentration camps, still living in "camps" on German soil, were waiting for the creation of a Jewish state in Palestine. The passengers of the "Exodus," symbolizing Jewish attempts to reach Palestine illegally, came from German DP camps. While the Jewish DPs had no political power, the moral power they represented should not be underestimated. The image of liberated Jews, confined to Germany but longing for a state of their own, was certainly a factor in the process of political decision making that led to the United Nations' partition of Palestine in 1947.

Fourth, the German factor should be mentioned. After all, what was an interlude in Jewish history was a postscript in German history. Between 1945 and 1950 there were, for the last time, a considerable number of Jews living in Germany. Although most of the Jewish DPs lived in their own quarters or in camps administered by the Allied armies, they were not isolated from the German population. Many were doing business with the Germans or living in apartments with German landlords, and a few settled down and married German women.

Fifth, the most important factor in understanding Jewish life in Germany after 1945 is the realization of its paradoxical character. In 1946–47 there was a mass movement of East European Jews who tried to reach the country whose death machine they had just escaped. It belongs to the ironies of history that Germany, of all places, became under the occupation of the Allied powers a sheltering haven for several hundred thousand Jews.

1

A short survey must suffice here to illustrate the situation of East European Jewish displaced persons in occupied Germany during the first postwar years. The term *displaced persons* referred to civil persons who were driven out of their home countries as a result of the war and relied on Allied assistance to return or to resettle somewhere else. Only a small percentage of the few millions of displaced persons who lived within the territory of the four Allied German zones in 1945 were Jews.[3] The various estimates of the number of Jewish Holocaust survivors who were liberated within the borders of the German Altreich differ substantially.[4] Taking the enormously high death rate immediately after the liberation into consideration, it can be assumed that not more than thirty thousand East European Jews were living in the occupied zones of Germany in the summer of 1945.

This number increased steadily between 1945 and 1948 when several hundred thousand Jews crossed the borders to the American occupied zone of Germany. Those Holocaust survivors fled from anti-Semitism in the East European countries where their lives were threatened by terror again.[5] They considered Germany to be the stepping stone to their ultimate destinations: America and Palestine.[6] As many crossed the borders illegally and were never officially registered in Germany, the exact proportions of this migration will never be known. Some spent only a few weeks on German soil; others stayed several years or even settled in Germany.

The term *camp* evokes an association with the concentration camps where these Jews had spent most of their recent past. The DP camps, of course, were not comparable to the Nazi death camps. However, some camps superficially resembled concentration camps in terms of the primitiveness of the housing. In some cases the new homes were stables or unheated barracks. Former Wehrmacht and SS barracks also served as new homes for the survivors. Others felt privileged to spend their time after liberation in former hotels, asylums, or regular apartment houses. The paradox of their situation may be illustrated by the group of Jewish Holocaust survivors who turned the farm of the most radical Jew baiter and editor of the *Stürmer*, Julius Streicher, into a kibbutz.[7]

---

3. Wolfgang Jacobmeyer, "Jüdische Überlebende als 'Displaced Persons,' " in *Geschichte und Gesellschaft: Zeitschrift für Historische Sozialwissenschaft*, vol. 9 (1983), heft 3, 422; Lynn Rapaport, "The Cultural and Material Reconstruction of the Jewish Communities in the Federal Republic of Germany," *Jewish Social Studies* 49, no. 2 (Spring 1987): 139.

4. Jacobmeyer (op. cit., 421) provides a survey of contemporary estimates, which ranged from 15,600 to 55,000 persons.

5. In the worst of the pogroms in postwar Poland, which occurred in Kielce in July 1946, forty-one Jews were killed. Cf. Bauer, op. cit., 81–82.

6. On illegal Jewish immigration to Palestine, see Yehuda Bauer, *Flight and Rescue: Brichah, the Organized Escape of the Jewish Survivors of Eastern Europe, 1944–1948* (New York, 1970), esp. ch. 2.

7. Schwartz Collection, *YIVO Institute for Jewish Research—Archives* (New York), File 160.

DPs had to obey "camp orders" as decreed by the Allied soldiers who served as officials in the camp administration. Many were not allowed to leave the camps without official permission. A "Report on the Situation of the Jews in Germany," compiled in December 1945 by American officials, emphasized that the Jewish survivors "are still deprived of their freedom. Human rights are systematically denied them. Nobody cares about their individuality or restores their self-respect."[8]

Despite their unfavorable living conditions, the Jewish DPs were quick to initiate educational and cultural activities. They organized schools, theater troupes, orchestras, lectures, chess clubs, and historical commissions. Between 1945 and 1950, they edited around a hundred, usually short-lived, newspapers and journals, most of them in Yiddish.

2

The East European displaced persons were the most numerous and visible group of Jews living in Germany immediately after the war. They were not the only ones, however. At the same time there existed a small group of German Jews who had survived the Nazi terror within Germany itself.

Some fifteen thousand German Jews who had survived in hiding or in concentration camps were liberated in April and May 1945. Most of them had had only very loose contacts with the Jewish communities before 1933, and a high percentage survived only because they had been protected to a certain degree by a non-Jewish spouse or parent. More than two-thirds of the seven thousand members of the Berlin Jewish community of 1946 were intermarried or children of mixed marriages.[9] In some smaller communities all of the members were either married to non-Jews or were Jews only according to Nazi definitions.

The years of persecution, however, had evoked or strengthened the Jewish consciousness of many assimilated German Jews. These people, whose knowledge of Judaism and experience in Jewish organizations were very weak, were now confronted with the difficult task of organizing some kind of Jewish life upon the ruins of formerly flourishing Jewish communities. The most urgent demands were for the physical and psychological care of the survivors, the establishment of contacts with

---

8. "Report on the Situation of the Jews in Germany," n.p., October-December 1945, 17.

9. Jüdische Gemeinde Berlin, appendix 1 to *Arbeitsbericht, 1945–1946.*

American-Jewish help organizations, the search for new community offices, and the restoration of damaged cemeteries.[10]

A considerable number of Jewish communities was officially reestablished as early as 1945. The Jewish community in Cologne resumed its activities before the end of the war, in April 1945. The first document, permission by the British authorities to hold religious services, dates from 11 April. The official reestablishment of the Jewish community and its first elections followed on 29 April.[11] In many other places where German Jews survived the war, the Jewish communities were reestablished shortly after liberation. This was the case in Munich on 19 July,[12] in Hamburg on 18 September,[13] in Mainz on 17 October,[14] and in Bonn on 3 November,[15] to mention only a few examples.

By 1948, more than one hundred Jewish communities had been founded, reaching from Berlin, with its eight thousand members, to Itzehoe, with eight. A total of some twenty thousand German Jews were registered in the newly founded communities in 1948. By that time they had also created a network of supracommunal organizations in the various Länder. In June 1947, these state organizations founded an Arbeitsgemeinschaft jüdischer Gemeinden in Deutschland, out of which grew the Zentralrat der Juden in Deutschland three years later.

---

10. The first president of the reestablished community in Freiburg, Nathan Rosenberger, summarized his first activities after the war as follows: "Meine erste Arbeit begann mit dem Besuch sämtlicher jüdischer Friedhöfe in meinem Bezirk und mit dem Vorstelligwerden bei den zuständigen Bürgermeistern, wo ich energisch die Wiederherstellung der von den Hitlerverbrechern verwüsteten Friedhöfe beantragte. . . . Die nächste wichtige Arbeit war die Zusammenfassung aller in meinem Bezirk lebenden Juden zu einer Gemeinschaft. . . . Meine nächste Aufgabe war nun die Errichtung eines Betraumes und wurden mir von den zuständigen Behörden dazu geeignete Räume zur Verfügung gestellt" (*Jüdisches Gemeindeblatt für die Britische Zone*, 5 February 1947).

11. Cf. Günter Bernd Ginzel, "Phasen der Etablierung einer Jüdischen Gemeinde in der Kölner Trümmerlandschaft, 1945–1949," in Jutta Bohnke-Kollwitz, ed., *Köln und das rheinische Judentum. Festschrift Germania Judaica, 1959–1984*, (Cologne, 1984), 446–48.

12. Juliane Wetzel, "Lebensmut im Wartesaal: Der Wiederaufbau der Israelitischen Kultusgemeinde und des jüdischen Lebens in München, 1945–1949," in Friedrich Prinz, ed., *Trümmerzeit in München. Kultur und Gesellschaft einer deutschen Großstadt im Aufbruch, 1945–1949* (Munich, 1984), 142.

13. Oskar Wolfsberg-Aviad, *Die Drei—Gemeinde: Aus der Geschichte der Jüdischen Gemeinden Altona—Hamburg—Wandsbek* (Munich, 1960), 138.

14. Alfred Epstein, "Nach dem Nationalsozialismus: 1945 bis heute," in Friedrich Schütz, ed., *Juden in Mainz* (Mainz, 1979), 93.

15. Pedro Wagner, "Neubildung der Synagogengemeinde Bonn," in Heinrich Linn, ed., *Juden an Rhein und Sieg* (Siegburg, 1983), 383.

3

We have, thus, the picture of two distinct groups of Jews living in Germany after 1945: a large number of East European displaced persons who came more or less by chance to Germany, many of whom lived in camps and expressed their wish to leave the country as soon as possible; and a small group of German Jews, most of whom had been highly assimilated and connected with their German surroundings because of their non-Jewish spouses or a non-Jewish parent.

The principal question that divided East European and German-Jewish Holocaust survivors in postwar Germany was: to stay or to go? The officially expressed attitudes of the two groups differed substantially. Jewish DP organizations, on the one hand, regarded their stay on cursed German earth as a short interlude before emigration to the Jewish state, which was to be built in Palestine and would need their support. The German-Jewish organizations, on the other hand, expressed their willingness to help in the process of founding a new Germany with democratic structures.

The position of the Jewish displaced persons was not surprising. As the term *displaced* suggests, this group had no roots in Germany. On the contrary, it was Germany and the German people that had caused them years of suffering and, in most cases, the loss of whole families. Unlike most other DPs, however, they could not simply leave Germany and go back to their homelands. The Jewish communities of Eastern Europe had been destroyed and a new outbreak of anti-Semitism and even pogroms had occurred in these countries. Moreover, most of them never viewed themselves as Poles, Russians, or Lithuanians. There were only two destinations open to most of the East European Jews: the United States, the traditional haven for immigrants, and Palestine, which would soon become the state of Israel.

The idea of a Jewish state was highly attractive to those people, even if they had never been Zionists. The immediate experience of the Holocaust and continuing anti-Semitism in Eastern Europe underlined the Zionist premise that Jewish existence was safe only in a Jewish state. Immigration to Palestine was, however, blocked by the British authorities who controlled the region until Israel's declaration of independence in May 1948. The impossibility of legal immigration to Palestine under British rule caused most Jewish displaced persons to persevere in Germany.

The tenure of Jewish life in the DP camps therefore lasted longer than anticipated by most of the East European Jews. As early as 1946, *Undzer Weg*, the official newspaper of the Central Committee of the Liberated Jews in Bavaria, expressed its hope that "the coming year will

be the last year on the cursed German earth."[16] The newspaper announced several times its liquidation, since "the dissolution of the German Diaspora is only a matter of short time."[17] It had to realize, however, that the process of dissolution was a rather complicated one.

Finally, in 1950, just before the newspaper disbanded, it had to
admit that not all of its readers were ready to leave. The Jews who
wanted to stay in Germany were sharply condemned: "Those are people
who one day, too, will understand that they have committed a terrible
mistake, against themselves as well as against their families . . . but it
will be too late—and nobody will be able to help them."[18] In even
clearer terms the newspaper commented: "To stay in Germany when
everything is dissolving and everybody leaves, means practically to be
lost for the Jewish people."[19]

This opinion was shared by most foreign Jewish organizations, which
urged all Jews to leave Germany.[20] Some expressed the even more radical
attitude that Jews remaining in Germany should under no circumstances
be supported since "the complete liquidation of the Jewish community in
Germany by means of emigration is therefore of vital importance to the
entire Jewish people. . . . Those who are tempted by the flesh pots of
Germany must not expect that Israel or the Jewish people should provide
them with services for their convenience in Germany."[21] Sometimes the
German-Jewish emigrants of the 1930s were among the sharpest critics of
any future Jewish existence in Germany. Shalom Adler-Rudel, who was
an active Zionist in Weimar Germany, was quoted as saying: "Let them
stay, where they are. Let them wait in their beloved fatherland, until they
[the Germans] will cut off their throats, too."[22]

By 1950, the vast majority of East European Jews had left Germany, leaving behind only around fifteen thousand Jewish displaced
persons who decided to stay for different reasons. Some were unable or
unwilling to move because of sickness, weakness, economic success, or
marriage to German spouses. In addition to those who never left Germany, a small number of the displaced persons who emigrated to Israel
returned to Germany during the early 1950s, disillusioned with war and
economic problems.

---

16. *Undzer Weg*, 5 September 1946, 3.

17. Ibid., 1 April 1949.

18. Ibid.

19. Ibid., 20 January 1950, 7.

20. See, for example, *Resolutions Adopted by the Second Plenary Assembly of the World Jewish Congress, Montreux, June 27th–July 6th, 1948* (London, 1948).

21. C. Yachil, "The Jews Must Leave Germany," *Jewish Frontier* (May 1951): 20.

22. J. Posner, *In Deutschland, 1945–1946* (Jerusalem, 1947), 115.

The situation among the German-Jewish survivors was different. Born and raised in Germany, deeply rooted in German culture and language, and often married to non-Jews, they always had regarded themselves as Germans. Some survived only because of the help of Germans who provided them with places to hide or supported them in some way or other. Thus, they had not only met the masses of Nazis and hangers-on but also the few who had the courage to resist nazism. It was these elements they wanted to help in building a new, democratic Germany in which a tiny Jewish minority should have its place, too. Some of the survivors even felt the obligation to participate "in the democratic education of the German people."[23] This opinion was expressed by the founder of the German-Jewish newspaper *Der Weg*, Hans Frey: "We German Jews have not only the right, but the obligation, to stay in Germany and to rebuild what was taken from us."[24]

There were also more radical views, which emphasized that the Nazis did not succeed in destroying German connections among the German Jews. One German Jew wrote an angry letter to *Der Weg* protesting the calls for emigration,

> since we believe to be good and true Germans; Germans who obtained their *Bildung* in German schools, who received God's message in German from our rabbis and still hear it [in German], and who are not ashamed to regard Germany as their fatherland and German as their mother tongue. I and people like me stayed in Germany, because we did not want to leave, because no crazy man and no seducer of our German *Heimat* could take from us our Germany.[25]

This statement is certainly not typical of the feelings of most German Jews who tended to express their willingness to stay in rather cautious terms. The demand of American Jewish organizations that all Jews should leave Germany, however, was clearly rejected by most official representatives of German Jews. Some reacted angrily, like the first postwar leader of the German-Jewish communities, Philipp Auerbach.

> What had American Jewry undertaken to prevent what has happened to us and how long did it take until we received the first aid of our brethren from abroad? They may talk easily as outsiders. They

---

23. *Der Weg*, 1 March 1946.
24. *Jüdisches Gemeindeblatt für die britische Zone*, 19 March 1947.
25. *Der Weg*, 5 June 1946, 3.

can forget what we have experienced. . . . You were sitting over there in front of your radios, you heard that six million Jews were killed, wept a tear, said "I am sorry" and switched to the music program. And now we are the poor relatives, with whom one does not want to be seen.[26]

However, there were also German Jews who expressed the impossibility of staying in their "fatherland" after all what had happened. Thus, Erich Nelhaus, a member of the Berlin Jewish community executive board, wrote: "Our community shall be a small *Heimat*, until our great *Heimat* Palestine opens its doors and we may enter the Promised Land."[27] In the same circles one could hear the opinion that "on a cemetery life can not prosper and people cannot live."[28]

The different positions taken by East European and German Jews concerning Germany and the Germans found their reflection in the treatment of intermarriage. The East European Jewish displaced persons who could not imagine a Jewish future in Germany were indignant at the prospect of Holocaust survivors fraternizing with their oppressors and marrying German women. In almost every significant settlement of displaced persons, there were cases of Jews living with or marrying German women, some of whom converted to Judaism. Certainly there was concrete cause for the Regensburg Yiddish newspaper *Undzer Moment* to publish in especially large letters on the title page of its 1947 editions the following message: "The Germans murdered your father, your mother, brother and sister. Eternal shame on those who marry German women! The Jewish public has to expel those who have married German women from the communities."

The question of mixed marriages existed in the German-Jewish communities, too, but with a different emphasis. A large percentage of their members, often the majority, were married to non-Jews. Calls similar to those published in *Undzer Moment* were unheard of in German-Jewish circles. One has to recall that non-Jewish spouses had in most cases enabled the survival of their Jewish partners and had also suffered under Nazi legislation. The problem in the German-Jewish community was not that of excluding Jews who intermarried but of ensuring that the large number of mixed marriages did not halt the future development of the communities. It was therefore demanded that children of mixed

26. *Mitteilungsblatt für die jüdischen Gemeinden der Nordrheinprovinz*, 24 May 1946.

27. *Der Weg*, 1 March 1946, 3.

28. *Allgemeine Jüdische Wochenzeitung*, 19 March 1947.

marriages should be educated as Jews. Many communities passed resolutions stipulating that Jews who were married to non-Jews and let their children grow up as non-Jews were not eligible for community positions.

The central rabbinate of the Jewish displaced persons in the British Zone asked the Jewish communities and committees to compile lists of mixed marriages "in order to obtain a complete genealogical survey." In the same resolution the rabbis drew exact lines to define the members of the Jewish communities: "For us there are no 'half'—or 'quarter'—Jews or so-called Christian Jews." The text goes on to refuse all subsequent conversions to Judaism, concluding with the following harsh words: "A Jew who today marries a non-Jew has no right of membership in any Jewish community or committee."[29]

The reference to conversion needs some further elaboration. Nathan Peter Levinson, a rabbi in Berlin between 1948 and 1953, remembers that one of his main tasks during these years was to deal with the flood of applications for conversion. "Suddenly, it was good to be Jewish, especially in Germany," Levinson commented. In the beginning, most of the "candidates" were former Jews who had converted, non-Jewish spouses of Jews, and their children. But soon there were those who would rather be identified with the victims than with the murderers and those who thought they might gain economic advantage from their conversion. Levinson estimated that only some 5 percent of the "candidates" were accepted by the rabbinate. He recalls that one person who was rejected subsequently tried to circumcise himself.[30]

In Berlin, where seven thousand Jews were living after the war, there were two thousand five hundred applications for conversion by June of 1946. The community had to create a special commission to cope with this phenomenon. The German-Jewish newspaper *Der Weg* scoffed at the high numbers of people looking for Jewish ancestors with the headline: "Black Market in Jewish grandmothers."[31]

Another group of Jews in postwar Germany has to be mentioned. The presence of Jewish returnees in Germany was felt soon after the end of the war. Although numerically this was a very small group in the immediate postwar years, some returnees were to play an important role

---

29. "Resolution des Zentralrabbinats zum 2.Kongreß der "Sherith-Hapletah" in der Britischen Zone Deutschlands: Angenommen am 22, Juli 1947," quoted in Zwi Asaria, *Die Juden in Niedersachsen von den ältesten Zeiten bis zur Gegenwart* (Leer, 1979), 559–60. Zvi Asaria (Helfgott) was the chief rabbi in the British Zone after 1945.

30. Rabbi Nathan Peter Levinson, interview with the author, 27 April 1987. See also Levinson's article on this subject: "Conversion or Camouflage? An Account of Proselytism in Post-War Germany," *Judaism* (Fall 1954): 352–59.

31. *Der Weg*, 22 March 1946.

in German public life—for example, the later mayor of Hamburg, Herbert Weichmann, and the labor leader Ludwig Rosenberg. This group included also persons who took up prominent positions in the development of future Jewish life in Germany such as the editor of the *Allgemeine Jüdische Wochenzeitung*, Karl Marx, and the secretary general of the Zentralrat der Juden in Deutschland, Hendrik van Dam. Returnees like Marx and van Dam initially provided the small Jewish communities with deeply needed leadership.

In many communities, however, the East European Jews who decided to settle in Germany took over positions of spiritual and political leadership. This was the case predominantly in southern German communities where East European Jews outnumbered the German Jews. They founded their own communities in towns and regions to which no or very few German Jews had returned. Their leadership in these communities was undisputed. This was not the case in the larger communities, especially in the north.[32]

Many German Jews, especially in the south, feared that they would be outnumbered by their East European brothers and therefore lose control over the communities. It must be recalled that conceptions of what a Jewish community should be and how religious life should be organized differed substantially between assimilated German Jews and East European Jews who had grown up in a traditional, often Hasidic, environment. The German Jews expressed their concern over what they called "southern German problems": "There exists the danger with respect to the small number of German Jews who returned from the concentration camps, that they will become a minority and thus the continuation of the tradition of the communities will be questioned. This development results in certain tensions which do not exist in other areas."[33]

The formerly much despised "Jargon," the Yiddish language of the East European Jew, now became the primary language in many Jewish communities. The German Jews still had no intention of identifying with a culture expressed in a language that many of them considered to be

---

32. One has to recognize the importance of the regional factor in the composition of the Jewish community. While the Eastern European Jews constituted 94 percent of the Jewish population in Bavaria in 1949, they were a minority of 14 percent in the northwestern regions of Germany (Maor, op. cit., 19). This uneven distribution explains the fact that the German-Jewish newspaper was edited in Düsseldorf, while several Yiddish newspapers were printed in Munich. It also accounts for the centrality of the Rhine region for the formation of the major German-Jewish organizations, while most of the Bavarian Jewish communities grew out of DP committees and preserved the structure of the immediate postwar organizations.

33. Hans Fabian, quoted in *Der Weg*, 26 July 1946.

"bad German." One witness recalls, "Again and again, the majority of those who were born in the country in some way or another found the East European Jews unacceptable socially and rejected their religious customs, and sometimes gave as a reason for their lack of participation in communal life their aversion to having anything to do with the East European Jews."[34]

Another potential for tensions between the two groups was the participation of some East European Jews in the black market, especially in Munich, where it centered around the Möhlstrasse, home to many Jewish refugees. In the minds of the German public the black market was generally identified with East European Jewish activities, while the involvement of non-Jewish Germans was often overlooked. It is interesting to note that some German Jews uncritically adopted this identification, while others were afraid to be identified with the activities of those Jews, a fear expressed in the following opinion: "If there is a God, why, after making us suffer so terribly much in the past, has he punished us with the Möhlstrasse, which is a disgrace to us before the world and which must make every decent Jew blush with shame?"[35]

The German-Jewish lawyer Alfred Mayer expressed a common opinion within the German-Jewish communities when he criticized Jewish black market activities and favored the quick dissolution of the East European Jewish population in Germany, which "is connected with this country neither by link of affection nor by obligation of loyalty [durch keine Bande der Zuneigung, durch keine Pflicht der Loyalität]." He juxtaposed their situation with the position of the German Jews: "It is here where we belong. Here we have a right of *Heimat* and here we have to prove that the men and women of National Socialism were wrong when they wanted to deprive us of equal rights. Yes, we few, only a hand full, may have to fulfill a mission [haben eine Sendung zu erfuellen]."[36]

On the other hand, many East European Jews, consciously or subconsciously, identified the language of the German Jews with the language spoken by their tormentors. Moreover, some of them openly expressed contempt for the tradition of assimilation among German Jews. This accusation had a twofold content. First, it implied that the German Jews were not "real Jews," but had abandoned the cultural traditions of Judaism. Second, it also implied that German Jews had

---

34. Quoted in Karen Gershon, *Postscript: A Collective Account of the Lives of Jews in West Germany Since the Second World War* (London, 1969), 81.

35. Ibid., 76.

36. Knud C. Knudsen, ed., *Welt ohne Hass: Aufsätze und Ansprachen zum 1. Kongress über bessere menschliche Beziehungen in München* (Berlin, Hamburg, and Stuttgart: n.d.), 158, 161.

been blinded to the threat of anti-Semitism by their continuous attempts to identify with German culture.

The tensions between the two groups found concrete expression in the deprivation of certain rights for non-German citizens in some Jewish communities. This constituted the revival of an inglorious tradition of the Weimar period when especially those Jewish communities that consisted mostly of Ostjuden did not grant them equal voting rights. The same demand was now made public in various communities reestablished immediately after the war by German Jews, whose membership by the end of the 1940s, however, consisted mainly of displaced persons who had settled in Germany. The community in Munich, for example, tried to restrict suffrage to those who "already belonged to a Jewish community in Germany in 1938."[37]

In Augsburg, the community of thirty-two German Jews refused until the mid-1950s not only to grant the sixty East European Jews suffrage but even to accept them as community members. The most that German Jews in Augsburg were willing to accept during the long conflict was the presence of two non-German members on the executive board of nine and suffrage for half(!). Finally, the German Jews, under pressure from outside authorities, had to give in and grant equal rights to all Jews living in Augsburg.[38]

A last aspect to be mentioned is the unequal distribution of care packages in the early postwar period. While the Jewish displaced persons received immediate help from international and American Jewish organizations, the German Jews in their newly founded communities were often forgotten. This can be partly explained by the policy of the Allied authorities, especially in the British Zone of Germany. Until the promulgation of "Zone Policy Instruction No. 20" in February 1946, the British authorities regarded the German Jews as Germans and treated them accordingly. The victims received the same food supplies as their former persecutors. It should also be mentioned in this connection that the British authorities prevented the British rabbi Moses Cohen from going to Berlin to serve the local Jewish community since British citizens were not allowed to give any support to Germans![39] British policy toward Jews in Germany was dominated by its possible repercussions on

37. Wetzel, op. cit., 143. In Stuttgart, non-German members of the community could obtain suffrage only after they had lived there for three years (Maor, op. cit., 19).

38. Letters of *Aktionskomitee zur Vorbereitung demokratischer Wahlen in der Israelitischen Kultusgemeinde Augsburg*, January 1954, Archives of the Leo Baeck Institute, New York, AR 5890/3.

39. Ursula Büttner, *Not nach der Befreiung: Die Situation der deutschen Juden in der britischen Besatzungszone 1945 bis 1948* (Hamburg, 1986), 16–17.

the situation in Palestine. Since the British did not recognize the existence of a Jewish people, they insisted on the strict separation of Eastern European and German Jews based on their different nationalities.

As mentioned above, international Jewish organizations, too, were cautious in their support of German Jews who planned to stay in the country of persecution. Philipp Auerbach, the spokesman for the German Jews, did not spare words in expressing his disappointment over the lack of help from international Jewish organizations. In his appeal to the Jewish world, Auerbach complained of the fact that German Jews received the same food supplies as non-Jewish Germans: "For 12 years we lived as Jews and today we suffer as Germans."[40]

Various attempts to unite the organizations of German Jews in Hanover and Jewish displaced persons in Bergen-Belsen under one roof in the British Zone, and thereby guarantee sufficient food supplies for the German-Jewish survivors, failed. Often the German Jews themselves did not welcome a common representation, being afraid that it would be dominated by the large number of Eastern European Jews. One of the main protagonists of the unification of both groups, the chief rabbi of the British Zone, Zvi Asaria (Helfgott), finally had to give up his efforts: "My appeal that we all suffered together and that the enemy did not know a difference between Eastern and German Jews . . . fell on infertile soil in Hanover. . . . The newly founded Jewish community of Hanover continued thereby an old tradition."[41]

4

I have dealt here with one chapter of the centuries-long encounter between German and Eastern European Jews on German soil.[42] The ambivalent relationship, as expressed by Steven Aschheim in the terms of "brothers" and "strangers" in pre-Nazi Germany, seems to be even more pronounced in the period following 1945.[43] As brothers the Jews were bound together by years of common suffering under Nazi terror. But, instead of eliminating the traditional tensions between the two groups,

---

40. Asaria, op. cit., 585.

41. Ibid. The Hanover Jewish community was one of the very few that refused to accept non-German citizens as members before World War II.

42. It should be remarked that it was not the last encounter of this kind. The emigration of Russian Jews in the 1970s created the basis for a new encounter between East European and German Jews in Germany. Today an even larger wave of Soviet Jewish emigration is having an impact on Germany and the German-Jewish community.

43. Steven E. Aschheim, *Brothers and Strangers: The East European Jew in German and German-Jewish Consciousness, 1800–1923* (Madison, 1982).

this common experience only served to focus them more clearly. In the aftermath of the Holocaust any assimilationist tendency exhibited by German Jews was condemned by the Eastern European Jews, while the German Jews continued to defend the German character of their communities against the Ostjuden. Such traditional stereotypes as contempt for the Yiddish language and traditional measures, and the deprivation of suffrage, continued after 1945.

Contemporary historiography is wont to declare the time between 1942 and 1948, which saw the greatest catastrophe of the Jewish people as well as the rebirth of a Jewish state, to be a Stunde Null, a total break in Jewish history. To be sure, these two events changed the Jewish world in an unprecedented manner. Still, one ought to be aware of the continuities beyond this decisive incision. The thesis that the Holocaust eliminated previous differences among Jews belongs to the realm of myth. In the case of Ostjuden and German Jews in postwar Germany we see the emergence of new conflicts, as well as the continuity of traditional ones, between the two groups.[44]

---

44. On the problem of continuity and discontinuity in Jewish self-consciousness and German attitudes toward the Jews in post-Holocaust Germany, see my article "Wider den Mythos der 'Stunde Null'—Kontinuitäten im innerjüdischen Bewußtsein und deutsch-jüdischen Verhältnis nach 1945," *Menora* 3 (1992): 155–81.

The Identity and Ideology of Jewish Displaced Persons

Cilly Kugelmann

Approximately 30,000 Jews are organized today in the Jewish communities of Germany. With the exception of a small number of Oriental Jews
who have arrived in the last twenty years from Israel and other countries
of Eastern Europe, the Jewish population of the Federal Republic consists of survivors of the Holocaust and their children. The Jewish community, organized in so-called Einheitsgemeinden (unitary communities), is
at pains to present a homogenous image of itself to the non-Jewish
public, an image that also reflects the group self-definition of its members as a community of common fate. Within this form of collective self-
representation as unitary community there nevertheless exist both conflict and distrust, and its members live to a large extent isolated from one
another. The groups and individuals that make up the Jewish community
interpret their Jewishness in completely different ways, both in terms of
their personal and familial situations and in terms of the role of Jews as a
group in Germany. Not only the geographical background of the community members and the degree of Jewish acculturation and other cultural
factors but also the individual experience of persecution and survival
under national socialism are significant for these self-interpretations.
From the time of the reestablishment of Jewish communities in Germany after 1945, the specific experiences of members have played a
dominating role in conflicts involving Jewish self-interpretation and orientation. Such conflicts were often barely contained by the felt necessity
to present a unified and harmonious image to the outside world. The
need to draw a border between the community and its affairs and the
environment has often displayed paranoic traits and is similar to the
group "politics" of families that disallow and even punish revelation of
intimate family matters to outsiders.

Such exclusionary politics can be observed, of course, in Jewish communities in other countries as well, but there they tend to be less acute than in Germany. In Germany the border drawn between "insiders" and "outsiders" depends not only on the distinction between Jewish and Christian culture, or of what might be termed "naive" anti-Semitism experienced by individuals in their daily lives, but rather, of course, on the collective experience of genocidal anti-Semitism: and both personal as well as structural continuities of this experience exist to this day.

The survivors of the Holocaust now living in the United States feel the need to solicit attention to and recognition of their specific experience; this extends even to their children, as shown by the establishment of the organization Children of Holocaust Survivors. In Germany this need, however legitimate, represents but one aspect of Jewish life in the United States. The situation is different. Jews in Germany are defined and define themselves exclusively with respect to their status as victims. To live as a Jew in Germany means, on the one hand, to represent all Jews murdered by the Nazis; this is a burden. On the other hand, it is precisely this status and this burden that provide legitimation, to whatever degree conscious or subconscious, for living in the country at all. The early definition of the survivors' identification of the DPs as "the last remnants [who] regard as their main task symbolizing the Jewish national tragedy . . ." became the paradigmatic self-definition of German Jewry (Samuel Gringauz, "Jewish Destiny as the DPs See It," *Commentary* [1947]).

To exist as a Jew after the Holocaust left little room for self-determination of one's Jewish identity. The threat to destroy all Jews meant just that: all Jews, irrespective of individual self-definition and of the facets of collective self-definition that existed beforehand, were to be destroyed. It included religious Jews and assimilated and Christianized ones, atheists and Communists, and it meant even German nationalists, as long as they were of Jewish ancestry. In the aftermath of genocidal anti-Semitism, it became extremely difficult to resist a corresponding ethnic collectivization: whether or not one had experienced a Jewish-religious socialization, whether or not one had profound knowledge of Jewish tradition, even whether or not one had a particular attachment to the culture and religion, it became imperative to document one's Jewishness, if for no other reason than to compensate for wounds inflicted upon one's self-respect. To be sure, assimilative tendencies within Judaism, even in Germany, were not eradicated by the Holocaust, but they were, especially in Germany, placed under ideological edict. In the aftermath of the Holocaust, only a unitary and normative Judaism seemed possible, and Zionism, quite apart from political and nationalistic factors, played the most prominent role in the suppression of individual and personal definitions of Jewishness. Ben-Gurion's pragmatic comment on the situation of European Jewry in 1944 was to become the general conviction of the survivors: "At all events, we will not revive the dead. But there is life. There are still Jews living in Eretz Israel" (Tuvia Friling, "Changing Roles: The Relationship Between Ben-Gurion, the Yishuv and She'erit Hapletah, 1942–1945," in *She'erit Hapletah, 1944–1948: Rehabilitation and Political Struggle* [Sixth Yad Vashem International Historical Conference, Jerusalem, 1990], 464).

After the Holocaust, Jews in Germany feel forced to accept and represent the Jewish heritage. What had only recently been a death sentence now became something that under no circumstances could be denied—or only at the cost of the loss of newly regained self-respect. As an early example of this attitude I want to quote a member of the Cologne Jewish community who argued for excluding Jews living in mixed marriages from the communities: "These egoists would go as far as to have their children baptized. They are traitors to Judaism. . . . The community councils should be obliged to exclude those Jews from being members of the congregation, because they are Jewish traitors. Who undermines Judaism today is not worthy of being a member of a Jewish congregation" (Moritz Goldschmidt, *Die Gemeinde Köln* [Jüdisches Gemeindeblatt, Düsseldorf, 1946], quoted in Harry Maor, "Über den Wiederaufbau der Jüdischen Gemeinden in Deutschland seit 1945" [dissertation], Mainz, 1961). The Swiss psychoanalyst Paul Parin (Paul Parin, "Die Homosexuellen und die Juden," *Psyche* [1986]) has spoken in this regard of the "over-emphasis of the Jewish habitus," which, according to Parin, acts as a kind of filler to cover the loss of Jewish substance. Moreover, the spectrum of Jewish self-definition that had existed before the Holocaust between the poles of the "non-Jewish Jew" and religious orthodoxy, had become intolerable for many victims of the Holocaust. Society, and especially German society, had come to expect of Jews that they be recognizable as Jews, that is, as victims of eternal anti-Semitism. A flood of publications on Jewish communities between 1933 and 1945 has been published in West and East Germany, mostly by nonprofessional, barefoot historians. As Monika Richarz, the head of Germania Judaica, has pointed out, more than 2,000 single studies have been collected since 1965 (*Babylon* 8 [1991]). Next to the archival material of cities and villages and information gathered from Jewish cemeteries, the primary source of information is survivors of the Holocaust. Schools and institutions for adult education started about ten years ago to depend on "time-witnesses" when teaching the Holocaust. So one might say that there is an increasingly strong interest in Jews—as far as they perform their roles as former victims.

Jews in Germany have been—and still are—denied recognition by international Jewish organizations. Before the negotiations regarding the reparations measures of the Federal Republic, and even afterward, the newly founded Jewish communities in Germany had their raison d' être put into question: the establishment of new centers of Jewish culture in Israel and the United States were now being seen as a triumph over the destruction of European Jewry and as the places of a renaissance of Judaism in general.

Numerous instances document the ostracism of postwar German Jewry. I wish to cite only one: an extraordinary session of the World Jewish Congress in Brussels in 1966 was to discuss the theme "Jews in Germany." This topic was rejected as out of the question by all representatives of the participating Israeli political parties. Members of Cherut told the Jews of Germany "to be ashamed to have helped the Germans to rehabilitate and to find a place in the family of man"; Mapam made it plain that all Israeli partisans' and veterans' groups were against any form of German-Jewish dialogue, and even the representatives of Oriental Jewry expressed regret at the choice of the theme. The rejection of the existence of Jewish communities in Germany could not, of course, fail to make its mark, as Jews in Israel had become the only emotional and intellectual focus for Jewish identity.

Liberation as Continuation of the War against the Jews

Since the situation of the Jews in Germany is deeply influenced by the turbulent conditions of the immediate postwar period, I will focus in the following on the displaced persons phenomenon. It was not immediately apparent to observers that the experience of persecution and genocide would have long-term psychological consequences for the victims. In fact, social scientists and psychoanalysts only began to recognize the long-term consequences of the Holocaust experience in the middle of the 1960s in the context of difficulties encountered in the application of the compensation measures undertaken by the Federal Republic. The law under which victims of Nazi crimes were to be compensated required proof of injury to health in the form of the diagnosis of current symptoms and the linkage of such symptoms to traumatizing persecution during the Nazi period. It was in this context that observers came to recognize the existence of long-term traumatization syndromes. A. Wilson and E. Fromm, for example, came to the conclusion that all heretofore applied interpretation schemes were inadequate for the analysis of the later experience of victims of the Holocaust. They came to understand the concentration camp experience in terms of immersion in a "foreign culture," in which all assumptions concerning the behavior of other human beings under civilized conditions had to be suspended, and they recognized this experience as the cause of deep-seated and lasting traumatization. The truth, however is that no one, immediately after the war or decades later, has adequately dealt with the experience of the survivors of the concentration camps.

While it is true that observers and participants found that camp survivors had greater difficulty adjusting to postwar conditions, no one seriously doubted that it was only a matter of time before the survivors would once again feel at home in the world. Often the survivors were not given much time to readjust, and their problematic and often asocial behavior was only barely tolerated for a given period. Members of Jewish and Allied assistance organizations observed with a degree of abhorrence that camp survivors "concerned themselves with the past to an extent that borders on morbidity," had little interest in anything else, and displayed "little or no social responsibility." It seems that the audiences subjected to reports about events and conditions in the camps found even these reports threatening and feared being thrown into moral chaos.

The denial of the psychic reality of the death camps through active amnesia and impatient interpretation of the social deficiencies of the survivors fulfilled a collective and ideological need on the part of those who had not experienced the camps directly. The image of human beings being taken to their death like lambs being led to slaughter, and connected with this the idea that cowardice and not courage had prevailed— these were hardly images conducive to the reconstruction of a collective identity. The political trauma, moreover, implied that the collectivity had failed to defend itself and its members and had failed to react adequately to the "Final Solution." This trauma resulted in extreme ambivalence toward the survivors and their suffering, and attempts to establish a collective interpretation of events did not focus on the surviving victims of the Holocaust but on the Jewish partisans instead. The fact is that for the vast majority of victims resistance to their destruction was not possible. The victims were also "victims of their belief in Mankind," of the belief that civilization itself places limits on the degree and form of persecution and degradation that human beings can inflict upon one another (T. Des Pres, *The Survivor: An Anatomy of Life in the Death Camps* [New York, Oxford University Press, 1976]). Or, as Jean Amery described this phenomenon in his book *Jenseits von Schuld und Sühne* (Munich, Szczesny, 1966), as a total collapse of confidence that made it impossible "to feel at home in the world" again.

In the course of the first months of 1945, when Allied troops liberated the camps on their way to Berlin, a terrible truth came to light that up until then no one had been willing to accept, despite numerous reports from escaped prisoners. What had been represented as propaganda and exaggeration revealed itself in its full horror to the troops of the Soviet, British, and American armies as they entered the camps at Auschwitz, Dachau, and Bergen-Belsen. Uncounted bodies were piled up in heaps: starving, filthy, living skeletons capable only of crawling, whose empty eyes failed to reveal whether they even comprehended the fact of their liberation. The victims were "physical and mental wrecks. With swollen feet, gloomy eyes, no teeth and dry hair they present[ed] a gloomy picture" (*Congress Weekly*, 29 June 1945, quoted in Leonard Dinnerstein, *America and the Survivors of the Holocaust* [New York, Columbia University Press, 1982], 28). According to Bill Lawry, a member of the propaganda unit of the British army and the cameraman of the film *Memory of the Camps* (produced by the Propaganda Unit of the British army during the liberation of the concentration camps in 1945),

> They looked at you and didn't notice anything. They didn't smile, they didn't cry. They didn't do anything at all. Their expression was motionless, their eyes had a glassy stare and I didn't know whether they saw me or not. Nobody shouted with joy: we are free.

At the end of hostilities there were between seven and ten million DPs in Europe. A part had been driven from their homes, others had performed forced labor, many were prisoners of war. Among the group designated by the Allies as DPs in the spring of 1945 were almost fifty thousand Jews who had survived the death camps. Twenty thousand died within weeks, apparently having had the strength to survive until, but not after, their liberation. Their physical constitutions were so weakened that it was too late for any kind of intervention. A survivor of Bergen-Belsen commented: "They ate and died, they died because they ate" (from the film *A Painful Reminder*, a documentary on the shooting-and-release politics of the film *Memory of the Camps* [BBC, 1988]).

Millions of DPs created a huge administrative problem for the Allies. First the Allied armies, and later the United Nations Relief and Rehabilitation Administration (UNRRA), were made responsible for relief and administration of the DPs. Between May and September of 1945, 6 million DPs were repatriated, while another 1.5 million, many of them Hungarians, Serbs, Croats, and Ukrainians, refused repatriation because they feared being prosecuted as collaborators by the Soviet occupation armies. A large number of Jews from Eastern Europe refused repatriation; they did not want to return to destroyed communities in a traditional anti-Semitic environment. There were more than 1 million DPs in nine hundred UNRRA camps at the end of 1945.

Despite the shocking conditions of the death camps, the Allied organizations had little understanding of the situation of the surviving Jews. Incomprehension about the consequences of the death camps for the survivors, a naive analysis of the character of Nazi anti-Semitism, and a measure of home-grown anti-Semitism together made possible statements such as "Military government action should stress treatment of Jews equal to that of other citizens of the Reich" in order not to create the impression that the USA "will tend to perpetuate the distinction of Nazi racial theory" (Civilian Department of the U.S. Army, SHAEF Document, 1 May 1944, quoted in Dinnerstein, *America and the Survivors*, 32).

A political situation arose that could only lead survivors of the Holocaust to the conclusion that their persecution was not necessarily at an end. German-Jewish survivors, along with Jews of Hungary, Rumania, and Austria, were reckoned as part of the populations of the Fascist alliance and treated just like other nationals of these states. Jews, on the other hand, who were citizens of the nations of the Allied alliance were given special privileges. Survivors not fortunate enough to enjoy such privileges were housed together with Axis prisoners of war, SS death camp guards, and Nazi collaborators. Moreover, German administrative personnel were often used in the DP camps, leading to the diversion of vast amounts of relief material intended for the camp inhabitants.

The catastrophic condition of the former death camp prisoners activated latent anti-Semitism within the occupying Allied forces. In a diary entry of 15 September 1945, General George Patton went so far as to deny that the DPs belonged any longer to the human race: "and this applies" he wrote "particularly to the Jews who are lower than animals." Earl Harrison, a special representative of President Truman, prepared a shocked report in which he compared the American treatment of death camp survivors with that which they had experienced in the death camps. He concluded: "As matters now stand we appear to be treating the Jews as the Nazis treated them except that we don't exterminate them." The Harrison report, as well as other protests, finally led to the separation of nationalities into different camps; one of the demands of the Harrison report, the recognition of Jewish nationality status, was thus fulfilled, at least in the U.S. zone. This reconstruction of the DP camps was instrumental in bringing about a new Jewish social life and especially facilitated the development of Jewish organizations in the camps.

This "new beginning" occurred at several levels. In the first weeks and months after capitulation, a combination of victor's pride, desire for revenge, and pedagogical objectives led the Allies to conclude that the Germans must be confronted with the crimes committed in their name and with their participation. The civilian population around some of the concentration camps was, for example, forced to visit the camps. This phase, however, passed very quickly, and the shock about conditions in the death camps was soon forgotten. Lists of Nazi opponents that had been prepared by German exiles working for the Allied intelligence services were soon routinely ignored, apparently on the theory that whoever had been renitent under the Nazis would presumably also be renitent under any regime that was to follow. Soon one came to rely on the same administrative apparatus that had functioned so well under the Nazis; the reconstruction (Wiederaufbau) of Germany along with the integration of the three western zones into the Atlantic bloc was given first priority.

The original intention was to dissolve the DP camps as early as 1946. In this respect, General Lucius D. Clay was merely following the directive to give first priority to the economic and political reconstruction of Germany, and the U.S. Army apparently believed that it had fulfilled its responsibility to the DPs after one and a half years of relief effort. The position of the occupying forces was that whoever resisted repatriation should be integrated socially and economically into German life as soon as possible. This policy, which also applied to the Jewish DPs, drove the latter even further into isolation. Indigenous Jewish DP organizations were in constant conflict with the Allied and UN administrations. Almost daily, demonstrations occurred in the camps demanding free emigration to Palestine—until 1948 still a British mandate. Moreover, black-market raids and conflicts with the German police necessitated the presence of military police within the camps. Many camp inhabitants rejected offers to emigrate to countries other than Palestine and demanded continued operation of the camps until mass organization there could be undertaken.

The UNRRA personnel, mostly Americans, had very little understanding of the mental constitution of the Holocaust survivors; indeed, even the representatives of Jewish organizations capitulated before the phenomenon. What the Allied troops, and later the relief organizations, observed during the liberation of the camps was only the surface of a problem whose duration and depth could not be imagined at the time. Only the survivors themselves appear to have had an intuition of the degree to which the death camp experience would separate them from others. A Dutch survivor of Auschwitz reported, for example, that "It stank of death and excrement. They [the soldiers] said now we've seen everything. I said you haven't seen anything."

UNRRA soldiers were irritated and appalled by the behavior of the survivors in the DP camps. The soldiers had the greatest difficulty in their attempts "to understand and like people who pushed, screamed, clawed for food, smelled bad, who couldn't and didn't want to obey orders, who sat with dull faces and vacant staring eyes in a cellar, or concentration camp barrack, or within a primitive cave, and refused to come out at their command." Psychiatrists defined the comportment of the survivors as asocial and an American observer at the Landsberg Camp made the following assessment in September of 1945: "I would say 90% of the camp inmates are neurotics. *How* they speak, *how* they roll their eyes, *how* they wallow in their sufferings, *how* they repeat and repeat their stories" (quoted in Dinnerstein, *America and the Survivors*, 64).

Negative assessments of the disturbing symptoms shown by the Holocaust survivors were made not only by UNRRA relief personnel but also by Jewish observers. Doubts were expressed concerning the circumstances under which individuals had been able to survive and whether they had been collaborators. Cynical comments were made as to the character of the "Scherit Hapleita," and the survival of individuals was seen as a kind of negative selection: "selection by the SS . . . bribery of the SS . . . accommodation [and] extremely egoistical attitudes . . . regarding the fate of others" (Samuel Gringauz, "Über die Aufgaben der europäischen Judenreste," *Jüdische Rundschau* 6 [1946]). Their embarrassment, earlier denial of the victims' situation, their shame about not having acted decisively to save as many people as possible—these things made it impossible for Jewish observers to empathize with or understand the mental situation of the survivors who for years were subjected to inescapable humiliation and brutality. In this context, the fact that the process of readjustment occurred only very slowly, or not al all, was registered with unease. Many of the survivors refused to accept work, especially if their work would benefit Germans. Many showed no interest in values such as order and cleanliness, and many refused to take part in official distribution schemes that had no illicit, "illegal" character. The functionaries of the Jewish organizations were as little able to comprehend the extent of inner devastation experienced by the survivors as were their UNRRA coworkers.

To go through hell and to then reemerge in a world in which nothing remained of one's previous life is an experience almost as devastating as the confrontation with the death camp itself. It is quite imaginable that the hope of being able to return to an intact existence after the camp was the only thing that kept the survivors from suicide or loss of self—the hope of returning to one's loved ones, the hope of returning to places of birth and existence, the hope, finally, of resuming the life from which one had been torn. The recognition that one's loved ones no longer existed and that there was no longer a place or a life to return to was an existence-threatening disappointment that made the thought of life after the Holocaust a torture for many survivors. The new experience of normality turned into the nightmare of the permanent outsider. Hugo Gryn, an Hungarian Jew who came to Auschwitz as a thirteen-year-old and survived in one of the forced labor camps on the perimeter, described the devastation of recognizing that he alone had survived.

> I think one of the most painful moments I experienced was in a camp in Silesia, called Groß-Rosen when we got permission to write a postcard. It was a Sunday afternoon when everybody received a postcard and something to write. You could have written where ever you wanted to. It was phantastic, I would be able to write. But then I realized that there was nobody I could write to.

The dilemma of the Jewish DPs had to do with the ambivalence of the very fact of their survival—an ambivalence regarding one's self and regarding the contradictory attitudes of one's social environment. Because they had survived, the Jewish DPs had become witnesses to the existence of previously unknown and unimaginable death machinery, and it was their historical responsibility to bear witness. For the world at large, they were a reminder of a morally decrepit civilization, and for the Jews they were the survivors of a national catastrophe. They called themselves Sherit Hapleita ("The rest of the saved") and thereby placed themselves in a historical context in which the survivors of catastrophe represent the new beginning of Jewish national history. The words *Sherit Hapleita* refer to a vision of the prophets Esra and Nehemia in which the Jews of the Babylonian exile are reunited with the "rest of the saved"—those who had escaped subjugation in Israel. Both aspects of this vision were projected onto and assumed by the Jewish displaced persons, at once as exiled prisoners and as the saved in the face of a terrifying judgment. For the very reason that they had survived Nazi genocide, they were seen as carriers of hope from whose ranks would emerge generations embodying a new Jewish consciousness. They were given the function of representing destroyed European Jewish culture in a Jewish state that was still to be established. And *Sherit Hapleita* was closely associated also with the Zionist conviction that Jews living outside of Israel could expect the worst: "O Lord God of Israel, thou art righteous; for we remain the saved remnants, as it is this day: behold, we are before thee in our trespasses: for we cannot stand before thee because of this" (Esra 9:13–14).

However painful the loss of parents, children, and relatives had been for the survivors, the fact of genocide and the inability to prevent it made the loss appear even more senseless. It was perhaps for this reason that the countless "historical commissions" that arose in the DP camps concerned themselves more with the fate of the partisans and ghetto martyrs than with the fate of the millions who had gone to their death in the gas chambers. The resistance was idealized and given a new interpretation: it was seen as being a part of the struggle for a Jewish state. Samuel Gringauz, an East Prussian economist and social scientist, himself a camp survivor, concerned himself with the ideology of the survivors. In the *Jiddische Caitung* of the Landsberg DP camp—edited by Gringauz—and in the *Jüdische Rundschau*, the only DP journal published in German, Gringauz dealt with the collective role of the Holocaust survivors. Because Nazi anti-Semitism knew no other category for Jews than to sentence them to death, the few who had survived should, according to Gringauz, assume responsibility for demonstrating to Jews everywhere that they are one people. He writes that "the Sherit Ha-Pleita must demonstrate to all Jews everywhere their involvement in the common fate" ("Jewish Destiny," 81). The Nazi persecution had finally turned its victims into Jews, and it was the function of the survivors to carry this message, thereby relieving some of the pain at not having been able to prevent the Holocaust: "Nothing must permit Hitler a final triumph by destruction of the Jews through the circumstances of the postwar world or through inner disintegration" (Gringauz, "Jewish Destiny," 81).

Zionism received a new emotional dimension with this formula, one that persists and has remained paradigmatic up to the present. Suddenly it was no longer the kibbutzim and the propagators of a new social order who determined the face of Israel; rather it was the survivors of the Holocaust who provided the "critical mass" with which the state of Israel was finally founded and for whom Israel was meant to provide not only a place but also meaning in life: "This is the basic foundation of the Zionism of the survivors. It is no party Zionism, it is a historical-philosophical Zionism felt as an historical mission, as a debt to the dead, as retribution toward the enemy, as a duty to the living" (Gringauz, "Jewish Destiny," 75). Whatever meaning was given to survival and the painful memories it may have suppressed, irrespective also of the political achievements that could be associated with it, survival as a category meant to create collective meaning could not eradicate all the feelings of inner distress, extreme agitation, angst, and depression experienced by the survivors.

The individual survivors doubted whether they would ever be able to find a place in the "normality" that was offered to them. They doubted whether they would be able to make themselves understood and doubted whether their surroundings, their Jewish as well as their non-Jewish surroundings, had any interest in that which they had experienced. In fact, they often went into some sort of coalition with exactly those who were not willing to listen and who were actively engaged in the denial of the past. In the words of a survivor of Buchenwald, "I survived a concentration camp but I regularly made the observation that people did not really want to talk about my experiences, and whenever I started they invariably showed their resistance by interrupting me, by asking me to tell them how I got out" (quoted in Martin S. Bergmann, and Milton E. Jucovy, eds., *Generations of the Holocaust* [New York, Columbia University Press, 1990], 6).

The survivors of the Holocaust played an important symbolic role; they had a collective function that brought about a revision of Jewish history and, among other things, gave Zionism new legitimation. Having arrived in their new home, Israel, they were expected to forget the devastating experiences that had led them there. Aharon Appelfeld, an Israeli writer and Holocaust survivor who came to Palestine after the liberation of the camps, writes in the context of wanting and needing to forget.

> After liberation the one desire was to sleep, to forget and to be reborn. At first there was a wish to talk incessantly about one's experiences, this gave way to silence, but learning to be silent was not easy. When the past was no longer talked about, it became unreal, a figment of one's imagination. The new Israeli identity, sun-burned, practical, and strong, was grafted upon the old identity of the helpless victim. Only in nightmares was the past alive, but then even dreaming ceased. (Bergmann, *Generations*, 5)

German-Jewish Relations
in the Postwar Period:
The Ambiguities of Antisemitic
and Philosemitic Discourse

Frank Stern

In a short story entitled "The Survivor," by Stefan Heym, a young German recalls why he did not resist and thus was able to survive. The following beginning of his self-righteous monologue can serve as a kind of motto for the social and spiritual dispositions with which this chapter intends to deal.

> If it's something you've never experienced yourself, you'll never understand it. It's as if you were from another era, or had come floating down to us from another planet. Your world of experience is different from ours, your reactions have no connection with ours. Which is why your questions are not to the point. And why our answers remain for you incomprehensible. Your behavior reminds me of that idiotic American lieutenant back then, 1945, the guy who saw me limping along the highway and asked me to get into his jeep. And then began to ask questions. 'Why did you Germans do all that—I mean, didn't you people know?' Naturally we did. All of us. Even the ones who pretended to their wives and kids—and to themselves—that they didn't know. There are things that a person simply knows. This was one of them. It split the consciousness of people apart and gave their immortal soul a false double-bottom. Like in a smuggler's suitcase. You remember how after the war everyone told you he'd always been against the brutality. And

Translated by William Templer.

against what they'd done to the Jews. And against attacking so many countries.[1]

The ambivalence in German postwar thinking, in collective consciousness, and in relevant patterns of attitude and behavior that is given vivid expression in the above passage is nowhere clearer and more pronounced than in respect to Jewish survivors in 1945 and Jewish topics in postwar political culture. In treating the complex interrelations between Germans and Jews after 1945, it is necessary to investigate problems of German political culture, its intellectual atmosphere, and relevant attitudes in a watershed period when the old had not as yet been fully transcended while the new was still in the process of crystallization.[2] The legacy of the Third Reich, the policies of the occupation authorities, and the reactions both of the Germans and of the Jews living at that time in Germany produced a multilayered metamorphosis of antisemitism and contributed to the emergence of a significant new phenomenon in German-Jewish relations: philosemitism.[3] This phenomenon, as it developed after 1945, is not identical with the Christian philosemitism of the seventeenth and eighteenth centuries, although it bears some resemblance.[4] It is, first, the notion that in any dealings with Allied institutions and officials Germans should show an emphatically and demonstrative pro-Jewish attitude; second, a position that developed gradually and—while turning away from, and rejecting, traditional antisemitic stereotypes—elevated the absolutized opposite of such stereotypes into the object of public activities and publications; third, a political instrumentalization of pro-Jewish attitudes and norms with the development of West Germany along the path toward sovereignty, in particular concerning Germany's foreign policy and international image. It has to be stressed, though, that the images and stereotypes of philosemitism are related to the impact of antisemitic continuities throughout the history of the Federal Republic. Antisemitism and philosemitism, therefore, can be viewed as the extreme poles in the context of existing social notions and practice in respect to Jews and things Jewish. Following, I

1. Stefan Heym, *Die richtige Einstellung und andere Erzählungen* (Frankfurt, 1979), 55.

2. See also Anson Rabinbach and Jack Zipes, eds., *Germans and Jews Since the Holocaust: The Changing Situation in West Germany* (New York and London, 1986).

3. For further elaborations on this subject, see Frank Stern, *The Whitewashing of the Yellow Badge: Antisemitism and Philosemitism in Postwar Germany* (Oxford and New York, 1992).

4. See Hans Joachim Schoeps, *Philosemitismus im Barock: Religions- und geistesgeschichtliche Untersuchungen* (Tübingen, 1952).

will deal with three aspects of German-Jewish relations in the immediate postwar period.

1. Ambivalence and imagination—antisemitic taboo and the confrontation with the Jewish survivors
2. Antisemitic continuities and "new style" philosemitism
3. The new moral credit and the decline of philosemitism

Ambivalence and Imagination—Antisemitic Taboo and the Confrontation with the Jewish Survivors

At the end of World War II, approximately 15,000 German Jews, and 50,000 to 80,000 Jews of east European origin, had survived persecution inside the Third Reich.[5] It was this remnant of the Jewish people that the allied forces, the German administration, and the German population were confronted with in the aftermath of the war. It was, in fact, a historic triangle, consisting of the Allied authorities—particularly the American military government—the postwar Germans, and the Jewish survivors.[6] At the time of liberation in 1945, patterns of a relationship between Jews and Germans began to crystallize and take shape, a relationship stamped by the collapse of the Nazi state and its aim of total extermination of European Jewry. With Allied victory, the German state had ceased to exist, yet only slowly did a new political structure begin to emerge out of the ruins of the Third Reich. The surviving Jews had to adjust to this situation in the midst of a population that was still much the same as before, although military, political, economic, cultural, and psychological conditions in Germany had undergone drastic change. Germany was in the throes of a profound crisis that permeated every segment of society, its social life, intellectual and spiritual climate, indeed, its very substance.

Jews began, in various ways, to take on a certain social significance at this watershed time against the background of their horrific experience at the hands of Germans under nazism and the profound crisis afflicting the defeated country. Surviving Jews now emerged as actors on the new stage of social reality, both in an individual sense and as a group,

---

5. There were approximately fifty thousand Jewish survivors from concentration camps in occupied Germany and Austria in June 1945, and of these some thirty thousand were in Bavaria. In addition, about fifteen thousand German Jews had survived, mainly outside the camps in the German Reich. See the discussion of these data in Stern, *Whitewashing*.

6. See Frank Stern, "The Historic Triangle: Occupiers, Germans and Jews in Postwar Germany," *Tel Aviver Jahrbuch für deutsche Geschichte* 19, (1990): 47ff.

and became a factor in social consciousness. On the one hand, this consisted of concrete encounters, individual and collective, between Germans and Jews and the more abstract confrontation with allied efforts to expose the truth about the massive crimes committed against the Jewish people.[7] On the other hand, that public exposure of Germany's guilt and responsibility stirred memories among the German population of individual participation, passive toleration, or even sympathy for the policies of massive and total racial persecution. The anti-Nazi measures introduced immediately at the beginning of the occupation, activities aimed at supplying provisions to meet the elementary needs of the population, as well as increasingly more detailed and widespread revelations about the "Final Solution" constituted general and encompassing elements in a new and emergent public sphere in early postwar Germany.[8] In personalized form, this was evident and manifest as Jews came forth from their hiding places inside Germany or returned to their former towns from the concentration camps or from their lives as emigrés abroad. Antisemitism, of course, continued to exist in, at least, one third of the population, but it is important to stress that the German relation to Jews in the period immediately after May 1945 cannot be reduced to some sort of antisemitic continuum and is far more complex.

Thus, the German-Jewish postwar relationship was decisively shaped in the first instance by the legacy of the Third Reich, political, cultural, and administrative. The official racist antisemitism of the immediate past was an evident factor that Allied officials, Jewish survivors, and Germans who were striving for a new democratic society all had to confront and deal with in some manner. The resolute endeavor of the Allied powers to denazify, democratize, and reeducate the German people focused intensively on the repudiation of antisemitism and its consequences. The American military government developed social and political activities to combat antisemitism and prejudice as part of their program to reeducate the German nation.[9] On the one hand, this

---

7. See Nicholas Pronay and Keith Wilson, eds., *The Political Reeducation of Germany and Her Allies After World War II* (London, 1985).

8. See Ulrich Borsdorf and Lutz Niethammer, eds., *Zwischen Befreiung und Besatzung: Analysen des US-Geheimdienstes über Positionen und Strukturen deutscher Politik, 1945* (Wuppertal, 1976); Klaus-Jörg Ruhl, ed., *Neubeginn und Restauration: Dokumente zur Vorgeschichte der Bundesrepublik Deutschland, 1945–1949* (Munich, 1982); Hermann Glaser, *The Rubble Years: The Cultural Roots of Postwar Germany* (New York, 1986); and Manfred Malzahn, ed., *Germany, 1945–1949: A Sourcebook* (London and New York, 1991).

9. See repeated references in Office of the Military Government, U.S. in Germany (OMGUS), Opinion Survey Section, Reports in 1946 and 1947, National Archives, Washington, D.C. (hereafter OMGUS, NA.Rg 260).

required insight into the evolving German political culture; on the other, it required the introduction and application of theories and methodologies that had proved useful in combatting antisemitism and group prejudice in the United States. The unique opportunity to make use of occupied Germany as a huge laboratory for applied social science was well understood. The American military government transferred know-how and manpower to its zone of occupation, with the result that an extensive program of social-scientific research accompanied the military and occupational administration of West Germany. To reeducate a whole nation—however questionable this was as a task for an occupying power[10]—entailed research on prevailing opinions, attitudes, behavior, and mental dispositions. Without first knowing the German mind, if such an entity existed, how could one change its political psychology?[11]

A detailed description of this research,[12] which went on for some ten years (until 1955 when West Germany gained full sovereignty), would exceed the limits of this article.[13] Rather, I would like to deal with certain of its salient findings, which are essential to any discussion of German-Jewish relations after the historical caesura of 1945. That historical rupture was not a "zero hour" but rather the beginning of a postwar era that began for the Jewish survivors with the liberation on German soil of the first concentration camps.[14] The negation of this caesura within the context of a more appropriate periodization of Germany in transition and its historization, as has been proposed by some German historians,[15] might help to shed light on various continuities of German history. However, in respect to the relation between Germans and Jews, such a revised periodization is of no assistance at all.

10. See Franz L. Neumann, "Re-educating the Germans: The Dilemma of Reconstruction," *Commentary* 6, no. 3 (1947): 517ff.

11. See Frank Stern, *Jews in the Minds of Germans in the Postwar Period*, 1992 Paul Lecture (Bloomington, Ind., 1993).

12. See the abstracts of related research in Anna J. Merritt and Richard L. Merritt, *Public Opinion in Occupied Germany: The OMGUS Surveys, 1945–1949* (Urbana, Chicago, and London, 1970); and, by the same authors, *Public Opinion in Semisovereign Germany: The HICOG Surveys, 1949–1955* (Urbana, Chicago, and London, 1980).

13. See Frank Stern, "German Postwar Antisemitism and American Military Government," paper presented at the Annual Conference of the German Studies Association, Washington, D.C., 1993.

14. See Robert H. Abzug, *Inside the Vicious Heart: Americans and the Liberation of Nazi Concentration Camps* (New York and Oxford, 1985); and Leonard Dinnerstein, *America and the Survivors of the Holocaust* (New York, 1982).

15. As, for instance, in Martin Broszat, Klaus-Dietmar Henke, and Hans Woller, eds., *Von Stalingrad zur Währungsreform: Zur Sozialgeschichte des Umbruchs in Deutschland* (Munich, 1988).

The caesura was truly incisive: for those Jews who were not murdered and managed to stay alive until May 1945 and in the difficult weeks thereafter, another era in Jewish existence had commenced—a period of new life and old guilt, marked by lingering hatred, searching, demands for justice, and the beginning of a very complicated process of psychological survival. Out of the ashes they came, a human and spiritual challenge for everything German.

How did Germans react to this challenge in the German postwar period? In the changed political framework of the immediate postwar period, antisemitism became taboo in Germany. People either "had not known anything," asked rhetorically "What could we have done anyhow," publicly deplored the cruelties of the extermination camps, or were silent about anything Jewish, avoiding even any mention of the words *Jew* or *Jewish* in public. It was a kind of national amnesia. This was an antisemitic silence, born out of a sense of insecurity, which cloaked itself in terms like "incomprehensible catastrophe," "standing at the edge of nothingness," and "blow of fate" among the vanquished. The glib reverse side of this coin were those anecdotes whose essence often boiled down to that familiar family remark—"Dad was in the war"—the domesticizing of wartime memory.

What is centrally important here is not the question of who knew about mass murders during the Third Reich or what segment of the population was reached by newspaper reports about the Nuremberg trials; that is, emphasis is not meant to be placed on the *cognitive* aspect of dealing with the persecution of the Jews. It is not a question of knowledge, of information. Rather, what is crucial is what was done with this complex on a psychological and emotional plane and thus how it functioned to shape mentalities and spontaneous behavior.

Official racist, genocidal antisemitism was now banned legally, politically, ideologically, and culturally. The reemergence of a postwar German political culture was supposed to contradict any aspect of the former racism, antisemitism, and group prejudice. The hegemony of such ethical, moral, and social values was imposed from above upon a whole nation; it was reasoned that such an imposition of new value orientations would lead the German nation back into the international family of civilized peoples. Such at least were the intentions of various programs of and proclamations by the Allies and those Germans who were endeavoring to bring about a profound change in German political culture.

It was obvious that the renunciation of antisemitism and the development of a new German-Jewish relation had to be two of the main targets for democratic reeducation. After everything that had happened, this task appeared to be one of greatest urgency on the agenda of German politics and culture. As a matter of fact, it turned out to be a true test case of political culture at the time, and it has indeed remained so, down to the present.

In an article published as early as 1946, an American occupation official summed up his experience and gave an evaluation that retains its relevance.

> Of course, German-Jewish postwar relations have not yet even begun to be tested in the crucible of experience. . . . At the same time, a new form of antisemitism may be arising in Germany. The Jews now in Germany, both native and foreign, are the corpus delicti, the accusers who haunt the Germans and will continue to haunt them until the thousands or millions of individual Germans who had a personal part in the extermination of the Jews are brought to justice. . . . As long as the Germans lack the moral courage to accept the consequences of the Nazi crimes against the Jews, they will seek to banish the accuser and they will denounce him as a disturber of their peace. . . . If the German Jews decide to remain and start life anew, their treatment by their neighbors will be the true measure of the German people's progress towards decency, progress, and democracy.[16]

This problem has indeed been at the very center of German-Jewish relations since 1946, extending down to the most recent present. Bitburg, the Fassbinder case, and other antisemitic scandals over the past decade, the revisionist turn of the screw by some prominent West German historians in the "Historians' debate,"[17] or antisemitic events after the Berlin Wall fell in November 1989 are by no means new revelations of a specific German Zeitgeist unique to the coming fin de siècle.[18] They are part and parcel of a broader set of postwar continuities, with a growing component of nationalistic sentiment at its very core. That "crucible" test of German-Jewish relations the American officer spoke about has not lost its relevance over the course of time, nor has it been rendered superfluous by the gradual withering away of a generation of

16. Moses Moskowitz, "The Germans and the Jews: Postwar Report," *Commentary* 1, no. 2 (1946): 12ff.

17. See Peter Baldwin, ed., *Reworking the Past: Hitler, the Holocaust, and the Historians' Debate* (Boston, 1990).

18. See Frank Stern, "Die deutsche Einheit und das Problem des Antisemitismus," *Österreichische Zeitschrift für Geschichtswissenschaften* 4 (1992): 515ff.

perpetrators. Rather, it remains at the very center of German political culture, now as in 1946.

Jews living in Germany since 1945 have been living witnesses to a past that had allegedly "passed away"—yet this past continues to permeate every strand and fiber of postwar German society. It is not simply an inconvenient shadow Germans can shake off and leave behind. That past is an ideological and social reality, not just a psychological burden on individual and collective memory or a bad conscience that has somehow been repressed. Every struggle for the opening of a new museum dealing with national German history or the history of the Jews, every debate and dispute over the reconstruction of a former synagogue confronts the public anew with this disturbing reality. It often leads to the denunciation of those supposed "troublemakers" who have chosen to raise these issues, either by verbal attacks on them, by totally exaggerated philosemitic praise, or by covering them in a deafening cloak of silence.

Even more than in the confrontations with those Jews who remained in Germany, there was an ever-present social memory, a historical burden that the individual could feel and with which the collective had to grapple. Without presenting a blow-by-blow chronology of German-Jewish antagonism over the five decades since 1945, one need but recall the controversial reactions to Bitburg in 1985 in order to realize that Jews in Germany can still be denounced as "disturbers" of this particular moral, political, and spiritual peace.[19] And, although Bitburg, with its crudely staged German-American reconciliation, was a rather paltry and dubious success at the time, today its basic failure can only be seen as an early indication of Germany's endeavor to reconcile itself with the criminal and horrifying aspects of German history. Since unification, in 1990, this attempt at reconciliation has become one of the main features of the newly developing German historical consciousness, and it has determined much of German historical writing.[20]

Be it before or after Bitburg, whenever public declarations relating to Jews or Jewish topics were made, these were framed within an attempt to bring about the "final and conclusive" German-Jewish reconcil-

19. See Geoffrey Hartmann, ed., *Bitburg in Moral and Political Perspective* (Bloomington, Ind., 1986).

20. See, for instance, Uwe Backes, Eckhard Jesse, and Rainer Zitelmann, eds., *Die Schatten der Vergangenheit: Impulse zur Historisierung des Nationalsozialismus* (Frankfurt am Main, 1990); Michael Prinz and Rainer Zitelmann, eds., *Nationalsozialismus und Modernisierung* (Darmstadt, 1991); and, in a more popular vein, Klaus-Michael Groll, *Wie lange haften wir für Hitler: Zum Selbstverständnis der Deutschen heute* (Düsseldorf, 1990).

iation. Jews as a collective were supposed to be bound by a presumed "duty" to engage in reconciliation.[21] The rather questionable term *reconciliation* has surfaced on repeated occasions since 1945 whenever Germans speak of their relation to Jews.

One of the well-known political figures who influenced postwar relations among Germans and Jews was the first president of the Federal Republic of Germany, Theodor Heuss. He coined the term *collective shame* as a substitute for the temporary Allied concept of collective guilt and responsibility, stressing the Jewish contribution to German culture and the necessity of reconciliation in his speeches. Hence, to work out some modus of "reconciliation" with the Jewish side became a public topic. Often, it was underscored as being a primary task of German-Jewish relations, as if the few survivors could speak for the millions of those murdered and act on their behalf. An analysis of public speeches relating to Jewish issues clearly demonstrates the presence of a recurring rhetorical pattern: anonymous crimes are hinted at, past Jewish contributions to German culture are mentioned in a rather pathetic vein, and the panacea of reconciliation, with its religious connotations, is held up as the remedy. In numerous speeches and declarations, governmental authorities were—and still are—ready to take on a kind of "proxy role" for the Jews who were murdered, or even for the survivors and their children, and to forgive the guilty in their name. The verbal stress on the desired reconciliation with the Jewish people is, in fact, nothing less than the ongoing reconciliation of Germany as a nation with its own past. This was and remains part of the broader public dimension.

Such attempts at presumed reconciliation become obvious, particularly when one looks at the efforts in contemporary political culture in Germany to instrumentalize Jews. In fact, that instrumentalization is one of the basic general problems for Jews living in Germany in the postwar decades. They are supposed either to keep quiet and say nothing or serve to assuage a bad public conscience and provide the society at large with a "clean bill of historical health." This basically is a manifestation of the brazen attitude adopted by many Germans in the immediate postwar period: namely, the unabashed insolence to request, specifically from Jewish survivors, a personal "Persilschein," a certificate washing away any brown stain from the past.

Jews in German postwar political culture are, thus, not linked solely with the Nazi past; they are closely bound up with the concrete, everyday facts of social and political life since that time as well. Martin Buber,

---

21. See Andrew Steiman, "Die Versöhnung von Bitburg in Frankfurt, " *Der Spiegel,* 31 October 1988.

Leo Baeck, and others were—although no longer living in Germany—important for maintaining the image prevalent in Sunday sermons and the ritualized Brotherhood Week. Nonetheless, it is likely that at the grass roots level of everyday life and interaction, the local neighborhood Jewish houseowner and landlord, the Jewish displaced person, and the Jewish critic of antidemocratic developments were a far more present and influential factor in West German public consciousness—less publicized yet quite effective.

Of relevance here is the concept of collective response based on the postwar taboo on antisemitism. Along with this collective aspect, of course, there is an individual, more private dimension. The confrontation of the individual Jew with the German administration after 1945 usually was an experience that went counter to the official line on resumption of German-Jewish relations. When it came to the rehabilitation of the Jews, the restitution of their rights, property, and social status, the gap between the new official and public attitudes, on the one hand, and everyday realities, on the other, was enormous.

In mid-May 1946, one year after liberation, the Representative Body of Jewish Congregations and Religious Associations in the western zones of occupation appealed to the state governments in Germany in an "open letter," noting that the returnees from the concentration camps "had still not obtained the property stolen from them when deported, or their movable possessions." Among other things, that letter went on to say:

> We will not allow the new guilt now being incurred by the present governments due to their hesitation and indifference to expand and grow. As long as we are denied our rights, our liberation remains incomplete. . . . Who gives you the right to tolerate a situation in which the Nazis look down from the windows of our houses, and we must stand aside? . . . Do not let the bitter thought arise in our hearts: that you would have preferred had we too been destroyed.[22]

One of the main experiences of Jews living in Germany after 1945 is that their encounter with Germans has always had at least these two, often conflicting, dimensions: individual contacts took place against the background of the high standards of public declarations of morality. In most instances, the everyday experience fell short of the collective proclamation, whether made by the state, the churches, or another relevant

---

22. *Jüdisches Gemeindeblatt für die Nord-Rheinprovinz und Westfalen*, 7 June 1946.

social and political body.[23] The early set of connections between public administration, official politics, and a Jewish new beginning shaped the German attitude toward Jews as well as the reactions of the Jewish minority. On this rather bureaucratic level, social and economic factors in the German-Jewish relationship, along with their perception, took on a distinctive ideological and political quality. The decentralized structure of public administration, continuities in personnel in the existing bureaucracy, and new anti-Nazi appointments affected the postwar relations between surviving Jews and the new order to the extent that Jews needed to seek out partners in official positions in order to address the staggering problems with which they were faced.

Nevertheless, it would not be adequate to inquire into antisemitic continuities merely in terms of traditional anti-Jewish attitudes or persisting stereotypes. These are only constituent layers in a social reality in which every Jewish issue was likewise a political topic from the very outset of new developments in Germany after 1945. The evolving postwar relationship of Germans to Jews and Jewish topics was rapidly extended from the realm of opinions, views, and individual relations to the institutional sphere. The state, churches, and, to a lesser extent, the political parties were the main institutions dealing with or responding to Jewish issues. This becomes clear if one recognizes the fact that even not being antisemitic or philosemitic was of immediate social or political relevance. However, this did not always imply a characterization of real relations with Jews in social life.

Antisemitic Continuities and "New Style" Philosemitism

It is crucial to note that these dimensions include a whole scale of attitudes, oscillating between antisemitism, philosemitism, and what I would call a humanist, democratic outlook. The first studies by the American military government on postwar German antisemitism in October 1945 and April 1946 indicated a continuity of antisemitic attitudes combined with a rise in nationalistic attitudes and sentiment, the veritable breeding ground of antisemitism. Since this is the first representative survey on German postwar antisemitism, it is instructive to quote its key findings.

> Results of an October 1945 survey made in the American Zone showed that a fifth of the people went along with Hitler on his treatment of the Jews. They were presented with three alternative

---

23. See Frank Stern, "Evangelische Kirche zwischen Antisemitismus und Philosemitismus," *Geschichte und Gesellschaft* 2 (1991).

statements for agreement or disagreement: 1) Hitler was right in his treatment of the Jews; 2) he went too far in his treatment of the Jews, but "something had to be done to keep them within bounds"; and 3) the actions against the Jews were in no way justified. A majority agreed with the third statement. However, 19% chose the second alternative and thus ranged themselves on the side of antisemitism.[24]

In a survey conducted in the first half of 1946 it was shown "that a clear majority of the German public holds some appreciable degree of ethnocentrism, and that about one-third of the public must be said to be not obviously tainted with an antisemitic disposition."[25] Different statistical data repeatedly refer to a rather high percentage of antisemitism, the lowest usually about 20 percent—figures that return more or less in all empirical research on antisemitism in postwar Germany.[26] It is obvious that one has to take this kind of attitudinal continuity into consideration—not particularly in the sense of statistical patterns but as a long-range social basis—when describing the development of German-Jewish relations and the relevance of antisemitism at the time. As early as 1946, OMGUS researchers maintained that "An antisemitic outlook is highly correlated with generalized appreciation of broad historical situation rather than with attitudes toward specific situations."[27]

Democratic or antidemocratic developments, nationalistic revivals, and continuing social and economic crises are indicators of such broad historical situations. In these tendencies in the immediate postwar period lie the roots and source of antisemitic phenomena that came to the fore in connection with Bitburg in 1985, in the German unification process since 1989, in the debate on Jewish immigration to Germany from the USSR in 1990, during the Iraqi rocket attacks against Israeli population centers in early 1991, and in the antisemitic and xenophobic attacks of today's right-wing extremists and Nazis. In short, the "yellow thread" running through German history still exists. Antisemitism in Germany was—and remains—more than just crude

---

24. OMGUS, Opinion Survey Section, Report No. 5 (1 April 1946), NA.Rg.260.
25. Ibid., Report No. 19 (19 August 1946).
26. Elisabeth Noelle and Erich Neumann, eds., *Jahrbuch der öffentlichen Meinung, 1947–1955* (Allensbach, 1956), 128; Friedrich Pollock, *Gruppenexperiment: Ein Studienbericht* (Frankfurt, 1955), 125ff.; Alphons Silbermann, *Sind wir Antisemiten? Ausmaß und Wirkung eines sozialen Vorurteils in der Bundesrepublik Deutschland* (Köln, 1982), 73; *SINUS-Studie über rechtsextremistische Einstellungen bei den Deutschen, 5 Millionen Deutsche: "Wir sollten wieder einen Führer haben . . ."* (Reinbek, 1981); Werner Bergmann and Rainer Erb, *Antisemitismus in der Bundesrepublik Deutschland. Ergebnisse der empirischen Forschung von 1946–1989* (Opladen, 1991).
27. OMGUS, Opinion Survey Section, Report No. 49 (3 March 1947).

racism; it is also a highly sophisticated and deeply rooted cultural and political phenomenon.

Antisemitic continuities in the German postwar period were not primarily racist but rather were bound up with social, political, economic, cultural, and religious anti-Jewish traditions. Jews were seen as bearing responsibility for the German catastrophe, occupation policies seemed to be dictated by some fictive "world Jewry," returning emigrés were mistrusted as strangers, the return of Jewish property was labeled as "revenge," and the publication of writings by Jewish authors was denounced as cultural usurpation. Significantly, existing antisemitism within the Allied armies appeared to be a kind of unofficial confirmation of widely held attitudes. Aside from sensational scandals and bureaucratic and authoritarian behavior against Jews, which aroused protest in some segments of the public, the antisemitic undercurrent was tabooed in the public sphere. But it was deeply inculcated in a semipublic sphere, and more especially in the private sphere, where nothing had to be said explicitly because everybody understood.

This kind of latent antisemitism by allusion and innuendo influenced the family atmosphere, the educational system, the emotional identification of the younger generation, and the ambiguity of the popular image of the Jew. One knew that there was some "negative" element present, one could hint at those "foreigners," the Jewish displaced persons living in camps, and at the owners of restituted property, but in public one was supposed to react in a totally positive manner when it came to Jewish topics. Private reality and public norms were in tension and at odds.

Much research conducted by the American military government, which could have led to an open discussion, was not published. The reason for this was that the results contradicted the official, and in the time of the Cold War "necessary," image of a democratic Germany that had to present a new attitude toward Jews. The *New York Times* commented more on this new antisemitism than did the German newspapers. In contrast, the Jewish press in Germany was full of reports and letters on this subject.

Already, in the late 1940s and early 1950s, antisemitic phenomena in the findings quoted are associated with philosemitic opinions and statements. Surveys indicated a figure of between 6 and 10 percent pro-Jewish attitudes for the years 1949–52 and emphasized the ambivalent character of philosemitic attitudes; these were to be placed on a scale ranging between "not-antisemitic, humanist and democratic" attitudes, on one hand, and what might be termed "latent antisemitic" attitudes on the other.

What were these philosemitic attitudes more specifically? What was the character and function of the instrumentalization of Jews and Jewish topics? As has been shown above, beginning in the spring of 1945, there was a growing recognition that attitudes in the German public toward Jews were going to play a crucial role when it came to the future of Germany. Many Germans were looking around for adequate expressions and associations that would make it possible for them to publicly identify with the new political repudiation of antisemitism. But the associated insecurities about what should be said in regard to Jews, and how, led to various exaggerations (if it proved impossible to avoid the topic altogether). Moreover, a strange dichotomy began to make itself felt in the western zones. The clear and evident discrediting of antisemitism in public life did not necessarily imply any concrete activity or action against antisemitism on the part of an individual or the group of which he felt himself to be a member. Indeed, another possibility existed: a positive, pro-Jewish stance could actually serve to substitute for open and forceful rejection and repudiation of those who were advocating and spreading antisemitism. Such a philosemitic declaration was duly recognized within the existing narrow range of acceptable political options, and was seen in analogy to formal avowals of support for democracy. At the same time, the social costs of such a stance were negligible, and a moral avowal of that type remained abstract, nonbinding—because it contained a certain distance: the Jews who were its object were, for the most part, not directly present on the scene.

> The files of the Special Branch sections of Military Government are stuffed with documents submitted by Germans in support of their claims to political reliability. These almost invariably refer to past social and business relations with Jews. . . . Was it mere opportunism that, after their defeat, prompted the Germans to advertise their "Jewish blood" and their Jewish "friends and associations," in the belief that it would help them escape some of the consequences of de-Nazification.[28]

The attempt to prove one had been a friend, or at least a helpful neighbor, of the persecuted now replaced, as it were, the former scramble to prove one's "Aryan descent." A new public philosemitic mode of behavior came into being, which had nothing in common with the Christian-motivated philosemitism of former centuries. In respect to the significance of antisemitism and philosemitism in social consciousness, it

---

28. Moskowitz, "Germans and Jews," 8ff.

should be stressed that it was not a question of false, illusionary content. Rather, what mattered was the social function, effectiveness, and political relevance of such attitudes. All opinion surveys demonstrate an ambivalent reality: side by side with the socially accepted, public philosemitic opinions, one finds similarly acceptable, nonpublic, antisemitic views. In the public sphere, an overtly non–antisemitic approach toward everything Jewish came into being. Instead of going about the difficult job of working out the social, cultural, and political consequences of individual culpability and collective responsibility, the former Jewish enemy was transformed into an abstract person—one who now had to be loved. *Anti* was switched to *philo.*

The search for formulations and the lapse into stereotypical images after 1945 can certainly be viewed in a positive vein as a process involving the change and formation of new attitudes and values. However, every laudatory mention of "decent and upstanding" Jews—as in the speeches of Theodor Heuss[29] or by conservative politicians—could also heighten feelings of anger and resentment about those Jews who weren't so "decent." Popular opinion about the thousands of Jewish displaced persons in Germany was extremely negative. That might then combine with newly forming prejudices: as in the case of the supposed "material-profit" Jews who were gaining from restitution. Another example is the cultural stereotype of the "Jewish contribution to German culture and science." It became a central theme for public, exaggerated presentation of the image of the Jew. The way in which major Jewish personalities of the past are placed in such presentations on a figurative pedestal—and thus monumentalized—contributed not only to their stylized depiction but to their neutralization and romanticization as well. The "conceptual constellation 'Jewish contribution,' which points to a notion of Judaization, is customarily utilized more to create a certain mood than to offer proof of anything"; it is not very far from talk about the "contribution of Jews to the cultural and intellectual life of Germany" to the "dictum of the 'Jew as a stranger' . . . , an alien who has only 'added' something to German culture in a good sense or bad, though without being a part of it."[30] Not to mention the fact that socialist radicals such as Rosa Luxemburg, of course, had no place in these exaggerated laudations.

The appraisal of Jews as bearers of culture, however, contrasted

---

29. See Theodor Heuss, *An und über Juden: Aus Schriften und Reden, 1906–1963* (Düsseldorf and Wien, 1964), 94.

30. Alphons Silbermann, *Was ist jüdischer Geist? Zur Identität der Juden* (Zürich, 1984), 22.

with the fact that on the level of government there was generally no attempt made—by means of a collective political appeal, for example— to actually ask Jewish survivors to return. Philosemitic expressions, as lacking in precision as the phenomenon is, remained eminently ambivalent; yet they functioned as a surrogate to block and supplant the real confrontation with Jewish past and contemporary history.

One of the most embarrassing features of philosemitism was the legitimating use German politicians made of returning emigrés. Usually no cliché is left out in the public speeches that greet and reintroduce those Jews into the conservative consensus of the Adenauer era. Take, for example, a few representative sentences from a speech in honor of a returned emigré, a newly appointed university rector.

> You have returned to your fatherland in an exemplary gesture of reconciliation, and have taken up your chair at this university again. Such loyalty demands loyalty in return. We all, therefore, feel that your election to the highest academic office at our Johann Wolfgang Goethe University has been the climax of our own duty to provide restitution and compensation [Wiedergutmachung].[31]

The two central figures of speech that characterize a recurrent philosemitic pattern are *reconciliation* and *restitution*. As if any returning Jew, any survivor, could serve as a "deputy" for the murdered. Or as if the return of a small number of Jewish scholars could restore the situation at the universities as it had been before the elimination of some two thousand Jewish academics after January 1933. The response of the newly appointed rector refrained from any critical remark, even from any reference to German postwar realities. He climbed up into the traditional ivory tower of the "mandarins"—as if that Jewish scholar had never been forced to leave Germany.

The first two decades of the Federal Republic were inundated by a high tide of philosemitism. It was a new phenomena in West Germany's political culture, and it symbolized the not yet accomplished democratic overhauling of a society in the process of transformation. It proclaimed a fundamental change in the German mind, notwithstanding the less pro-Jewish realities of the German postwar period. Philosemitism had little to do with the *unwanted*[32]—those refugees of the German postwar era, over 230,000 Jews living in West Germany in 1946, or the 20,000 to 50,000

---

31. Quoted in Rolf Wiggershaus, *The Frankfurt School: Its History, Theories, and Political Significance* (Cambridge, 1994), 447.

32. See Michael R. Marrus, *Unwanted: European Refugees in the Twentieth Century* (New York, 1985).

resident in the country at the end of the 1950s. Rather, it was an instrument for the moral and political integration of West Germany into the West, a salient factor of foreign policy. Public philosemitism had to demonstrate an attitudinal change that was not social reality but could serve to demonstrate and "prove" Germany's new democratic character to a doubting world. It was a substantial moral instrument for rehabilitation—not of the Jews in West Germany but rather of the young Republic itself.

Philosemitism in the early 1950s, then, was transformed into an officially ordained element of politics, which was complemented by the negotiations between Germany, on the one hand, and international Jewish organizations and the state of Israel on the other. These negotiations led to the 1952 Luxemburg Agreement on reparation and restitution. It seemed to be possible to pay off the bill of "first guilt"; the account of the so-called second guilt—the failure of the Germans to grapple properly with collective responsibility, individual guilt, and the Jewish presence in postwar Germany—apparently did not bother anybody.[33] The result was the reconstruction of Germany's respectability—with the Jews living on in Germany as the moral hostages.

Within this particular element of West German political culture, philosemitic forms were combined with traditional antisemitic content and modes of reaction. That point must be stressed, considering the fact that the period after 1945 was an exceptionally short span of time and that no relevant philosophical or other systematic explanation was developed that conceptualized philosemitism as a fundamental form of the attempt to overcome antisemitism in Germany. Even the concept of philosemitism does not appear until a relatively late juncture in West German political culture, although the term *new style philosemitism* is utilized as early as 1946 in analytical reports by OMGUS.[34] Thus, the concept is generally employed after the fact to characterize a context that many persons who reacted or react in a philosemitic manner were not fully aware of. Philosemitism is more a product of experienced reality and a form of response to the assumed ideological necessities of this reality than a direct outcome of reeducation or fundamental change in social consciousness and behavior.

Consequently, it is the contextual change in the prevalent image of the Jew that we have to consider when talking about antisemitism or

---

33. See Ralph Giordano, *Die zweite Schuld oder Von der Last Deutscher zu sein* (Hamburg, 1987).

34. The Office of Military Government for Bavaria refers in its *Trend: A Weekly Report of Political Affairs and Public Opinion*, no. 23, 11 November 1946, to the political opposition to antisemitism of a large group of Bavarians "for opportunistic reasons" and elaborates upon this "new style 'philosemitism.' "

philosemitism. When many Germans, immediately after May 1945, discovered that they had had a "Jewish neighbor" or "friend" whom they helped, and who could prove their political reliability, but who was unfortunately gone or dead, then they were not simply lying; rather, they were expressing a behavioral amalgam of distorted memory and utilitarian adaptation to the new situation. The problem was that there were Jews still living in Germany or recently returned whose vivid memories contradicted the "cordon sanitaire" of German memory, as Primo Levi characterized this German attitude.[35]

It was in this early postwar period that the ambiguity of real and imagined relations toward Jews began to evolve. Side by side with the concrete Jewish individual, another Jew existed in postwar German imagination, a kind of abstract Jew. That Jew could be the accuser, the excessively good and wise sage (Lessing's *Nathan the Wise*), the "rich Jew," or the "wandering, homeless Jew," but also the "anti-German conspirator," or even the member of "certain circles" that were supposedly "too powerful," "too influential." These idealized and stereotyped images of the Jews were at the center of the new postwar German imagination. In public, however, there was only the image of the good, wise, decent, and assimilated Jew who had returned to German culture. The real antagonism between Germans and Jews had its counterpart in the abstract antagonism between the Jews living in Germany and the officially ordained image of the Jews. That later image was often in stark contrast with the legacy of lingering antisemitic prejudice. Such ambivalence is important for an understanding of the content, functions, and political utility of Jewish issues in Germany.

If one looks at the emergent political culture in the first few years after defeat, one can recognize a transition in the relation toward Jews: from a self-evident antisemitic standpoint to a crumbling and tabooed racist worldview, then on to philosemitic expressions of opinion that were waiting for some sort of reaction, and finally to collectively confirmed pro-Jewish attitudes and views. The anti-Jewish stereotype does a full reverse in public (in contrast to the semipublic and private sphere): it shifts into a pro-Jewish stereotype. This marks the emergence of the philosemitic syndrome. Philosemitism, to a significant degree, became "a German self-therapy: the attempt to free oneself a bit from the terrible past—a German remedy for a German pain."[36]

---

35. Primo Levi, *The Drowned and the Saved* (London and New York, 1988), 17.
36. Ludwig Marcuse, "Wie Philo ist der Philosemitismus," *Tribüne* 3, no. 10 (1964): 1059.

The New Moral Credit and Its Decline

At the first supraregional meeting of representatives of Jewish congregations in the summer of 1949—shortly before the establishment of the Federal Republic—U.S. High Commissioner John McCloy stated that the "behavior of Germans toward the few Jews in their midst is a touchstone of their moral disposition and of a genuine democratic will for reconstruction."[37] All previous experiences in the relationship between occupiers, Germans, and Jews are concentrated as in a prism in this statement. At the same time the tone is set here for further developments affecting this relationship and the character of West German political culture. After 1945, the relationship between democracy and the attitude toward the Jewish minority must be viewed explicitly as an element of evolving political forms in postwar Germany. The declared public rejection of antisemitism, the emphasis on a pro-Jewish attitude, was increasingly postulated as identical with a democratic attitude. Against this backdrop, an intensifying political functionalization—and finally instrumentalization—of philosemitism evolved from West German political reactions to efforts at denazification and democratization.

In order to avoid any misunderstanding about this problematic strand of continuity in the German-Jewish relationship, a remark make in 1946 by a former chairman of the Christian Social Union, the Christian Democrat sister party in Bavaria, is worth quoting at length. Departing early from a party meeting in August 1946, he told his colleagues:

> Unfortunately I have to leave now, since I've got an important meeting with the rabbi of Munich. . . . We've agreed that there is just as much place in our party for a decent and upstanding Jew as for a Catholic or Protestant. You can well imagine that this will have a very positive effect tending in a certain direction for the party.[38]

Leaving aside another basically anti-Jewish stereotype, that of the so-called decent and upstanding Jew (implying that most others are not), it is quite instructive to consider another instrumentalization, for example, that of Jewish members of the Federal German parliament

---

37. *Die Neue Zeitung,* 1 August 1949; *Allgemeine Wochenzeitung der Juden in Deutschland,* 5 August 1949.

38. Quoted in Klaus-Dietmar Henke and Hans Woller, eds., *Lehrjahre der CSU: Eine Nachkriegspartei im Spiegel vertraulicher Berichte an die amerikanische Militärregierung* (Stuttgart, 1984), 92.

when the negotiations on restitution and indemnification with Jewish organizations and the state of Israel were taking place at the beginning of the 1950s. Finally, in the process of unification since 1989, German politicians have been eager to quote Jewish voices in order to improve the German image internationally, which was somehow damaged in the light of foreigner bashing and antisemitic scandals.

This political use of philosemitism is based on the years 1945 to 1952—the formative years of West Germany—when an attitudinal and social-psychological factor was transformed into an ideological and political instrument. Philosemitism became the moral legitimation for the development of the new German body politic. If the new, positive attitude toward Jews was to make public the new, positive quality of West German democracy and prove this to a skeptical world, then it was necessary for the government to present this in corresponding form. Philosemitism served to whitewash yellow and brown stains in the political culture whenever the ordained, democratic, anti-Nazi character of the Republic was questioned. This state-based, political-ideological dimension dominated all other philosemitic tendencies at the beginning of the 1950s. It developed into officially sanctioned philosemitism and was used as an international moral credit, which seemed to be backed by material payments, restitution, and indemnification.

Though philosemitic manifestations on this level did not necessarily need the actual presence of Jews, their connotations always refer to Jews. No other population group in Germany was so directly connected with political conditions, with decisions on domestic and foreign policy affecting the development of Germany's path to power. That was obvious in the negotiations, which led to the Luxemburg agreement in 1952. This aroused international public opinion at the time of the antisemitic wave 1959–60 and later during the Eichmann trial.

In the 1950s and 1960s, philosemitic stereotypes were accompanied and strengthened by a totally exaggerated public image of Israel. In the West German media, Israelis came to be seen as the veritable "Prussians of the Orient," though in a positive sense. An Israeli military victory was celebrated by segments of the West German press as an indication of the latter-day success of the "Blitzkrieg" strategy. Hence, the search by many young Germans since the late 1960s for historical answers beyond the scope of philosemitic pathos should not be denounced as being merely antisemitic when it is associated with a critique of politics in Israel. The point here is that the decline of philosemitism left a social-psychological void, which, under the circumstances of rising nationalism, could slowly be filled with antisemitic attitudes, both old and new. Leftist worldviews seemingly neutralized historical consciousness and lent a mental and cultural distance to any serious attempt to intellectually work through the collective antisemitic past of the German people.

The second half of the 1960s was a period marked by the beginning erosion of the philosemitic syndrome. The patterns of explanation common to the integrative postwar consensus were increasingly called into question as segments of the liberal public and a new generation of students and academics searched for new approaches to their identity and perspectives. Their questioning, though generally not based on serious reflection and an effort to come to fundamental grips with the history of German antisemitism, was also directed at the prevailing philosemitism of official policy. The generation of their parents had lost its credibility, and this seemed to hold for philosemitism as well. A further change occurred in the 1970s and 1980s when the general discourse on Jews and things Jewish became more and more related to finally overcoming the weight of the past, and—as it was pronounced by the Bavarian conservative Franz Josef Strauss—to step out of Hitler's shadow. For many Germans it seemed to be annoying that Jews particularly were not eager to accept this process of cultural "normalization." Thus, it was not astonishing that numerous Germans instead "of working through their Judeophobia, the questions of guilt, oppression, and crimes . . . reversed the relationship of victim and victimizer and accused the Jews of causing them to suffer."[39]

Looking back at the history of antisemitism and philosemitism after 1945, it is obvious that philosemitic phenomena did not develop in a linear manner. As Elenore Sterling wrote in 1965, philosemitism had "less to do with Jews and more with reasons of state and foreign policy." It signified "the exploitation of a symbol, which by proxy is supposed to certify as already completed a process and product as yet only in the stage of emergence: namely, a true democracy and a positive attitude toward the Jewish minority. Philosemitism—like anti-communism—is part of the confessional character of the as yet unrealized German democracy."[40]

Thirty years later, one comes to realize that the philosemitic impact of the late 1940s and 1950s has largely lost its relevance. Other western countries are now grappling with their own manifestations of antisemitism and racism. The world does not consider Germany's attitude toward "its" Jews particularly alarming, although there have been disturbing events since the begin of the unification process. Philosemitism as a symbolic substitute act in the context of domestic and foreign policy

---

39. Jack Zipes, *The Operated Jew: Two Tales of Antisemitism* (New York, 1991), 23.

40. Eleonore Sterling, "Judenfreunde—Judenfeinde: Fragwürdiger Philosemitismus in der Bundesrepublik," *Die Zeit,* 10 December 1965.

helped West Germany to achieve sovereignty in the immediate postwar period—and as such it was quite successful. But, in terms of its original content, it was not effective in overcoming and eliminating antisemitism as an element in Germany's postwar political culture. It is clear that philosemitism proved unable to bring about an "immunization" of the German populace against antisemitism, or did so only temporarily and to a limited degree. However, antisemitic attitudes and expressions did not reenter the public sphere, the center of political culture, in intensified form as a potentially acceptable value until the 1970s and 1980s. There was a process underway in which taboos were removed from the image of the Jew. The extent to which this might be possible or acceptable highlighted the entire debate on Fassbinder's play about the "Rich Jew" in Frankfurt.[41] This process, in which socially accepted philosemitic views and attitudes are replaced by others, which are free from any historical responsibility toward the Jews and which seem to indicate the ongoing process of German "normalization," sheds light on how philosemitism is mediated and thus on its limited effectiveness in individual and collective consciousness. Nevertheless, the attitude toward Jews and Jewish issues has been a touchstone and remains so. Contemporary antisemitic phenomena in German society should not only be viewed as part of the nationalistic and xenophobic wave in unified Germany but also as the historical response to the philosemitism prevalent during the establishment and restoration of the Federal Republic. Today, philosemitism and antisemitism coexist in contradiction.[42]

---

41. See Janusz Bodek, *Die FASSBINDER-Kontroversen: Entstehung und Wirkung eines literarischen Textes* (Frankfurt am Main, Bern, New York, and Paris, 1991).

42. See Frank Stern, *German Unification and the Problem of Antisemitism*, ed. American Jewish Committee (New York, 1993).

3

Identity Formation in the German Environment

From Nowhere to Israel and Back: The Changing Self-Definition of Periodicals of German-Jewish Youth Since 1960

Martin Löw-Beer

Introduction

The Project

Some time ago, I discovered that friends of mine had published a Zionist youth magazine in Frankfurt during the sixties. I became curious and wanted to know what had been on their minds at the time. But it was the invitation to a conference on "How Jews can live in Germany today" that gave me the idea that one could be interested in Jewish youth magazines for different reasons: to learn about the relationship of the young to history, to their lives in Germany, to Israel. Of particular interest to me were the questions: who do these young people speak to? What public role do they want to play?

I began to study the periodicals from the sixties, the seventies, and the eighties to determine what might have changed in the ways these young Jews saw themselves and how they related to the public. I was less interested in comparing or sketching developments than in describing different models of social integration. From the sixties I examined a project, which reduced the Federal Republic to a railroad station where

Abbreviations used in this chapter are as follows; M9/12: *Meoroth* 9:12; S3/12: *Schofar* 3:12; T3/21: *Tachles* 3:2; *ZJD*: Zionistische Jugend Deutschlands (Zionist Youth of Germany).

Translated by Harold Ohlendorf.

after some to and fro people say goodbye. It was a matter of establishing an exclusively Jewish public domain. From the seventies I studied a magazine that reacted to the public debate at the universities dominated by the "New Left." It became within this debate a moral advocate for Jewish concerns. As to the late eighties, I read journals in which the young authors made their own circumstances the basis for discussion. They are informed by a desire for empathetic recognition of Jewish history and intend, at least in the beginning, to play a role as Jews in a multicultural society.

Method

I use the texts as virtual conversation partners.[1] I ask myself with whom the authors want to establish contact. What are they reacting to? Such inquiry cannot avoid evaluation. It also implies a point of view. Thus, I submit that the history of the Holocaust is a topic of importance for young Jews throughout the last thirty years. But, if this history is thematized only indirectly or stereotypically, as happened during the sixties and seventies, it is my task to shed light on this public silence. The evaluative position is that something of relevance for the lives of Jews was excluded from public discourse. Moreover, I have come to the conclusion that the young Jews of the sixties had ideological rather than empirical notions of Germany and Israel. Such findings only make sense if I trust myself to criticize the accounts in the magazines. To characterize a statement as a cliché implies as much a point of view as labeling another as insightful.

Meoroth

During the sixties, the Zionist Youth organization of Germany (ZJD) published the magazine *Meoroth*. An older member recollected that the organization had been founded at the end of the fifties with the help of Israelis in order to "save young Jews, to awaken in them a feeling for the land of their fathers and a love for the home country, and, in the end, to return them there" (M9/6, 1962).

Not only is the name of the journal in Hebrew, but the reader who is unfamiliar with the language stumbles over such sentences as "Among the madrichim of the seminar the moledeth had the strongest representation"; earlier in that article I had learned that until half a year ago

---

1. The concept of such dialogical historiography can be found in J. Renn, "Dunkle Vorstellungen unterwegs zu klaren Sätzen," 1990, 16–31, Ms.

"the moledeth were overshadowed by the esheth." Luckily, by the way, "the va'ad has been helping the madrichim recently." However, my fears of not being able to understand are allayed with further reading. Hebrew is not used as a means of communication but rather as a symbol of orientation toward Israel. The Hebrew vocabulary is confined to names of groups, indications of status and function within the hierarchy of the youth organization (*madrichim* = group leader) and the references to institutionalized activities (*mishpath* = discussions modeled after court procedures). The Hebrew sprinklings are frequently borrowed from the nationalist vocabulary (homeland, flag, soil). A good illustration of the psychological function of Hebrew are the bylines to articles. Thus, an editor signed her first article "Michal/Maria" (M9, 1962). In the next two issues she does without her German first name, signing "Michal" (M10/11–12, 1962; M11/5–7, 1963; M12/16–17, 1963–64). Finally, her last article for *Meoroth* (M13/7–8, 1964) is signed "Maria Beckmann." The only indication that it is the last is the use of the German name.

The Hebrew vocabulary points to an identification with Israel. At the same time, it reveals that the journal only wants to reach an exclusive group. It wants to encourage the exchange of ideas among young Jews who want to emigrate to Israel and to convince others of the ideas of Zionism (M9/1, 1962).

What do these young Jews cite as the reasons for emigration? Does life in the Federal Republic appear intolerable? Or is emigration the lesson they want to draw from the annihilation of the Jews? Or do they believe that to live an authentic life as a Jew is only possible in Israel?

Presumably, the young readers would have answered all of the questions affirmatively; I say "presumably," since elaborate rationales for the intent to go to Israel can hardly be found in the journal. An exception is Michal's portrayal of a biographic model in the first issue of *Meoroth*.

1) Ruth was born in Germany, German is her mother tongue. . . . She has personally never experienced anti-Semitism for the simple reason that the children she plays with are too small to comprehend the implications of the word "Jew." Ruth's parents had been in concentration camps; they lost their entire family. They anxiously watch as Ruth becomes more and more alienated from her Jewishness. They tell her about the murder of the six million Jews. This plunges Ruth into her first profound conflict. She cries, she refuses to believe the horrific facts. For several years yet, she will accept only the mere facts without recognizing their true meaning.

2) Ruth has grown. She is ten years old and attends a German high school. She has long since grown accustomed to Jews from abroad asking as their first question: "Well, do you get a lot of anti-Semitism?" Also, she senses more and more in school that she is different from the rest of her class . . .

3) Ruth has made friends with a Jewish girl who is growing up under similar circumstances as she is. The girl tells her about Israel where she spent the summer holidays. Ruth waxes enthusiastic about this land which to her is a utopia. She can barely grasp that the milkman, the mailman, the teachers, in fact everybody, would be like her. There she would not be "different."

4) One day it happens. An anti-Semitic remark flung at her by an incensed classmate wounds Ruth deeply. She runs home in tears. . . . At this moment she knows she would always feel like a stranger and almost accidentally the thought of this land "Israel" crosses her mind. . . . At this point in the narrative, her parents are somewhat held to account. To be sure, in Israel her parents would not have been able to provide their children right away with the same high living standard as here. One thing is certain, though: a child in Israel would never shed tears because of anti-Semitic remarks! I ask these parents: What is more important, to be well-off among strangers, or to feel at home among people like myself?

5) Ruth's story continues. She joins the ZJD. . . . She has an easier time now with her environment because she has a goal. . . . Ruth's parents witness the changes in her. But, instead of being delighted at her becoming a free, independent human being, they feel Ruth is becoming a stranger. Arguments crop up. They forbid her to belong to the ZJD any longer. Ruth fights them tooth and nail . . . (M9/7, 1962)

The reader is presented with a mosaic of connected conflicts to which the way out leads to Israel. The elements of the conflicts are:

1. The "natural" integration into the German environment mediated by language and childhood ambiance. The parents' unease in light of this integration. They inform the child of the mass destruction of the Jews.

2. Reproaches from abroad. The child is asked how she can stand it in such a murderous environment.

3. The youngster experiences herself as a stranger in her German

surroundings. This sense of alienation is contrasted with the vision of a society in which she would be among equals: Israel.

4) The long-awaited injury of an anti-Semitic experience, from which the youngster draws the conclusion that she can exist in the Federal Republic only as an outsider.

5) The orientation with like-minded friends toward emigration to Israel. Fear of the parents that they will lose their child and the resulting conflict with them. The alternatives for the youth appear to be not so much between Israel and Germany as between Israel and her parents. After all, the alienation from, and the distrust of, Germans are shared by parents and children.

The ZJD offers a way out of a schizoid and limited existence. Jews have settled in where they least want to be. Their children are to have nothing to do with their German environment. Nonetheless, the parents fear that their children will turn their backs on Germany.

Many of the articles in *Meoroth* confirm on the whole the pattern of motivations in the story I summarized. An exception is (4), the thesis that anti-Semitic experiences function as triggers for the wish to emigrate to Israel, does not appear to have been typical. No other article between 1962 and 1968 refers to encounters with anti-Semites.[2] The texts do not allow the conclusion that the young distance themselves from the society of the Federal Republic because of anti-Semitic experiences. Distancing presupposes an earlier proximity. The account by Michal that I have summarized is the only one in *Meoroth* describing someone turning away from German fellow students in disillusionment. Disappointment in German friends was not typical for young Jews in their orientation toward Israel. Rather, the circle of Jewish friends was from the very beginning taken for granted as the only point of reference. To be distant from Germans was an attitude that had been handed down by parents and was expected by them. The question was not Germany or Israel but rather staying with the parents, in a familiar but narrow circle, or venturing into Israel, a place where one can move freely but where it is also dangerous (war) and materially difficult.

I assume that is the reason why one can hardly find any explanations in *Meoroth* as to why one would leave the Federal Republic. Within the Jewish community, it was a matter of course to reject a Jewish

---

2. This is true if one disregards the complaint about "an excessive interest in Jews," which is attributed to guilt feelings. This could give rise to problems, the author speculates, which she, however, does not have, because she does not enter into such close contact with Germans (M10/9, 1962).

existence in Germany. Leaving did not require explanation, staying behind did. A commentary to a report in *Der Spiegel* on "Jews in Germany" bears that out (M12/9f, 1963). It is entitled "At Home on Cursed
Soil!!!" Its first sentence is cited with approval: "They live in Germany
and mistrust the Germans." The author continues with the thought "that
the meaning of this introductory sentence contains a paradox, for how
can a conscious person live in a country whose inhabitants he distrusts
and from whom he distances and separates himself. After all, that is how
the presumed "living together" basically has to be seen" (M12/9, 1963).

The bylaws of the ZJD, framed in 1961, do not contain the word
Germany. It is only emphasized in general that "it is an essential feature
of members of the ZJD that they reject the Golah" [life outside of
Israel]. Michal, the editor, reacts to this paragraph with a remarkable
minority vote, to be sure. The decision to emigrate, she writes, should
not involve contempt of Jews who did not want to live in Israel. There
was no obligation to emigrate. "We reject life in the Golah for ourselves.
But that does not devalue the Jews living in the Golah. . . . Israel is
home not only to Israelis, but to all Jews everywhere" (M10/12, 1962).
That Israel is the homeland of the Jews is beyond question. What Michal
means to say is that those who do not live there should not be scorned.

The Alternative between Self-Realization (Israel) and Material Well-Being (FRG)

Blaming and, at least hidden, self-blaming are part and parcel of Jewish
existence in Germany. The letter of a young emigrant illustrates how
massive the reproaches were. He reports about his first days in Israel.

> I run almost daily into people who view being German as a crime,
> who view being a Jew in Germany to be the worst crime in the
> world. Of course, these people suffered greatly under the Germans,
> of course one cannot forget that, but one might expect perhaps
> enough objectivity that the attempt is made at least to accept the
> Jews in Germany as much as the Jews in France, Russia, and South
> Africa. . . . It is unbelievable, yet to some there are no Jews in
> Germany because none are allowed to exist there. (M21/11, 1968)

The alternatives of a life in Germany versus a life in Israel are dealt
with, if addressed at all, as personal comfort versus morality. It is economically easier to live in Germany, but one should live in Israel. Self-
realization is possible only there. Thus, the ideals of the simple life that
characterized the German youth movement after World Was I gain re-

newed significance. The battle against consumerism, make-up, alcohol, and nicotine becomes a test of strength in the face of the material temptations, which block emigration (M18/13f., M19/19, 1966).

What do these young people mean when they write about *self-realization*? The term resonates with meanings culled from the Zionist tradition. Only in Israel would one be an equal among equals and that is the precondition for self-realization. Israel would be the haven to all who are exposed and subjected to indignities. Of course, there were threats, but one could stand up to them and fight, one need not let oneself be led to slaughter as happened under the Nazis. *Self-realization* is also associated with self-preservation, and nature, and, in turn, is associated with agriculture. Working one's own soil is sanctified labor. So says the ideology of the kibuzzim (M23/19–21, 1968). Why do these young people accept without question that self-realization is possible only collectively and only in Israel? Building your own country represents a daring challenge, to be sure, and a state of your own must appear as an adequate response to the foreign state, which had intended to annihilate you. Yet there was, I believe, a further reason: the isolation in German society. The vast majority of the Jews of the sixties could not even imagine an integration into that society. The Jews had no acceptable model of togetherness with Germans, not even one that was deemed worth discussing. Therefore, the wish grew for a social sphere within which mobility, discovery, and social participation were possible. Israeli society appeared as the opportunity for freedom of movement and change, as an end to stewing in your own juice. Israeli society may have appeared as a blow-up of the Zionist youth movement. The equation of emigration and self-realization was solved for the young Jews so easily because in the FRG they lacked even minimal conditions for social development, that is to say, a model of mutual recognition and acceptance between Jews and Germans. That Israel was marked so exclusively as the destination of emigration—emigration to other countries is not publicly discussed—may well have been a conclusion drawn from the Shoa and the insight that Israel was the appropriate reaction. At the same time, though, we have to differentiate between published opinion and actual action. It remains to be tested empirically whether Israel was in reality or only ideologically the preferred destination of emigration.

The Youth Movement and the Parents

Many members of ZJD had trouble with their parents. Michal indicated as much in the biographic model cited above. The young tended to feel contempt for their parents' decision to live in Germany. The parents feared abandonment by their children. This conflict is only hinted at in *Meoroth*. Perhaps it could not be displayed openly since the views of the parents and those of their offspring did not differ. The parents had personal motives but no moral justification for living in Germany. There existed, within the Jewish community, no acceptable model of integration into Germany. That is why there is no discussion in *Meoroth* of views that argue against emigration. There was no ideological or cultural difference between parents and children. Both lived in the same no-man's-land. But, while the parents only dared to live, the children weighed in with ideals and hopes. In a certain way, the writers of *Meoroth* seem to be the parents of their parents. They distanced themselves from them by identifying with their superego. The children stood resolutely for their parents' ideals. Emigration was seen as a moral decision, but it was also a reflex reaction to the isolation and confining self-restriction within German society.

I can only speculate about what it might have meant for the parents when their children decided at the age of twelve or thirteen to leave because this did not become a topic of discussion within the closed cosmos of the youth movement. I would suspect the parents had socially no more to lose than did their children, whose departure began when they joined the ZJD. It must have increased their sense of isolation. This conflict is dealt with in *Meoroth* ideologically only, not psychologically. The parents are criticized for their inconsistencies in that they view Israel as home yet do not live there. But nothing is said about the forms the conflict takes. The picture of life in the ZJD, which we are given, is made up of accounts of group evenings, of training courses, or of tours during the holidays. Somewhat later we read of travels to Israel. The *youth movement* adhered to the ideals of the parents, but was at the same time *an instrument of emancipation*, perhaps even of renunciation of the parents. The world of the young is distant from the German world surrounding it; it seems a closed cosmos from which even the parents are excluded. They are hardly mentioned. Perhaps the hierarchical structure of the youth movement functioned somewhat as a surrogate parental home. The ZJD was being led by adult kibuzniks, many of whom had had prewar experiences with the German Zionist youth movement. The leaders (*shlichim*) selected the group leaders (*madrichim*). Still *Meoroth* does not present an authoritarian picture of the youth movement, even though the functionaries of the organizations were picked by the leadership. To become a group leader you had to consent. The journal presents a broad spectrum of opinions, in which criticism of the administration and the leadership are not exactly rare. The relationship to the group leaders may well have had something of a parent-child structure. A satire is entitled "Your Madrich—the

Superman." The relationship to the Israeli leaders of the organization as a whole seems throughout to be of importance and imbued with admiration and tenderness. The leaders are role models since they also did what the parents did not do: emigrate to Israel.

To emigrate is exemplary and yet one loses friends that way. The "sign-offs" are as much success stories as they are bad news. *Meoroth* prints these farewells pointedly as "obituaries," literally 'calling after'— *Nachrufe* (M13/3, 1963): "We say farewell to M. with a laughing and a weeping eye. We lose such a [great] 'madrich,' but then again Israel gains such a [wonderful] human being." The ambivalence of the farewell is thematized only in terms of parting from the youth group, not in terms of leaving the parents. That corroborates the thesis of the youth organization as a surrogate parental home.

The hierarchical structure and the farewells of the seniors may have appeared, from the inside, as the changing of the guard of generations, between whom there was hardly any age difference. At any rate, this confusing telescoping becomes the theme of a little story, which for its literary merit alone should be cited, at least in excerpts. It's called "The Song of the Grandfather."

> I could, just as an example, still think of a family with a grandfather sitting around. This grandfather could, of course, sit behind the stove, smoke a pipe, and pat a cat. Yet the problem "grandfather" would not be solved in the least.
>
> He isn't even a nasty old man let alone a dirty old man, no, he is an understanding, wise old man. So the problem is getting more difficult, especially when I keep in mind that only three weeks ago grandfather had his twentieth birthday.
>
> The reader will recognize from his age alone that the problem is becoming more and more difficult. Grandfather is very reasonable and all his wisdom and laughter have brought a thousand crinkles to his face.
>
> He shares in all our cares and worries, in all our games and fun. That's the kind of grandfather he is.
>
> That's the kind of grandfather I am. I share in all their fun and am in spite of my age astonishingly alive and fresh. I know all their cares and worries, but, for myself, all of that is behind me, in spite of my age!
>
> I don't know what kind of a grandfather this person is, or what kind of a human being this grandfather is; perhaps both, the human being and the grandfather, the grandfather and the human being, are a person and a grandfather, could be, no? After all, we are all

only twenty years old. But still, what kind of a person are you, you
human being?

Perhaps a grandfather? At twenty? No way. But that's my problem. . . . The little story ends on the same helpless and absurd note
as it began. He or she, man or woman? Easter or pentecost? Well
now, gentlemen, who is that sitting behind the stove? And it is at
that one grandpa that all logic founders. (M20/18–19, 1967)

Thematizing the Destruction of the Jews

We have seen that Germany appears in *Meoroth* as a chiffre for "materially carefree existence." But it also occurs as a euphemism for "cursed
earth." The Federal Republic is regarded as the dangerous and infamous
world outside, against which one protects oneself as best one can. Only
news that has something to do with the fate or the endangerment of
Jewish existence is taken notice of. Thus, there is an interview in 1964
with Dr. Bauer, the impressive prosecutor in the Auschwitz case. The
following excerpts from the interview throw a glaring light on the hostile
atmosphere in which these cases were tried but also on the remoteness
of the Jewish students from the world surrounding them.

> Question: We heard that these court cases may have adverse effects
> for Jews.
> Dr. Bauer: Unfortunately, people overlook that the majority of
> witnesses so far have been Poles and Tchechs. The case does not
> only deal with the murder of Jews, but also with the murder of
> Poles and Russians. Unfortunately, it is not known in Germany
> that towards the end of the war Hitler gave the order to annihi-
> late the entire German population in case of defeat. Bormann,
> who is allegedly dead, was put in charge. To execute the plan, he
> needed the support of the armed forces, who did not comply and
> suppressed the order. A warrant has been issued for the arrest of
> Bormann on the charge of the attempted annihilation of the en-
> tire German people.
> Question: Why has that not become known to the general public?
> Dr. Bauer: It's being covered up in Germany. People don't want to
> hear about that. Germans don't like to have their noses rubbed in
> the past. (M14/5, 1964)

Bauer's argument sounds far-fetched and seems more like a desperate
attempt to deal with the hostile mood against the trials: if the Germans
had only been aware that only their army protected them against the

same fate that befell the Jews, then they could distance themselves as potential victims from the Nazi murderers and the trials would be less problematic for them. *Meoroth* only takes notice of the hostile reception of the Auschwitz trials. The interviewers do not criticize Bauer for his peculiar argument. The young Jews inform themselves about the hostility with which the legal proceedings are received as one would about adverse conditions with which one has to live. The Jewish students did not seem to have expected anything better and they do not harbor any missionary ambitions toward the Germans, to whom they do not want to talk. For them, the Germans are a passing, rather unpleasant, secondary condition of their existence. That is why they want to know if there are likely to be anti-Semitic reactions in the wake of the trials.

The interview indicates how unwilling German society was to recognize the injustice done to Jews and others. The isolated Jewish community faced aggressive silence and an unwillingness to take issue with German history. Many Germans wanted to repress the history of Jewish annihilation. The Jews may well have appeared to them as ghosts from a past they wanted to banish.

But the Germans are not alone in their preference for silence about the mass destruction; the young Jews hardly thematize it either. To be sure, there are articles in the style of seminar papers about anti-Semitism and hatred of Jews: the scapegoat theory, discrimination of the foreign, and finally some nonsensical racial doctrines based upon which the destruction of the Jews is almost a logical end. The uprising in the Warsaw ghetto is mentioned as well but only as testimony for a militant Jewish worldview. It is presented as a luminous contrast to the passive march of millions to their destruction. The history of the annihilation is scarcely even referred to indirectly in *Meoroth*. There is no mention of the camps or the gas chambers. The organization of the mass murder and its description are nontopics. The space given to the Holocaust could be compared to the space on a board game where you are instructed to move immediately on to Israel. "The annihilation of the Jews in the Second World War pointed like a bloody arrow in one direction: towards Israel" (M23/7, 1968). This may readily suggest that the coherence of the youth movement, its life-inspiring character, is psychologically linked to the repression of history. One lives in a world with surrogate parents and with the prospect of life in a country that was created to prevent the recurrence of the fate that befell the parents. The conflict with the parents is shifted to the omnipresence of the departure, planned or actual, from the surrogate family. Emigration is viewed as a task and as a sign of hope for self-realization, which I interpret as a promise of social integration. This counterworld may perhaps help also to keep history at arm's length or at

least out of consciousness. The knowledge is there that Germans organized the murders, and the suspicion perhaps, too, that they could again
become enemies of the Jews, but there is no formulation of either biographic or sociologic access to the destruction. Accordingly, the rise of the
fascist National-Demokratische Partei Deutschlands (NPD) in 1966 is
interpreted quite naturally as the threatening return of the Nazis and a
reason to leave Germany (M19/17, 1966). It seems as if history is to be
undone by drawing conclusions from it.

And yet, problematic issues of the destruction are never far from
the minds of the writers. There are indirect signs. We know that the
Nazis tried during the persecution and destruction of the Jews to dele-
gate tasks to their representatives. Jews were induced with death threats
and vague promises of survival to hand over, even to kill, fellow suffer-
ers. *Meoroth* documents an impressive mock trial (M13/7–11, 1964), in
which the young people debate aspects of the horrific dilemmas the
Jewish councils were forced into by the Nazis. Does a community have
the right to sacrifice any of its members in order to survive?

The students mask the history. They discuss the bind the Jewish
councils were put in with reference to a country they call Pont, whose
capital is named Uglaia.[3] The administration as well as the economy of
this fictional country were in the best of shape, however; it was not
prepared for war. Therefore, it could fall victim to a brutal invasion. The
invaders confront the government with a demand "which was the most
inhuman one could pose." They demand of the government the execution of one member of each profession, for a total of fifty-nine people. If
refused, they threatened to kill the 200,000 inhabitants of Uglaia. After
intensive deliberations, which the invaders limit to one day, the government decides to agree to the deal of death. "All of a sudden the piercing
scream of a woman ruptured the silence: 'Murderers!' she screamed
'Murderers!,' till she collapsed" (M19/8, 1966). After the execution, the
lives of the rest are spared, but all of them are sent "as slaves to the
east."

The charge against the government is that of the murder of fifty-
nine people: "Murder is the deliberate killing of a human being; the
facts of the case justify the charge."

The reasons: (1) "The life of a human being in inviolable. Nothing

---

3. Michal Bodemann pointed out to me that these fictional names evoke certain
associations. Uglaia made him think of "ugly," while Pont reminded him of the French
pont meaning "bridge." Together they suggested the metaphor "bridge to ugliness." This
play with words should, of course, remain just that, play. The students, most likely, would
not have invented the names but would rather have drawn on a legend. The crucial
questions are: why did the students select this story and how did they treat it?

justifies the killing of a human being"; and (2) the government agreed to a humiliating fate, sacrificing the honorable memory of its people. The Warsaw uprising, for example, shows that there is merit in dying with dignity. Perhaps a similar uprising in the capital might have ignited the whole country and would have been successful.

The defense argued that it is the task of the government to look after the welfare of the people. It was therefore the duty of the government to prevent the death of 200,000 citizens. Moreover, it was not dishonorable to lay down one's life for the good of the community. Agreeing to the inhuman demand had nothing to do with passivity and humility; rather it was a matter of saving lives at the risk of one's own. Acceptance of the execution was comparable to the willingness to lay down one's life for the sake of the common good. The sacrifice was to be justified in analogy to military duty. Furthermore, one would have to stipulate the consent of the victims. After all, their lives were forfeited in any case. Accordingly, preference was to be given to the kind of death that would have better consequences such as the survival of the rest of the people. The defense summarized its arguments concisely with the following two theses.

1) One could assume that the 59 people, as responsible citizens, were prepared to give up their lives for the freedom of their threatened people, since they knew the demands of the invaders according to which noncompliance would have led to their death in any case.
2) Responsible political leaders had not only the right but also the duty to sacrifice the minority for the sake of the majority, because they knew that if they did not, the majority as well as the minority would perish. (M19/10, 1966)

The courts absolved the government of Pont of the charges on the following grounds: "The government of Pont executed the order of a belligerent, numerically superior tribe which demanded the death of 59 men from all professions only after long deliberations. There are no grounds for a charge of murder" (ibid.).

I admire the defense when they characterize the consent to execute. What seemed at a first glance to be the passive acceptance of a humiliation reveals itself as the highest activity, as the attempt to rescue others at the cost of one's own life. Impressive is also the court's exclusive focus on the question of murder. The question of guilt is uncoupled from the question of whether life under the brutal regime of the invaders is worth living. The latter question no government can answer for its people. Of course one can ask such questions as: is it worthwhile to live in slavery and with the tormenting memory of friends who were murdered? Would it not be better to die in battle even it the battle seems hopeless from the start? Can one trust people who demand such terrible things? The Nazis could not even be trusted as blackmailers. The students recognized that such questions, weighty as they may be, had nothing to do with the responsibility of the government. The execution of 59 citizens is not murder if it is undertaken under the credible threat of death against 200,000. Maybe the sacrifice was not the best solution, but it can never-theless be seen as a responsible act of the government. Moral guilt must be distinguished from feelings of guilt that arise from tragic entangle-ments. The mock trial differentiates impressively between guilt and intol-erable conflicts.

If one were to disregard this unique indirect thematization of the problems connected with the Holocaust and were to focus on the ideo-logical side of *Meoroth,* one would find that the discussions can barely be distinguished from those of the Zionist youth movements before World War II. The annihilation only plays the role of a presupposition insofar as it appears to be simply ethical, a matter of course, to turn your back on Germany.

Israel

Do the students actually know where they are going? What is their picture of Israel?

Perhaps one should speak of three phases. In the *first phase* the writers deal with Israel mostly as an idea. They want to recapitulate the heroic decision to found a home country for the Jews, and they want to identify with the spirit of the pioneers. They recall the heroic experi-ences of the settlers (M9/3–5, 1962). The real problems of the country are seen only as distractions while they embrace the Zionist traditions that explain why Jews need Israel as their home. In the first issue already we hear of a group that is engaged in self-criticism because their pro-gram deals mainly with actual problems—"such as Israeli-Arab ques-tions and the death sentence for Eichmann, whereas we hardly concern ourselves with Zionism. We are going to make up for that now with Jehuda's help" (M9/3, 1962). The speakers have to admit that Zionism is somewhat out of date insofar as its goal, the foundation of Israel, has been reached. Still, they say, there remains the moral task "to show the Jews of the diaspora the true way to Israel" (M11/19, 1963).

Dealing with Zionism at the expense of Israeli reality was consistent in that it faced the reality of the young, for they wrestled with the decision to emigrate. To make such a decision at the age of twelve or thirteen is a big thing. The pioneers of Zionism were useful cult figures who could help carry the weight of the decision.

The orientation toward Israel was first and foremost ideological. At issue was the search for the right Jewish path to lead one's life. The first response to the conflicted experience of life in Germany was the decision to emigrate. But what does Israeli identity mean? Is it possible to be a Jew without being religious? The ideological adoption of Zionism as a collective project corresponds, on the personal plane, to the question of the nature of Jewish identity (M15/2–3, 11–15, M16/22–25, 1963). The case of "Pater Daniels" therefore created a heated debate in 1963. He was a Benedictine monk of Jewish ancestry who settled in Israel and sued for the right to be given Israeli citizenship. The question was: can ancestry and history alone grant the right to the status of a Jew? What is the position in Israel to the development of a secular Jewry? Tendencies toward a separation of state and religion are characterized by one writer as an Israeli "Gohla complex." Israel, he says, would like to be like other modern states, unfortunately, and accordingly exhibited a tendency to separate religion and state (M12/27–28, 1963).

To found a country is so much more than to merely travel there! However, to emigrate was made heroic when those about to go identified themselves with the fathers of Zionism. In 1966, a writer warns that "Israel should cease to be a name for a country about whose realities and difficulties nobody within even the ZJD knew anything (M17/2, 1966). But, in the meantime, on account of the cumulative experiences of emigration and travel, contact with the real Israel had deepened.

The *second phase* in the relationship to Israel begins in 1964 with travel reports from Israel. Now questions on how to realize the emigration project are being discussed (1964; M17/1–5, 1966). A group of candidates for emigration is created (Garin Aliah). A network of communication is established between those who have arrived and those who have remained behind. The problems facing new arrivals are being discussed: is it better to come alone or in a group? Should one first go to a kibbuz or into a city?

The *third phase* begins in 1967 with the Six Day War. They react to the war with trepidation and subsequent relief at the outcome. The real problems in Israel shove the ideological discussions aside (M21/7, 1967). From now on, Israel is seen no longer through the eyes of either the emigrant or the immigrant but rather through the eyes of Jews living there. The occupation of the Gaza strip and the West Bank move the Palestinian problem into the foreground. The relationship to Israel shows three phases: (1) Israel as a (Zionist) project; (2) the practical problems connected with turning the decision to emigrate into reality; and (3) *Meoroth* has arrived in Israel. Israeli problems dominate.

Summary

Meoroth shows an active Jewish youth group in the sixties whose members have as little contact with the Federal Republic as possible and whose contact with Israel for a long time is purely ideological. Together with their parents they live in a no-man's-land. They detach from their parents to move into the closed cosmos of a youth movement, which through its hierarchical structure assumes the function of a surrogate parental home. They make big decisions, think profound thoughts, and lead an active social life. The journal addresses itself to young Jews who are to be swayed to emigrate to Israel.

Schofar

In my time travels I would like to take a brief side trip to Vienna, where between 1968 and 1974 Jewish university students issued a lively journal entitled *Schofar*. As the ram's horn calls the Jews to prayer on New Year's Day, so *Schofar* wants to awaken Jews and non-Jews to Jewish problems. Young Jews in Germany and Austria are so small in number that they cannot fritter their energy away by publishing many journals. Accordingly, their respective projects reflect the way they see themselves in their environment. In *Meoroth*, young Jews write for young Jews. In *Schofar,* they write to participate in Austrian public life. The differing orientations are indications of different models of social integration.

Schofar can be seen as an attempt to initiate a structured dialogue. It is not so much that non-Jews are writing for the journal but rather that much of its space is devoted to the discussion of the positions of others in the public life of Austria. *Schofar* is giving young Jews a voice that participates and is heard.

The most important thing the Jews in Vienna and Frankfurt share after the war is that they live among people of whom some were involved in the extermination of the Jews. Austrian Nazis were no different than their German party comrades when it came to the persecution and elimination of Jews. These Austrians, moreover, understood themselves to be acting as Germans for Germany. But after the war, while the Federal Republic assumed responsibility for what had happened, the Austrians could persuade the Allies that they were victims of nazism. With regard to the responsibility for the extermination of the Jews, at least, the Austrian position, that it was an invaded and occupied country, is hypocritical and opportunistic. This interpretation was, however, so powerful in rewriting history that Austria emerged symbolically with a clean vest. Blood and dirt were successfully hoisted from the Austrian onto the German nation. From now on, the debate over historical interpretations that signal dismay at, or proximity to, nazism becomes a culture clash between 'Austrian' Austrians and 'German' Austrians. Identification with an 'Austrian' nation represents symbolically a distancing from national socialism. I would guess that this maneuver eased the way of young Jews into Austrian society. In addition, the student movement of 1968 signals with its happenings the ascent to power of the younger generation. Students who were born after the Nazi period create public space around the university. Their social engagement removes taboos and ignores geographic and temporal barriers. This unburdened yet tormented generation of students also makes the history of their parents part of their reexamination. Even though most of that is done in terms of abstract social criticism, the resulting climate may well have been infectious for young Jews.

The New Left, above all, becomes the audience addressed by *Schofar*. *Schofar* criticizes the single-mindedness of the leftists in their fixation on the critique of capitalism and materialism. The journal points to the repression in Eastern Europe and argues that the fight against Israel cannot be presented as legitimate anti-imperialism. It clarifies the dimensions of scale in the Near East, comments satirically on the notion of Israel as an imperialist superpower, and documents the introduction of classical anti-Semitic conspiracy theories into the ideologies of the Arab states (S5, 1969). The journal informs of the profoundly serious consequences these ideologies have for the Jews in Syria, Iraq, and Egypt. It reports the permanent nightly curfews, the denials of exit visas, the prohibition on shopping in Jewish stores, the ghettoization. All of this is news that Austria did not have at the time. In 1969 (S9), *Schofar* publishes a special issue on the history and present situation of Jews in the Soviet Union. Reports on the repression of opposition in the so-called real socialism are a constant feature of *Schofar*. In 1974, for example, it publishes a letter smuggled out of an insane asylum, which was written by a dissident and addressed to Angela Davis, who had been unjustly charged with terrorism in the United States. The dissident compares her life amid stench and injections with the opportunity to defend oneself publicly against false accusations.

It would be wrong to say that *Schofar* had a right-wing bent, if for no other reason than that it is impossible to sum up its views. It is a journal that characteristically displays a spectrum of contradictory opinions. One author, for instance, holds that a Zionist orientation makes for callousness vis-à-vis the Vietnam War and other problems throughout the world (S15/29, 1971), whereas another maintains that Zionism is an integral feature of being Jewish (S10/13, 1970), and a third pronounces in the name of the right to national self-determination (including that of the Palestinians), "Zionism is dead—long live Israel!" (S7/14, 1969)

The New Left was not a monolith. Not only did some of the contributors of *Schofar* belong to the left, but *Schofar* relied on documents of the discussions within the left. An example is the publication of a declaration of twenty representatives of the German left to the conflict in the Near East (S2, 1968).

The political niche of *Schofar* is partially determined by its critique of the one-sidedness and blindness of the New Left when it comes to Jewish problems. But what is its *cultural niche*? Its first issue contains a charming feuilleton entitled "Kaffee und Zionismus." It begins: "The Viennese spend most of their time in a coffee house, the Jews spend all of their time there, it follows that Viennese Jews cannot exist without coffee houses" (S1/32, 1968) The author paints the moving scenario of a prohibition on coffee houses in Vienna. At the height of this (Jewish) catastrophe, "Herr R." receives a letter from Tel Aviv, which begins: "I am sitting in the café 'Rowal' " (ibid.). The consequence of this news is a mass emigration of Jews to Israel. If a Jew in Vienna is injured playing a sport, he has to put up with his friends admonishing him: "Where does the Jew belong? In a coffee house!"

As you can see, Viennese Jews identify with the best feature of Viennese culture, the coffee house. That makes for cultural integration. The only question is with whom they associate there, only other Jews? In 1970, an article, which almost sounds like a manifesto, appears and bemoans such ghettoization. It leads off with a look back.

> 25 years ago, allied liberators released the minds of our parents from the terrible pressure of a life threatening power. . . . There they stood all of a sudden, face to face with this freedom, saw the collapse of a continent and took advantage of the opportunity to accommodate themselves. . . . of course they knew about their Jewishness, of course they needed to live like Jews! But they kept their thoughts to themselves, fitted in, went about their business— attempted to exist side by side with all the disguised oppressors and felt uneasy in spite of it all. . . . Material arrangements were not sufficient to [allow them to] forget what had happened, to overcome the past. They lived with their unease and once again created their own ghetto. . . . They were not prepared, let alone able to forgive, and yet they extended their hands to be partners . . .

The second section describes what life was like for the children, including the author.

> Gradually, after 25 years, we begin to take control of our own lives as Jews. Stuck in a ghetto we built ourselves, we can barely develop our individuality. We choose our friends, make our social world from our own small circle, and in each new acquaintance we first look for the Jew, then for the person. The unmastered past is now 25 years back, when shall we ever master it?. . . . We will not accomplish it here where we are a miniscule minority burdened with our parents' complexes. Only where we can experience a free Jewish society can we come to life, can we master the unmastered past, which is not ours! But what about those who need these complexes so much that their disappearance would leave them with a festering sore? They are truly unfortunate. Not even zionism can help them! They are condemned to become the "eternal Jew" of our time. . . . (S13/6, 1970)

This "manifesto" echoes in its content some of what was in Michal's Zionist-model biography, quoted above. It is unclear to what extent the description of Jewish life in Vienna is correct. The critique may well serve instead as a draft for an Israeli "counterlife."[4] But, even after we make allowances for its pathos, there remains the finding of troubled social relationships between Jews and non-Jews. There is no conception of interaction. Last, but not least, it seems as if Jewish self-hatred is rampant. The "eternal Jew burdened with complexes and sniffing around for the traces of new anti-Semitism" could have walked out of a textbook for anti-Semites.

Intellectually, *Schofar* attests to the integration of Jews into Austrian society. But, when it comes to emotions and friendships, the distance between Jews and non-Jews still seems to be great. It would be premature, however, to draw the conclusion that the Jews are culturally isolated. The literary contributions alone contradict that conclusion, for they are a mirror of Viennese virtues: the authors of the prose pieces display self-irony, sneering black humor, grotesqueries, in short, the screamingly funny feuilletons of *Schofar* are very Viennese. Still I did not find that the focus was on Jewish life in Austria. The coffee-house story is an exception. *Schofar* is abstract insofar as it does not thematize a "Jewish lifeworld." There is no trace of local Viennese-Jewish atmosphere in it such as could be found in the chansons of Georg Kreisler, for example.

---

4. See Philip Roth, *Counterlife* (Penguin, 1988).

The "manifesto" just cited identifies the annihilation of the Jews as the reason for the erratic contacts with other Austrians. The silence about national socialism was what struck us in *Meoroth*. *Schofar* is similarly devoid of any references except for the schematic mention of biographies and memoirs of the parents. Nor do we hear anything about how people in Vienna treat their memories. There are no accounts of actual experiences from the Nazi period. I did not find any attempts to explain the destruction of the Jews, any theories about national socialism, or even a word about the history of Vienna's Jews or the postwar migration of Jews from the East. Once *Schofar* did call for reports of anti-Semitic experiences, but the response was very meager.

Tachles

After this side trip to Vienna, let me return to Germany, to the period that by now is called reunification, even though the GDR was attached to the FRG by administrative fiat. Such periodization suggests itself quite readily, yet for our purposes it is somewhat misleading. At least the two youth magazines I want to deal with now, *Tachles* and *Nudnik,* can in no way be regarded as reactions to the process of unification.[5] They owe their existence to the concept of a multicultural society, a mollycoddled favorite of the political culture in the FRG during the eighties.

An oddity of the road to unification, which had "no speed limit" (T4/5, 1990) was the suddenness with which it opened up. Until the fall of 1989, even the notion of German unity was nothing other than a rather tired part of armchair ideology. Nobody believed it would ever happen. In 1988, when the Jewish youth magazine *Nudnik* appeared in Munich for the first time, "unity" was as much a nontopic as it was a year later when *Tachles* saw the light of day in Frankfurt. When unification forced itself on the West German consciousness early in 1990, *Nudnik* had already ceased to exist, and since unification became a fait accompli I have been waiting in vain for the next *Tachles*. I shall examine some of the reasons for the delay presently. Drawing on cultural contexts to explain the death of such a journal as *Nudnik* is a rather risky business, since frequently the psychological, personal, and financial problems of the editors may play a role as well. After all, it is only a small group of

---

5. In what follows I will only deal with *Tachles* since the elements I want to profile are stronger there. *Nudnik* also represents Jewish culture in Germany, but Jewish social life plays such a large role that one gets the impression at times that Jews are only writing for Jews.

people who would be involved and the mobility of the young, the speed with which their lives change, is high. Not the demise but rather the reasons why such a publication would appear are worth exploring. And here the cultural climate of the late eighties may have been a stimulant with its general interest in the history and evaluation of national social-ism, its appreciation of a narrative perspectivism, and the idea of a tolerant multicultural society. Young Jews found interest in and space to write about how they felt.

Tachles and *Nudnik* were indications that a new generation of Jews was speaking out. The children of some of the contributors to *Meoroth,* for instance, now write for *Tachles.* The names already contrast with *Schofar* and *Meoroth.* The new journals have names with which even Germans are commonly familiar. Most people know that "to talk tachles" means "to speak plainly," and, if someone does not know what a nudnik is, the subtitle, "the Jewish grouch," clarifies the matter. On the other hand, the word *schofar* means something only to those who are familiar with Jewish religious ritual, and that *meoroth* is the Hebrew word for "enlightenment" has to be explained to non-Hebrew speakers. *Meoroth* did not address itself to Germans, and the Jews who did not know the meaning of the word were thus given their first lesson: orienta-tion toward Israel was the order of the day and that meant to learn Hebrew. The name *Tachles* indicates that the publishers identify them-selves in public as Jews living in Germany.

Public Spaces

The young Jews in *Meoroth* all shared in the notion that Jewish self-awareness could only be gained by identification with Israel. Accord-ingly, Jews could only live in dignity as Israelis. This perspective changes already in *Schofar,* where Jews change from facing an internal Jewish public to dealing with the society in which they live. The journal func-tions as an advocate for Jewish problems. It is not necessary to be a Jew in order to point the finger at anti-Semitism in the Eastern bloc and the Arab states or to declare that it is unacceptable for former Nazis to be politicians again. It is sufficient to apply universalist moral standards to the situations of Jews. That, for *Schofar,* is the most important source of self-esteem. The grievances *Schofar* airs always deal with the partial or distorted reception of Jewish problems by the Austrian public. Typically, *Schofar* has two foci: articles about the Jewish community and theoreti-cal discussions about Jewish identity are addressed to an internal Jewish readership, whereas information and commentaries on Israeli politics or the persecution of Jews in the world always serve also as platforms on which to take issue with leftist stereotypes, which were en vogue among students at the time.

The different public arenas where *Meoroth, Schofar,* and *Tachles* operate, are only to a little extent created by the journals. They reflect changing social realities. The audience for *Meoroth* is a function of the goals of the Zionist movement: to organize the emigration of young Jews to Israel. *Schofar* encounters the discourse of the New Left, which moved international political and social problems into the arena of political responsibility and made the universities into centers of protest against the Vietnam War and the manipulation of public opinion. *Schofar* turns against the one-sidedness of leftist ideologemes. *Tachles,* too, finds its public space: it is identified on the one hand by the concept of a multicultural society where homogeneity and nationalism have lost their place as wellsprings of pride; on the other hand, *Tachles* can take advantage of the interest in the eighties in the history of national socialism. *Tachles* tries to define a place for Jews in Germany that reflects the Shoa and respects Germans who distance themselves from ethnic nationalism. One would want to be a Jew in Germany without becoming a German. At least to be German in the ethnic sense of the word is forcefully rejected, though it is equally unacceptable to regard oneself as a member of a foreign community. It is the normative interpretation of the historical tradition that accounts for both the proximity to and the distance from the Germans. The painful events of the history of the Jewish diaspora, culminating as they did in the Shoa, are the road signs to understanding oneself as a Jew.

Getting to Know the History of the Holocaust

In *Tachles,* contrary to *Meoroth* and *Schofar,* the history of the destruction of the Jews becomes central. The emphasis lies not so much on the collection of facts or theoretical investigation but on biographic representations. Indeed, one author even sees danger in too much theory about national socialism, since this would only lead to distance and desensitization (T2/17, 1989). The readiness to assume responsibility for history could only grow in a person who shared emotionally in the historical process. What *Tachles* wants are family novels, which often contain sections in which Germans and Jews face each other as perpetrators and victims. How are the narratives to be continued?

This dealing with the Nazi period in the categories of family history and the cultural importance of debates about national socialism are not a Jewish invention. *Tachles* reflects, rather, a great interest in these matters that was pervasive during the eighties in German society as a whole.

There was, for example, the heated debate among historians of the question of whether the crimes of the Nazis were unique. *Tachles* also shares in the general research interest in everyday life under the Nazis. The question of how national socialism invaded family life stirred historians as much as pupils, film directors, and others. Lay historians[6] investigate local histories to see how Germans related to their neighbors.[7] Pupils try to find out what went on in their school during the Nazi period (T1/5, 1989). *Tachles* is not alone in interviewing eyewitnesses (T2/10–12, 1989).

The question, then, of why *Meoroth* and *Schofar* by and large ignore the Holocaust, whereas it becomes a decisive focus for *Tachles,* cannot be properly posed with reference to internal Jewish developments alone; rather it has to be answered within the context of developments in the whole of society. I can only venture a speculative response: so long as the persecutors and persecuted confronted each other en masse, memories would have turned into tribunals for the persecutors, while the persecuted were ashamed to live among their persecutors.

Let us recall the shy question in *Meoroth* put to Attorney General Bauer: whether the Auschwitz trials would be damaging to the Jews in Germany. This question rests on the conviction that Jews in Germany embody the memory of the Holocaust whether they like it or not. A presupposition of remembering is that the period to be remembered has become past. The question "what was it like" can only be put by those for whom what has happened has become the past. Only distance lets the voices of victims and perpetrators become tolerable and only for the ears of later generations.

He who has no memory cannot deal with the past, cannot change. A poem in *Tachles* persuasively criticizes an attitude that turns toward the future in order to escape the past: "Don't look for the shadows, the lights are so bright, I have to care for you with the future in mind, tell me, will you remind me when I am gone" (T2/16, 1979).

It is in this sense that psychoanalysis opposes "repetition and memory." *Tachles* demonstrates this thesis with an interview of a radical right-wing city deputy who directs his eyes "always toward the future" and who relinquishes the past as a research field for historians (T1/17–21, 1989). The easy, personable tone of the interview shows that these Jews are not afraid of contact, even with political enemies. They are interested in "getting to know exactly the manner in which a radical

---

6. See M. Richarz, "Schwierigkeiten der Heimat forscher mit jüdischer Geschichte," *Babylon* 8 (1991): 27–33.
7. See e.g., A. Schleindl, *Verschwundene Nachbarn* (Groß Gerau, 1990).

right wing member of city council speaks and argues and to publish that" (ibid., 17). *Tachles* owes much of its liveliness to the thesis that history reveals itself through the memories and conversations of its participants.

The first two issues of *Tachles* show that the journal intends to play a public role in the Federal Republic. This intent is tied to the concept that as a group its associates are at home there culturally. The popularity of the idea of a multicultural convivium supports this concept: they hope to integrate as Jews without being forced to assimilate. Further encouragement is garnered from the broad interest in, and recognition of, the injustice of Auschwitz. It is from here that a cautious feeling of "we" of young Jews *and* young Germans, grows.

Tachles can be read like an experiment of the young to determine if they can live openly in the FRG. They pose questions: can we play a different role than to legitimate that Germany has become inhabitable for Jews? Can we deal with reproaches like the one of the right-wing Israeli quoted in *Nudnik*: "The majority of Jews stayed in Germany after the war, because life is easier than in Israel and these people see the golden calf. A dance around the golden calf" (3/44, 1989).

As German unification becomes a reality, skepticism increases. Germany is increasingly viewed from a distance. Perceptions like those published in *Meoroth,* which interpreted Germany as a hostile environment, seem not to be dead but only submerged. Now they appear again.

Phases of *Tachles*

The development of *Tachles* can be divided into three phases: The first two issues try to determine the place of Jews in the Federal Republic. "Who are we, and with whom are we?" The contributions strike a personal tone, sometimes taking the form of confessions. They challenge Jews to put an end to the denial of living in Germany. They appeal to Germans to understand how difficult it is for Jews to say yes to living in Germany. And they hope that a common desire for remembrance and empathy will rise out of German-Jewish history. They imagine being citizens of a German state whose inhabitants agree in the interpretation of the Nazi past and distance themselves from cultural and ethnic homogeneity.

The second phase consists of commentaries on the rapid process of German unification. *Tachles* criticizes the repression of historical self-reflection by national moods and problems. There was a sense throughout Germany that the war, which had the division of the country as a consequence, was now finally over and that the past should now be left alone. That, however, would mean that the Jews would lose their symbolic importance.

The third phase of *Tachles* coincides with the Gulf War and is marked by sustained silence. A few leaflets and a conversation with two editors lead me to believe that the silence is connected with the German peace movement against the Gulf War. For its members came precisely from that segment of the public *Tachles* had accepted as partners in communication. The movement against the war was interpreted as lack of interest in the threats against Israel and as a sign of an irresponsible attitude toward the Jewish people. The image of Germany as a hostile environment, so well known from *Meoroth,* was recovered.

In what follows, the focus will be primarily on the first phase of *Tachles,* since Jews, then, wanted to play a new role in the public arena. They turned their personal histories, their feelings, their lives in the FRG into a topic of public interest. Abstract questions about Jewish identity gave way to concrete descriptions. A young Jew, for example, tells of his reaction to a letter from the armed forces, which calls him to appear before the draft board. Can he imagine serving in a German army? He knows that as a child of survivors he has a right to be exempted from the draft (children of war dead, by the way, have the same right). Still, the letter reminds him that, nominally at least, he is German. Is that merely a passport entry or can he accept it fully?

> The first moment, holding the letter in my hand, was something like a shock. I was embarrassed to have received this communication with the federal emblem on the letterhead. . . . Yes, I am German, that was brought home to me only too clearly on that day. It embarrassed me before my relatives in Israel, I felt uncomfortable with myself and before history.
>
> In the past, I could always reply to probing questions that some time down the line I would emigrate to Israel and that I didn't feel at ease in this country. And I don't, even today. But I have to admit that I am prepared to spend the next years of my life here and probably the rest.
>
> A dream shattered. Probably the dream of a whole generation who have finally settled down, are raising their children here and have built a life for themselves in this country. The days of "next year in Jerusalem" are over. (T2/13, 1989)

On one hand the article turns to the Jews in Germany with the request that they should stop pretending they are only there temporarily. They should admit that they want to live in Germany. This opinion is awkward for the author, because the tenet (as held by *Meoroth*) still echoes in the background that Jews should not live in Germany. On the other hand, the article asks the Germans whether Germans and Jews could share a "normal" life together. The author denies that because he feels Jews are still faced with stereotypical anti-Semitic expectations. The last time he experienced them was at the draft board: "In answer to the question of profession of mother and father the nice gentleman across from me entered on his own without any prompting from me 'housewife' and 'merchant'" (ibid., 14).

The author concludes that a Jew should not join the Armed Forces, although it would be "quite correct to say that this country now has a democratic constitution . . . that a new generation has grown up. But constitutions can change, history cannot. Generations can come and go, but the memory lingers . . . and the time is not yet right to be accepted by this country as an integral member of its society. The time is not yet right to regard all wounds as healed" (ibid., 14).

To conclude, it is inappropriate, at least out of regard for the occurrences in recent history, to trust the Germans. Then there is the episode at the draft board, which further illustrates the grounds for distrust. And yet there is the optimism that one is well on the road to being accepted in Germany as a Jew.

It is not so much that convictions have changed since the time of *Meoroth;* it is rather that the orientation and the perspectives have changed. Completely new matters move into focus. In *Meoroth*, descriptions of group evenings or other communal activities were the only references to everyday life. "Everyday life" was defined in a Jewish context. The writer in *Tachles,* on the other hand, begins with the letter from the draft board. The point of departure is thus an experience common to Germans and Jews. The Jew now explains to the German what this call to military service means to him: that the month of September, when he received the letter, reminds him of that September when World War II broke out, and that he cannot overlook the continuities between the Federal armed forces and the German Wehrmacht. Reflections on personal experiences lead back to historical events, especially to those in the history of Germans and Jews that were deadly to Jews.

The peculiar brand of pathos and the description of personal experiences, which is so characteristic of many of the articles in *Tachles,* is perhaps better appreciated against this background. The editors have a twofold mission, and carry therefore a double burden. On one hand they want to demonstrate to other Jews that one can live in Germany without self-denial. On the other hand, *Tachles* wants to make it very clear to the Germans that the annihilation of the Jews was a crucial phase in their history. It followed from that history that even those who were born later have a responsibility toward the Jewish people. Contact points of German and Jewish history, even negative ones, are nevertheless contacts. The positive change in German history is tied to an altered attitude toward the Jews. The history and the fate of the Jews has, therefore, an important place in German consciousness.[8]

"In spite of it all, we want to play a role in German society." Such a slogan could characterize *Tachles.* Let me give two more examples for this cautious tendency toward integration.

The writer of an article entitled "Das Ghettosyndrom" writes with concern about a classroom of students he has heard about, where twelve of the students were Jews. He warns against such a constellation since it would hinder the integration of the Jewish children. He has personal memories of "little ghettoes" in the schoolyard, which interfered with making friends with non-Jews. He stresses the difference between assimilation, which would be tantamount to surrender, and integration, which nourishes friendships on the basis of mutual acceptance. He closes with the appeal that "we should abandon our spiritual ghettoisation, which binds Jews of all ages as if with red ribbons" (T2/47, 1989). These observations deserve special attention since the author identifies himself as a *madrich,* a leader of a Zionist youth group. The change from the sixties, the time of *Meoroth,* is striking: at that time there was no doubt that the encapsulated Jewish group was the desired option. At the time, a gathering of twelve Jewish children in one classroom would have been more than alright.

The second example is an article with the catchy title "Deutschland, der Lack ist ab" (Germany, the Lustre is Gone). The topic is the resurgence of German right-wing radicalism at the end of the eighties. A similar development in the sixties had elicited from *Meoroth* the laconic comment that it was time to leave Germany since the Nazis were coming back (M19/17, 1966). The opening of the article in *Tachles* seems to strike a similar note. Verbal trumpets sound at the ominous surge of the brown movement: "They are here. Everybody talks about them, everybody is horrified. The politicians of all parties are speechless. . . . And while the elefants lick their wounds, everything clicks on the other side. . . . Every evening meeting during the elections this year presented the same picture. The brown column crashed onto the stage with a bang" (T1/22, 1989). But the first impression one gets of the article is deceptive. The message is not "The Nazis are coming, Jews save yourselves!" Instead the make-up of the right is closely examined. The

---

8. Dan Diner, "Negative Symbiose," *Babylon* 1 (1986).

author points to the social groups that are left out of the distribution of wealth and who are not given social recognition. The crisis of the farmers and the lack of housing for the lower middle class ought to be dealt with, and the levels of recognition and security of the police should be increased. In short, the radicalism of the right is not regarded as German nationalists running amok but rather as a bunch of quacks addressing groups that have been marginalized by developments in society. The writer refuses to isolate the radicalism of the right as a specifically German problem, which as a Jew he could only address as a threat. Instead he feels called upon to participate in the efforts to improve the lot of the disadvantaged in society. "There is only one answer in the final analysis to the question as to who is responsible for the rise of the 'Republikaner': All of us" (ibid., 23).

This feeling of "all of us—together," based as it was on trust in a democratic public consciousness aware of its historical obligations toward the Jews does not survive the year 1989. The rapid integration of the GDR into the FRG is viewed with skepticism and commented on polemically. In a poem, which alludes to Germany winning the world championship in soccer, the author sketches the dreaded changes: "Once upon a time / There was a time / When you could rhyme / final match with final victory. / There flickered in the hindmost / Left cranny of your skull / a tiny red lamp, / flickered and got excited, / began to flash excitedly, / the two gold-black lamps / had long since died, / And it flickered, got excited, / Until it noticed that it was only half-time" (T5/ 52, 1990).[9] It is feared that economic and social endeavors will replace historical reflection. The dissolution of the GDR, and the recognition of Germany as a sovereign state, removes the last elements of the aftermath of the war. The memory of its victims, it is feared, may now disappear also. The author of the following polemic says what so infuriates him about the more recent historical developments.

> This "peaceful revolution" is the worst that could happen. The Germans suffer from the illusion that they have acquired a halo which radiates away with its bright glare the dark shadows of the German past. . . . First they had to suffer under Hitler, then under Ulbricht, Honecker and company, and today they are free at last for Kohl and "coal" [slang for "money"]. After a long ordeal during

9. "Es war einmal / Da gab es Zeiten, / Da reimte sich / Endspiel auf Endsieg. / Da regte sich im hintersten / Linken Eckchen des Gehirnkastens / Ein rotes Lämpchen, / Regte sich und regte sich auf, / Fing aufgeregt an zu blinken, / Die beiden gold-schwarzen Lampen / waren längst erloschen, / Und es regte sich, regte sich auf, / bis es merkte, daß es erst Halbzeit war.

which they were equally abused by brown shirts and Reds the Germans have finally emerged victorious in their fight for freedom: Resistance has won! (T4/5, 1990)

The article ends with the observation that "all attempts at therapy for the age-old German sickness of collective amnesia" have been abandoned.

The Gulf War

A German-Jewish dialogue, *Tachles* seems to say, entails the presupposition that there are Germans who mourn the victims of Auschwitz and are prepared to accept a historical responsibility toward the Jews. The touchstone for this attitude is the positive answer to the question of whether one is prepared to help the Jews in their hour of persecution and danger. An important reason for the long-lasting silence of *Tachles* during and after the Gulf War was the disappointment with its German dialogue partners, who, in the camp of the peace movement, had opposed the war against Iraq. They would not have passed the test, which should have shown their empathy with the destiny of the Jewish people; for Iraq had threatened Israel with poisoned gas and had attacked with rockets. Whoever would not stand with Israel in those circumstances could not lay claim to friendship with, and responsibility to, the Jewish people. At best, such a person would appear indifferent. These, at least, were the views of the two editors of *Tachles,* with whom I had a conversation. The solid ground on which they supposedly conducted their dialogue with Germans had turned out to be sand. They felt that the Right had used them in their inner political battles with the Left, and that the Left gave its respect only to dead Jews.

The responses of the editors of *Tachles* were not just expressions of disappointment. That was there, to be sure, but there also was the kind of calm one experiences after a strenuous journey during which one has gone beyond one's psychological limits. The time has passed, it seems, when the worldview they inherited from their parents could be shaken. Again they feel like an enclave in a hostile environment: "Now would be really the time to leave Germany, his father had said," one of the editors remarked with agreement, as if he had finally absorbed his parents' lesson that there is nothing for Jews to learn about Germany.

Summary

The public role and self-awareness of three Jewish youth magazines were to be investigated. The Zionist periodical *Meoroth,* which appeared in the sixties, perceived the society of the Federal Republic as a negative environment from which it was desirable to get away. What was published about everyday life was limited to reports about the activities of the Zionist youth movement. The journal aimed at creating a Jewish public in order to initiate the emigration of the young to Israel. On the pages of *Meoroth,* history becomes a means of painting a vision of the future. Israel is seen through the eyes of its founding generation. The main foci of *Meoroth* are the future, when Israel will have become one's home, and the present, as it is constituted within the closed world of the youth movement. The past is seldom referred to except when it explains the role of the youth movement as a surrogate parental home with its unquestioned orientation toward Israel.

Schofar, a magazine published by university students in the seventies, wants to play a role in Austrian public debate. It reacts to the lack of awareness of the distorted view of the situation of the Jews in the world. It becomes a forum on which proposals for solutions to the problems of Israel and Jews in general are being discussed. In *Schofar,* too, national socialism and individual biographies are seldom brought up. The articles are written from an ethical perspective on Jewish problems, which leaves the discussions of Jewish identity somewhat abstract.

By contrast, *Tachles* lets young Jews at the end of the eighties and in the nineties vent their problems with German history and society. The focus is on Jewish life in the here and now of the Federal Republic and on the relationship with the German environment. The question of how one can live here as a Jew loses its ideological, moral, reproachful quality for a while and becomes rather concrete. The memory of the Holocaust and empathy for the victims of German history become a measuring stick for a German-Jewish dialogue.

While *Meoroth* was read exclusively by Jews, *Schofar* was politically integrated into Austrian public life. *Tachles,* in turn, contains attempts at a cultural-historical integration into German society. The articles are written for Jews and Germans. But recent developments in Germany may mean that these attempts will come to naught.

Identity, Exile, and Division: Disjunctures of Culture, Nationality, and Citizenship in German-Jewish Selfhood in East and West Berlin

John Borneman

1. Who Is a German-Jew?

A major contention in contemporary debates about identity politics is that theories of modernity have led to an overemphasis on the aspects of coherence, unity, and continuity in identities. Significance, or even health, is attributed only to those identities that display coherence around single characteristics (such as, for example, ethnicity, sexuality, or nationality), appear unified between domains of experience (such as work and family), and can be narrated in a continuous history (usually around tropes of suffering or production). This overemphasis results in neglect, if not in a pathologization, of identities that are disjunctive and not easily narrated as part of a continuous history. In this chapter, I examine the autobiographies of a small number of German-Jews who left Germany before 1939 and returned to one of the Berlins after 1945. German-Jewish identity in this century has been marked by a series of disjunctures in categories of belonging, in particular by discontinuities between culture, nationality, and citizenship. I shall address the question of the meaning and significance of these disjunctures

Much of this chapter is drawn from my introductory essay in John Borneman and Jeffrey Peck, 1995, *Sojourners: The Return of German-Jews and the Question of Identity* (Lincoln: University of Nebraska Press).

for German-Jewish selfhood among the small group of German-Jews still living in Berlin.

This chapter is part of a larger project, which I completed with Jeffrey Peck, entitled *Sojourners: the Return of German-Jews and the Question of Identity*. In June 1989, we began ethnographic interviews—some of which we later filmed—with formerly exiled German-Jews in order to address three questions. We asked: "Why did some German-Jews voluntarily return after 1945 from exile in one of the Allied occupation countries to East and West Germany, more specifically to East and West Berlin? Did postwar experiences change the way in which people imagined themselves to be German-Jews? Who in fact is a German-Jew? History intervened in this project: the Wall opened on November 9, 1989; the East German state dissolved and its territories and people formally united with the Federal Republic on October 3, 1990. The extreme flux of this period, now called "die Wendezeit," during which we both regularly visited or intermittently lived in Berlin, continually dissolved many of the divisions and tensions that we were studying, only to replace them with newer and emergent ones not immediately identifiable. It forced us to continue our research for several more years.

We began by trying to identify all German-Jews living in Berlin who had lived in exile in one of the Allied occupied countries and returned to Berlin. No one, of course, keeps such lists. Moreover, the very category "Jew" or "German-Jew" has been a politically contested one, by the Germans in the East and West, by the various members and organizations of the international Jewish community, and by the different Allied occupation forces. For obvious reasons many Jews did not want to identify themselves as such, least of all for the purposes of citizenship or statistical quantification. Subject positions are always also political stances, placing an actor in an historical tradition and a present-oriented field of power and interest. Thus, the number of "Jews" one cites will always be partially determined by polemical, political, and factual considerations. With these caveats in mind, how did we, how might one, identify a German-Jew?

A census published in June 1933 registered 500,000 Jews living in the German Reich (around 1 percent of the total population), of whom approximately one quarter were foreign (non-German) Jews. Approximately another 100,000 people who were not registered had at least one Jewish grandparent. Of those registered by the government, around 72,000 lived in Berlin. Between 1933 and 1945, approximately 270,000 were able to leave Germany; more than 165,000 were murdered; about 15,000 survived the camps, and another 2,000 survived underground (Benz 1991, 10). In the spring of 1945, "as many as 100,000 Jewish survivors [the majority not being German-Jews] found themselves among the eleven million uprooted and homeless people wandering throughout Germany and Central Europe" (A. Peck 1991, 5). Between 1945 and 1950, the number of Jewish "displaced persons"—the official category used by the Allies—rose to nearly 200,000 (Jacobmeyer 1983, 421–52). International Jewish agencies then engaged in a massive and relatively successful effort to remove the Jewish population from Germany, so that by 1950 the number of Jews in Germany had dwindled to around 15,000. Of this small group, 6,000 were displaced Jews from Eastern Europe who settled in Germany, another 2,000 were Jews from other countries, and only the remaining 6,000 were German-Jewish emigrants or returnees (Yahil 1971, 496–500). Those who remained in or moved to Germany after the war became a pariah people in the eyes of groups such as the World Zionist Organization, the World Jewish Congress, and the Jewish Agency, all of which issued "ultimatums" to the effect that all Jews must leave Germany (A. Peck 1991, 9).

The relation of Jews to the Allied occupiers and to German authorities was entirely different. Within weeks of the defeat of the Third Reich, exiled Jewish Germans began returning to Berlin to serve—initially the Soviet Union, shortly thereafter the other three occupation forces—in rebuilding Germany. The great majority of these returnees were highly skilled, politically motivated, Jewish anti-Fascists who had worked in the opposition during the war. Some had begun this oppositional activity on the side of the Republicans during the Spanish Civil War; they saw the fight against Nazi Germany as a continuation of these earlier battles and the return to Germany as part of an international anti-Fascist struggle. Many identified themselves more strongly as Communists and members of the German Left than as Jews, and many were prominent personalities whose return to Germany was expected and hoped for by a small group of non-Jewish German friends and anti-Fascists who had also survived the war. On the whole, however, Jews who returned within the decade after the war report that most people living in, or occupying, Germany at that time treated their return—and their Jewishness, to the extent they revealed it at all—with total indifference.

In this chapter, I will illustrate my arguments by citing five of the twenty-three autobiographical interviews we completed, which is approximately half of the people we identified as German-Jews who also fit the categories of this project. We selected people based on categories that revealed a particular range of experiences and differences in age, gender, nationality, and county of exile; we did not select them randomly. We also maintained a nearly equal balance between those living in the East and West, between women and men, and between two generations. I will limit myself here only to a discussion of members of Generation I, who were born between 1904 and 1926, raised in Germany, left between 1932 and 1939, and were in exile during the war in one of the Allied occupation countries (USSR, United States, Great Britain, or France). They returned between 1945 and 1956 (except for one, who returned in 1979) to either East or West Germany, and eventually to one of the Berlins.

For the purposes of our study, we identified people as German-Jew either because they "subjectively" identified themselves that way or because they were so identified by ancestry, from the "outside" through shared blood on the male side (a category employed by the Nuremberg race laws) or through shared blood on the female side (according to Jewish religion). Thus, several of the participants in this study who had been labeled Jew at various times in their lives insisted that they were not Jews. Obviously, we are aware of the danger in hypostasizing an identity for someone who insists that they do not belong to the group in question. We recognize and respect the right of people to represent themselves as they wish. On the other hand, our goal is not to prove people's belonging against their wishes but merely to indicate the relation of subjective identifications to the two definitions of belonging listed above.

Our open-ended, autobiographical discussions extended anywhere from one to six hours at a time. In eighteen cases we returned for a second interview, in eight cases for a third. The discussions were taped and carried on in the language chosen by our partners, either German or English. About one month into the interviews, we decided to make a video documentary about these people, in addition to our book project, and thus selected nine people for filmed interviews. Since August 1989, we have met again either singly or together all of the people now included in our book. After transcribing, translating, and editing the initial interviews, we made the resulting protocols available to the interviewees for further corrections and comments.

2. The Decision to Leave

Specific reasons given for leaving Germany ran along two axes of comparison: those who returned *from exile* in the Unites States or the USSR and *to citizenship* in the Federal Republic of Germany (FRD) or the German Democratic Republic (GDR). My purpose here in citing these interviews is not to demonstrate a typical experience but to illustrate the range of responses to any particular issue. Half of the individuals of this generation whom we interviewed belonged to the Jewish Gemeinde (community) in East or West Berlin, all of those in the East except two were members of the Socialist Unity Party (SED), while only one of all those in the West whom we interviewed belonged to a political party. Among the reasons for leaving Germany, approximately half singled out fear of discrimination/persecution/murder because of their Jewish identity; one left to join a boyfriend in the USSR the year before the Nazis came to power; one left both because he suffered from an occupational blacklist (for political and ethnic reasons) and in order to fight in the Spanish Civil War; many said that they left out of political opposition *and* because they were Jewish. Concerning the country of exile/ emigration, no one went to the United States out of political conviction; two went to the USSR to work for the revolution. The others ended up going to countries that agreed to take them in, with no prior preference for refuge there.[1]

Case 1. Ruth Benario was born in Berlin in 1910, left for the USSR in 1932, and returned to East Berlin in 1954.

> I had a friend who was world-renowned in physics. He was in Genf and Lucern, was general-director there for five years. [Today he's] a very famous man, also with respect to East-West relations, and he's made a name for himself in the peace movement. I've recently found him again, after thirty-three years. I can tell you about that later. That's always funny and really accidental, how everything plays itself out in life, especially with our generation. He was supposed to go to take someone with him, and said, "Good, you come along." I said, "No. I'm not going along." I'd just begun working in a photography studio. That was 1932. And we cabled back and forth to each other, daily, until one day I suddenly said to him, because something funny had happened in the meantime, "Okay, that's enough of this story. I'll come along."

Like many women we interviewed, Frau Benario offers an explanation for leaving that, despite her independent spirit, makes her decision contingent on the life of a male friend. Although she designs her entire life story as one motivated by accidents and by unintended consequences of intentional actions, she also attached particular significance to events in which she ends up going along with men, particularly boyfriends and lovers. It may well be that freedom of movement for women at that time, even for relatively wealthy and independent women like Frau Benario, was limited by the extent to which they

---

1. All translations of the cited interviews are mine.

could attach themselves to men who had mobility. Earlier in her story, Frau Benario had described to us the circumstances of her childhood: raised in a private villa in the wealthy Dahlem section of Berlin, painted by Kokoschka; she drove a car and took private flying lessons. Yet perhaps the most fateful decisions of her early life, the move to the USSR, was a result of following a boyfriend there. The year after she arrived in Moscow, with Hitler firmly in power in Germany, she decided not to return. Though her boyfriend (the famous physicist Viktor Weiskopf) moved on to Denmark (and later to the United States), she made a life for herself in Moscow.

Case 2. Ernst Cramer was born in 1913 in Bavaria, emigrated to the United States in 1939, and returned to West Germany (as an American citizen) with the Allies in 1945: "Hm, you know that as so often in life, very much, very much is naturally accident, isn't that so?" After explaining that he had rejected his first offer to leave Germany in the fall of 1934 because it was to go to Israel, he continues,

> After I rejected this first offer to emigrate, I had approximately three other offers to emigrate to South Africa. Finally, I decided, after, after the ordinance, after they passed the Nuremberg Laws, that a young person simply couldn't live here any more. I then began working in agriculture—and that through the youth movement in which I had worked. In 1937, I formally joined one group. We didn't want to join the Zionist group because we said there were too few positions there and too few licenses to go to Palestine back then. . . . We then tried to find places elsewhere in the world. We wanted to find a place where we could remain together as a group and then settle together in South America. That also proved impossible to realize, and then came 1938. . . . After that the motto here was: just save yourself if you can. And I had a possibility to emigrate to Kenya, as well as to America. I went to America. . . . I was in Buchenwald in '38, and then in the summer of '39 I emigrated directly to America."

The specific circumstances that finally led to Herr Cramer's exile are unique. He told us that a Gestapo man finally convinced him to leave but in the most unexpected way. The man offered him the position of heading the Reichsvertretung der Juden in Deutschland (the official body said to represent all Jews living in the Third Reich). But the man offering him the position also assured him that even if he accepted it the Gestapo would soon arrest him. It was only a matter of time before they got to him and the other Jews. Therefore, Herr Cramer said, he was ironically thankful to the man for so clearly outlining his options, and he immediately left for the United States.

Case 3. Goetz Berger was born in 1905, became a lawyer and a Communist during Weimar, left Germany in 1934, went to fight in the Spanish Civil War in 1936, and was imprisoned in a concentration camp in France before "escaping" to the USSR in 1943. He returned to East Berlin in 1949. "In 1933, I was kicked out of the lawyer's profession, naturally. There was a law that forbade anti-Facists as well as Jews from practicing this occupation, called the Berufsbeamtengesetz. [Though this law was aimed at civil servants,] it was also applied to private occupations such as law. I had to leave the republic, illegally." Herr Berger explains that his association with Jews at that time was a symbolic one, that he did not identify himself subjectively as a Jew.

> Now, you have to look at it as follows: Before Hitler, we had many Jews, relatively many Jews were in the so-called free occupations, lawyers and doctors, for example, above all this was true for Berlin. In other places, it wasn't so concentrated. That connection had much to do with German history. The Jews were not allowed to enter the military in old Prussia, nor in the Weimar Republic. They weren't allowed to enter higher levels of administration, nor diplomatic service, and they were practically not represented at all among the farmers. . . . And now it came to a very negative decision, in my opinion, that in commerce the Jewish element was very strong. In the '30s, even already in the '20s, the large commercial centers, shopping houses, were well developed. These stores were nearly exclusively in Jewish hands. . . . Now the Nazis had an easy time playing with this, especially among the petty bourgeois, among the commercial interests and the small dealers. They felt, and objectively they were correct, threatened by the large concerns. And through this, Nazi propaganda, the racist Nazi propaganda using these categories, fell on fruitful soil.

Herr Berger then makes a similar argument for the intelligentsia, which also had a high proportion of Jews. During his narration, he always refers to the Jews in third person, though much of this history is one in which he is personally positioned, given his own family history, political orientation, and occupation.

As to why so many Jews did not leave Germany, Herr Berger explains,

Well, I see the primary, the most basic reason why Hitler came to power is that the German people, especially the intellectuals who were not politically sophisticated and did not want to be politically informed, that they always said, "Politics is something ugly. Politics spoils the character. We don't want anything to do with politics. We are suspended in spiritual/intellectual spheres [schweben in geistigen Sphären]." Therefore, they didn't bother. This became the fate of many Jews. . . . I knew several myself, who had remained in the Hitler period, long after they could have left, when they had the means to leave, but they said, "Good God, what we see in the newspapers, that can not be reality. In the end, after all, Germany has produced Goethe and Herder. Germany is a civilized country. And besides, there are laws and we have rights, and we haven't really done anything to anybody." What they failed to see were the political relationships behind it all. This unpolitical thinking, this rejection of all that is politics, this was very widespread among the Jewish middle class.

Several aspects of Herr Berger's explanation are striking. First, in substantiating his own cosmopolitan identity, one that in the Enlightenment tradition transcends religion, race, and nationality, he works within the same categories as the apolitical Jews he criticizes: he posits politics as a domain divorced from culture rather than culture as the very site of politics; he differs from those he criticizes only in that he emphasizes politics over culture, whereas they prioritize culture over politics. Second, he differs from the other two individuals cited above in deemphasizing coincidence and contingency as motivating his history and instead resorts to objectively identifiable structures in his arguments to explain history, of which his own history is only a specification. Third, his insistence on referring to Jews in the third person and refusal to position his own history as one interimplicated with Jewish history can be explained again partly by reference to his cosmopolitanism as transcendence of race and religion. Also he firmly believes the personal is the opposite of the political, with the former being trite and the latter significant. Fourth, "the political" for him is antifacism.

Case 4. Hilde Eisler was born in 1912 in East Galicia, at that time part of Austria, later Poland, currently part of Ukraine. When she was six months old, her family moved to Antwerp, Belgium. Two years later the First World War broke out. Her father was drafted into the Austrian army, and her mother, labeled an enemy foreigner by Belgium, resettled in Frankfurt, Germany, where her mother's parents had been living for many years. Frau Eisler grew up, then, in Frankfurt, in a fairly integrated wealthy family—her father was a banker in Poland and her Belgian relatives were in the diamond business—though as an Ostjudin (Jew from the East), she was never fully accepted by the Westjuden (Jews from the West) in Germany. After spending a year in prison for underground activities against the Nazis, she began her exile from Germany in 1937, landing in New York in 1941. She was deported from the United States during the anti-Communist hysteria of the McCarthy purges in 1949 and resettled in East Berlin.

> I was placed on a visa as the quasi-engaged woman of my husband [Gerhart Eisler]. It was like this: I didn't get a Mexican visa from the people there, those who organized it all from Paris. Why? To this day I still don't know. Something didn't work out, and then he [Gerhart] offered to put me on his visa. I had worked in the resistance in Germany; I was imprisoned. I worked illegally, giving out illegal literature against the Nazis. I was arrested, spent a year in prison, was then deported to Poland. . . . From there I went to Czechoslovakia, and from there I was able to go to France. I worked with Gerhart Eisler in Paris. I first met him there working with anti-Fascist radio programs. And he passed me off as his fiancée, so that I could get his on his visa. But I wasn't engaged to him. We were only friends. We later married in America, in Connecticut.

Much like Frau Benario, Frau Eisler ties her fate to that of a man with whom she was initially "quasi-engaged" and later married. She insists that her reasons for going into exile are both because she is Jewish and because she was in the political opposition.

In accounts of the circumstances of leaving or escaping Germany, the two German-Jews cited here who took refuge in the Soviet Union were, so they maintain, driven by circumstance and political convictions. Hence they offer political explanations, including a political explanation for German racism, for Hitler coming to power, and for their forced exile. For those German-Jews who took refuge in the United States, explanations for leaving tend more frequently to emphasize Jewishness and German racism without placing this in a political context—unless, that is, they would end up returning to East Germany instead of the Federal Republic after the war. Those who returned to East Germany from exile in the United States also offered accounts for leaving Germany similar to those of their peers who were in exile in the Soviet Union. I suspect that there exists a strong positive correlation between the degree of politicization and exile in the USSR, and between this politicization and the decision to return to the GDR from exile. These

accounts also seem to indicate that the politicization occurred most frequently before leaving Germany, not during life in exile. Why some
returned to the East Zone/GDR instead of the West was most dependent on a disposition to see the party and world ideology as movers of
history. Compared to their counterparts who went to the West, those
who went to the East were less convinced of personal fate as determinative of their own lives.

3. The Decision to Return

Decisions to return, when, and to what country were equally varied. I
shall present five examples.

Case 1. Frau Benario returned in 1954 to East Berlin after twenty
years in the USSR and two in China.

> We asked the Red Cross to repatriate us. I had been in the Soviet
> Union long enough. I wanted to go back to Germany and help with
> the rebuilding of Germany. I took that step, and I asked that the
> man Hart, Dr. Hart, Dr. Camillo Hart—he was my third husband,
> so to speak, all without papers—and I asked them if I could take
> him along with me. However, he was either supposed to go back to
> Romania (where he'd been imprisoned in a concentration camp
> before the Russians freed him) or to Vienna (where he was born).
> He wanted to come with me to Germany, but the Russians didn't
> want to release us from our duties [for me that was because I
> worked] as translator for the radio.

Why return to the GDR, we asked.

> For me it was clear. My husband said, "We're not unpacking. We're
> going immediately on to West Germany, to West Berlin." I said,
> "Without me." The people there [in West Germany], I really don't
> like them. But especially important is that I'm in agreement with
> what they want here, by and large, not in the narrow sense but with
> socialist democracy. I'm for that. And still more specifically the
> people [in the East] protected me from the concentration camp, so
> that I couldn't just simply turn my back on them. I cannot do
> that. . . . The thing is, this [going to the West] was taken for
> granted when one comes out of the Soviet Union. But I couldn't do
> it. I couldn't immediately go on over to the Federal Republic.
> That's exactly the opposite [of where I was at]. And back then there
> was the Cold War, and everything was much worse than now, still

more antagonistic and less friendly for the people who came back from the East. That all fit tightly together. For me it wasn't an option. I didn't have to do what all the others were doing—go West.

We asked whether as a Jew she had second thoughts about returning to Germany. "I've never had inhibitions [because I am a Jew], for at the time I went [to the Soviet Union] such a thing didn't really exist. There were Germans, you know? But there weren't Jews, and Christians, and Catholics, and all of that. And when I came back, I went about exactly the same way that I did before I left." Frau Benario remembers pre-1932 Germany as one where German identity was not exclusively inhabited by non-Jews, where Jewishness was not an icon for difference. "Jews, and Christians, and Catholics, and all that," meaning other particularistic forms of identity, were neither seen as coterminous nor in opposition to Germanness. Although she herself does not use the word *cosmopolitan,* she is remembering a time, at least in the circles she frequented, when that kind of identity was preferred. She hoped that she could resume this kind of identity after her return to Germany. Her reason for returning to East rather than West Germany she explains variously throughout our interviews with her: because she didn't want to shock her daughter, because she owed something to the Russians since they saved her from the Nazis, because she sympathized with socialism. Ultimately, she often came down to the conclusion that she felt more comfortable with those in the East because her own history in the intervening twenty-two years was more closely tied to theirs, and she did not want to be alienated from this history.

Case 2. Herr Cramer returned to West Germany with the Allied occupation army in 1944 after six years of residence in the United States. "We wanted to stay in America, but the positions they offered me there interested me so very little. And there was so much to do here, things that were very close to my, no, not my heart, that sounds so. . . . I had the feeling I could do more here than [in America]. I got a job [that enabled me] to remain in Germany." In contrast to Frau Benario, whose reasons for return often focus on concerns of loyalty, belonging, and Cold War ideological fights, Herr Cramer offers a kind of explanation that stresses contingency, accident, a dependence on circumstance. We never encountered any Jews who returned to West Germany out of conviction, though some, like Herr Cramer, developed a positive sense of belonging in their work and interactions in the intervening years.

Case 3. Albert Klein, the oldest of our discussion partners, born in 1904, returned to West Berlin in 1979. He initially went into exile, because of fear of persecution because he was a Jew, in 1935. His exile led him through Vienna and Riga, ultimately landing him in Lithuania, which was shortly afterward annexed by the USSR. He remained in Lithuania working in the theater until 1979, when he emigrated to Israel. "For me, to return was always a task [Aufgabe]. I always thought that I would come back to Berlin. Berlin is where I grew up and I have certain obligations here. [He explained how he had promised his first wife, who was murdered in a concentration camp, that he would return to Berlin.] [In all these years] I've been in no political party, have wanted no privileges, because I knew that somehow I'd come back to Berlin." Albert Klein remembers the decision to return as made before he left. He remembers having made a pact with his first wife about an obligation to return. He never portrays his Jewishness as being in opposition to other identities or even to different citizenships—German, Lithuanian, Soviet, or Israeli. Perhaps more than the other people we interviewed, Herr Klein embodies the idea of a cosmopolitan identity that did not seek to transcend any particularities but rather combined them in different, idiosyncratic ways.

Case 4. Herr Berger returned in 1949 after fighting in the Spanish Civil War, four years' internment in a concentration camp in France, and six years exile in the USSR. After mentioning that he came from a politically engaged family, that his father was a pacifist, he explains his decision to return.

> We said, it concerns eliminating the roots of fascism in Germany for all time. We fought against fascism before the war, during the war, and we wanted to [do that] also after the war after we returned to Germany. And we all shared the perspective to return to Germany. For we wanted to help build a democratic, anti-Fascist, and, from this perspective, a socialist Germany. Now, it was our task, since we were all old Socialists, old anti-Fascists, with experience, with knowledge of an international nature, now it was our task. . . . We looked at our task as a political one, an ideological, humanistic one. . . . First, we had to drive this antihumanism out of the German people, yes, and we wanted to help do that. And because of that, it was clear to us that we would return to Germany.

This particular explanation is a distinctly East German one, especially in the way in which democracy, antifascism, and socialism are linked as part of an Aufgabe: task, mission, obligation. This Aufgabe is not the same as that of Herr Klein. Herr Klein's mission was a personal one, to honor the memory of his murdered wife, to reclaim home, to deny the Nazi victory of a Judenfrei Germany. In contrast, Herr Berger sees himself as part of a historical mission (political, ideological, humanistic)—thus, his use of "we" instead of "I"—to eliminate fascism.

Case 5. Frau Eisler left Germany in 1936 and returned in 1949 to East Berlin. She had been deported from Ellis Island in New York after three months' imprisonment for refusing to inform on her husband, Gerhart Eisler, who, in addition to his anti-Fascist work, had also been a leader in Communist party organizing in the United States during the war.

> [I did not want to return] but I didn't have any other option. There were no options for me because, first, I was married, and my husband definitely wanted to return—he was politically engaged. And second, I would have found no sympathy with my American friends if I would have, so to speak deserted. There would have been a big scandal had I remained. The Americans would have exploited that. They would have made a big deal out of it.
>
> So it was clear to me that I would return. . . . I didn't have a permanent visa. . . . The Americans offered me one so I could stay—if I would have betrayed him, betrayed how he managed to leave the U.S. [He had escaped as a stowaway on a Polish ship.] But I didn't do that.

Much like her counterparts who went to West Germany, Frau Eisler's decision to return was not one made out of loyalty to a cause or ideology but was contingent on circumstances. In her case, the decision was to follow her husband to the East. To this day, Frau Eisler, whose American citizenship was revoked when she left, cannot visit the United States without being arrested. Although she claims to always have had Communist sympathies, her return was perhaps more attributable to gender (we found only one example, that of Frau Benario's "husband," in which a man followed a woman back) than to political convictions.

In sum, we could not isolate a primary reason for return that holds across all or even a majority of the cases. It may be that Jewish Communists were more eager and enthused about returning to the East because they and East Germany were more anti-Fascist than those who returned to the capitalist West where a consistent ideological explanation was unavailable. Yet this conviction may often have been an ad hoc, ideological justification for material circumstances that made the return to the East the best of the relatively few choices available to German-Jews at that time. In most cases, practical considerations—offers of work, McCarthyism in the United States, Stalinism in the USSR, deep ties to German language and culture, ties to place—were determinative of who returned and to where.

4. Division and Identity

Initially, Jews who had returned to Berlin were not radically affected by the division of Germany by the Allies. In fact, many wanted this division—as just punishment of Germany for the war, as a necessary lien on European security, and, especially for those in the East, as an opportunity to eliminate fascism and construct socialism. The Jüdische Gemeinde (Jewish community) in Berlin remained united until 1953. A majority of the early returnees to the Soviet Zone/GDR settled in the Pankow area of East Berlin. Officially acknowledged as "victims of fascism," and treated the same as other categories of victims, they received priority in apartments (only 8 percent in Berlin of which survived the war undamaged; see Luize and Höpfner 1965, 574), and many were immediately incorporated into high-status political, cultural, and administrative work. For most of these people, political identity was more important than religious and ethnic aspects of Jewishness. In any case, political authorities in the East encouraged the development of nonreligious and nonethnic identities, and most residents, Jews and non-Jews alike, accommodated themselves to this norm. At the same time, the state did recognize the principle of "freedom of religion." The community organized itself accordingly, along religious lines, and some people did practice a Jewish identity—much as others practiced Catholic or Protestant identities—within the state-approved and controlled confines of the confessional community. Given no alternative but a Jewishness reduced to religious practice, many East German Jews suppressed parts of their own histories, in the extreme case even hiding aspects of a Jewish heritage and history. Hence their children were often left on their own to rediscover or nurture relations to Jewishness or the Jewish community if they were so inclined. In 1986, a group called Wir für Uns (colloquially, "for ourselves"), comprised of approximately two hundred "members," began meeting regularly in East Berlin to cultivate a broad range of primarily nonreligious-based Jewish traditions (Kirchner 1991: 35; Ostow 1990: 47–59).

As the Cold War heated up in the early 1950s, people in the East and the West, including Jews, were increasingly asked to take sides against the other half. In 1952–53, a wave of persecution of "cosmopolitans" and "Western immigrants" in Prague and Moscow had repercussions in East Germany: Jewish Gemeinden were searched; the Parliamentary representative and chairman of the Jewish communities in East Germany, Julius Meyer, was arrested. Five of the eight leaders of the East Berlin Jewish community fled overnight to West Berlin in January 1953. The result of the exodus was a call from the rabbi for greater Berlin, Nathan Levinson, for all Jews in the GDR to move to the West. Many responded to this call, and on January 19, 1953, the communities were officially divided (Beigel 1953; Ostow 1989, 1–9).

Despite this turbulent political history, approximately 1,500 Jews were registered as living in greater Berlin in 1956. But the number of Jews in the GDR (with the vast majority in East Berlin) continued to decline dramatically, even after the building of the Berlin Wall in 1961, whereas the community in the West somewhat stabilized. By 1986, the number of Jews registered by the community in the East had declined to 350, with 200 registered in the Berlin community (Richarz 1988, 20). Approximately half of those with whom we became acquainted, either personally or through hearsay, were not registered by the community and thus not part of the official statistics. Most came from professional classes and worked in the same, or related, occupations from which they had been banned during the Nazi period. By the 1980s, the East German regime, in search of the international recognition already accorded the Federal Republic, began to curry the favor of international Jewish organizations and thus granted most Jews in the GDR a relatively privileged status, with more travel and business opportunities and better access to political authorities.

For West Berlin Jews, 1952 was also a decisive year, for at that time the Federal Republic began actively encouraging some prominent Jews to return. In its striving for international recognition and its desire to isolate the GDR, it formulated a reparations policy, not primarily oriented to the Jews who had suffered under the Nazis or to relatives of those who had been killed but focused on the state of Israel and the Jewish people as a group. Through policies earmarked as antifascist in the East and Widergutmachung in the West, both German states, but especially the Federal Republic, gained prestige and legitimation in the international community. In this light, Y. Michal Bodemann (1983) has argued that the major "function" of Jews in postwar Germany became one of doing "ideological labor" for the two new states. Because the Federal Republic was more successful at this game of international politics—until 1973, only thirteen states refused to go along with West Germany's Hallstein Doctrine and recognized the GDR—it experienced a net gain in Jews during the Cold War. From 1955 to 1959 alone, six thousand Jews migrated to West Berlin/West Germany; more than 60 percent came from Israel, with most of the rest from Latin America. It should be stressed that most of these immigrants were either of Sephardic ancestry or Ostjuden, not German-Jews; they were not "returnees" but new to Germany and to German culture. The Jews in the GDR, on the other hand, though smaller in number than in West Germany, were primarily German-Jews, either the products of so-called mixed marriages, concentration camp survivors, or returnees from exile (Kirchner 1991, 30). Following the logic of the Cold War from the other side, the GDR developed a different, often contradictory, policy regarding Jews. Initially it supported Jewish claims for indemnity but after the summer of 1952 suspended all outstanding restitution claims. Its policy toward Israel, initially extremely supportive, also became increasingly hostile over the years. Additionally, as pointed out above, official anti-Semitic persecutions in the Eastern bloc, especially but not exclusively under Stalin, caused a steady flight west. The West German Jewish community, under the leadership of Heinz Galinski from 1949 to 1990, worked closely with the FRG in welcoming those from the East.

By the time of our study, Jews (with minimally two Jewish grandparents) living in the two Germanies were estimated at 70,000, although only about half of them were registered as members of the Jewish community. If one includes converts to and others closely identified with Judaism, this number might approach 100,000. Of those registered by the communities, approximately 5,000 lived in the East, 25,000 in the West. Of this total, about 2,000 lived in East Berlin, 6,000 in West Berlin. Included among those in West Germany were approximately 10,000 to 12,000 Soviet Jews who had immigrated since the 1970s (see Bodemann 1993; Bodemann 1983, 28; Ostow 1989; and Richarz 1988, 25). Today more than 50 percent of all Jews registered with the community in West Berlin come from the former USSR (Hammer and Schoeps 1988). Of these numbers, only a small fraction are "German-Jews." Of this fraction of German-Jews, we were concerned with only those who had lived in exile in one of the Allied countries and returned to Berlin.

Living in East or West Berlin altered the way in which Jewishness and Germanness were articulated over time, and unification has again forced a rearticulation of this relationship. New German-Jewish identities were formed in dynamic interaction with East and West German state and social patterns of integration and postwar identity formation. To oversimplify the major differences, Jews who returned to the East were assimilated into a nationality based on a universalistic ideology of antifascism and socialism. Theoretically, anyone could become East German if they believed in this ideology. Jews who returned to the West were assimilated into a nationality based on a particularist ideology of membership in a blood-based German Volk. Theoretically, only those who were German by blood—and this included German-Jews—could become West German. However, West German citizenship was also guaranteed to anyone who had been a legal resident in the former Reich, as well as to all Volksdeutsche, Germans by blood, living in the East bloc. Moreover, it was West German practice to offer citizenship to all European Jews, many of whom were stateless after the war, regardless of their nationality or cultural background. Thus, German-Jews who returned to the West fit into a larger category of European Jews in which the German part of this hyphenated status became a sign of citizenship alone, and the Jewish part became a sign of cultural distinctiveness, if not radical otherness. As mentioned above, German-Jews who returned to the East tended either to omit the reference to Jewishness altogether, to downplay its relation to otherness by emphasizing its secular qualities, or to reduce it to a religious practice and membership in the Gemeinde. I submit five cases to illustrate these differences.

Case 1. In August 1989, Ruth Benario, who returned to East Berlin in 1954 after twenty-two years in the USSR, responded to our request to explain how she relates Germanness to Jewishness: "I am a German-Jew." To the question "Do you find that burdensome," she responded, "No. God, you sense things, sometimes there's a trace of something or other. But where don't you find that in life? That doesn't matter. . . . But I will say it, for I am it, and I'll remain what I am. I'll always be a Jew."

In the summer of 1989, we asked her about her relationship to the Federal Republic.

It's really seldom that I meet people over there whom I like. The size of the people over there, I feel, isn't right. And their attitude, the way they behave, the way they speak, the things about which they're interested. I am not like that! I'm not that and I don't like that kind of person. . . . It's frightfully difficult for me to get used to these people. . . . It's precisely that way with a woman, a friend of mine whom I've known since our childhood. I just recently began to think about why that is so, just the beginning of this year. I say, "Well, how's it going? What have you gone through?"

"Nothing at all," she says. "I'm always fine."

We were in Zurich back then. She went from exile in London to Zurich. I was so perplexed that she didn't go through anything at all during this period when we had to deal with Herr Hitler and Comrade Stalin, and where so many have gone through so much, such hard times. And that people are first really formed through this experience—that's something they don't at all understand. You see, it's the same for Frau X and her husband in West Berlin. They were in America. They also didn't live through anything that happened, who we were back then, and what we had, and how it all began. And that was for me really remarkable, how I came to this understanding, that they naturally lead a totally different life than we are

able to, because we see it from a totally different standpoint. . . .
And they are very nice and all, but they don't understand anything,
what happened to us because of what we've lived through, how that
penetrates us. Or it appeared to me that way. They're very loving
and nice, kind, but that's not the point.

Frau Benario expresses the relation of Jewishness to Germanness as
something experiential, as part of her personal history. Her history, she
reminds us, was made possible only because Stalin saved her from
Hitler. Later, of course, she explains how she was also terrorized by
Stalin while in Moscow, even exiled in Siberia during the war. Throughout our interviews with her, she stressed her desire to help others, to feel
for and live with and for others, as the major motivating force in her life.
She feels closest to those people with whom she shares the same experiential history. Her strongest criticism is reserved for her German-Jewish
friends who are unable to share with her this history, an inability she
attributes to exile in America and postwar life in West Berlin.

In an interview two years later, in 1991, she reformulated her relationship to the newly unified Germany. "The Jews aren't well-liked in
Germany. And the idea of a Jewish state is even more unpleasant. It's
difficult to explain to them that other people want to live just like the
people here." Her unstated reference was to German xenophobia and
the growing violence against foreigners, in particular asylum seekers and
Turks, that accompanied unification. With respect to her own identity,
she states, "I don't feel German. I feel Jewish. I am not a German. I
don't have anything in common with the whole German people. I was in
fact rubbed the wrong way when I came back from the Soviet Union. At
that time a friend asked me if I wasn't happy to be back in my home
country again. And I said, I am sorry I came back. I find nothing homey
here. I'm here to help. That's all."

Between 1989 and 1991, something had indeed changed for Frau
Benario. In our first interview, she cried several times in reciting the
events of her return, of how, after years of cramped living quarters in
Moscow, she was given a large apartment with a kitchen, living room,
dining room, and separate bedrooms. Nor she is beginning to remember
this return as something she regrets—and regretted as early as the
1950s. In the enlarged Federal Republic, she is already beginning to
reformulate Jewishness and Germanness as oppositional identities.

Case 2. Herr Cramer returned in 1944–45 with the American army
after six years in the United States. About his identity, he said, "I am a
German-Jew." When we asked about his decision to stay, he replied,

It wasn't a decision, no, it didn't work out that way. I didn't say one day, like Hitler said, that I'd decided to become a politician. I never decided to live here in Germany. Rather, it just presented itself that way. You accumulate so many things like that, like how I entered the American army. I feared that it wouldn't again be possible to build some kind of Jewish life [in Berlin] because I couldn't imagine that during the Hitler period there were still people who thought otherwise here in Germany. Then I came back and suddenly I noticed that, like so much in life, it's not always black and white. Nothing is black-white. It's all various shades of grey, everything is a little faded.

Herr Cramer's initial return to Germany was with the press division of the army. After several years, he returned to the United States, where he had obtained citizenship during his exile. Realizing that there were few career opportunities for him there, he returned to West Germany a second time, this time as a civilian working to establish the West German press (for Springer Verlag). He did not expect full integration and now attributes early problems to his own aloofness and distance from most people. Eventually he joined the Christian Democratic party and worked his way to the top in Springer Verlag. Today he is very proud of the way West German political institutions have developed, and he sees himself as having made a significant contribution to this through the development of an independent press. His personal aloofness never hindered his career, for neither the Federal Republic nor West German society required the kind of ideological integration or agreement demanded by the GDR. In fact, both of his children have left Germany, one for Norway, the other for the United States. He sees their decisions as exercises in freedom of choice, not as rejection of what West Germany offered them. For Herr Cramer, Germanness and Jewishness were never and are not now oppositional identities. Although one might suspect that Herr Cramer served an alibi function for the right-wing German press for whom he worked and for postwar West Germany—a single Jew serving prominently—Herr Cramer never experienced his work for Springer and his life in West Berlin, or so he told us, as those of a Jewish outsider treated as a token by the insiders. Indeed, as we interviewed him in the executive suite of the gold-capped, glistening Springer building, he appeared to us very much an insider.

Case 3. Albert Klein, who returned to West Berlin in 1979, after thirty-six years in exile (most of the time in Lithuania) and eight years in Israel, told us, "Naturally, I am a Jew, but I am also German." He explained his decision to return to the West as an obligation to his past, his ties to Berlin as a place, as well as for career reasons. He considers himself both German and Jew by birth, and like Herr Cramer, does not see the identities as opposed to each other. Although he complained bitterly of not being welcomed back by the Germans, he attributed this to being a late-returnee Jew, and to his return from the Communist East (via Israel). This lack of official welcome is ameliorated, however, by several other factors. First, his elected position as representative of the foreign press in Berlin brings him into constant contact with the international press and the artistic community, which has also enabled him to continue making documentary films. He also sees the move to Berlin as benefiting his wife's career as an artist. Second, he indicated that his ties to Berlin as a place have enabled him to reconnect the present to his life in the 1920s.

Case 4. Herr Berger, who returned in 1949 to East Berlin from an internment camp in France (via the USSR), denied altogether any links between his subjective self and either Jewishness or his life in exile.

> I am not Jewish. Isn't that clear? I was a Lutheran until I left the church. That was self-evident for me. . . . I'll be quite honest with you. In the old socialist community, where I saw myself as a Social Democrat and a Communist, sometimes as a Socialist, we shared a word, just once a word from Marx: "Religion is the opium of the people." On the other hand, the *International,* in which it says "No higher being will save us, no God, no Kaiser, no tribunal." And then we have to look at the entire history of Prussian Germany, where the church has always stood on the side of reaction.

For Herr Berger, there was no alternative to socialism, and, as he explained to us elsewhere, to anti-Fascism. Judaism was religion—here he agreed with the official definition of the East German state—and religion cannot save people. In German history, religion, as he sees it, had always served the forces of reaction. But Herr Berger has another criticism of German-Jews, which he goes into in explaining why so few returned to Germany. "I beg of us to judge them with care. But many Jews didn't come back for economic reasons. After 1945, Germany was a field of ruins, and it was difficult to make a career here. On the other hand, I believe that the politics of Stalin, in which one can certainly see definite anti-Semitic tendencies, worked to scare away many. It was worse in the Soviet Union, but that is Stalin, please. That's not socialism [we are talking about]; with Lenin it was the opposite." Herr Berger then explained how Lenin had many well-known Jews in his close circle of friends and advisers.

The line of Herr Berger's argument goes as follows: Jewishness means above all religion as ideology—and he distances himself from all religion. Moreover, neither Jews nor any other group can be delineated by blood or race. The fact that he and members of his family were identified by the Nazis in this way seems to have strengthened his resolve not to subjectively identify with the categorization Jew. (In a discussion with a close mutual friend, he once confided how his aunt was forced to give up her house pets once laws were passed making it illegal for Jews to keep domestic animals. Yet he refused to give us even this memory of Jewishness.) Much like Marx in "On the Jewish Question," he appeals for a nonreligious, nonethnic, nonracial identity based on international solidarity. Marx went further, of course, and also argued that Jews would never achieve selfhood and equality within Europe unless they were freed of the stereotypes attached to Jewish culture: greed, money, haggling, and commerce.[2] This criticism is also implicit in Herr Berger's explanation of reasons why German-Jews did not return.

Case 5. Frau Eisler returned to East Berlin from the United States in 1949. In our interview in August 1989, she explained, "The GDR gave to me for the first time in my life the feeling that I was a citizen with equal rights. I could vote in the GDR for the first time in my life. I feel like an absolutely equal member of the society here. I feel cared for and secure, ever more now. . . . And, as I said, my journalistic work was a great source of satisfaction. I also sit on the board of the Committee of Anti-Fascist Resistance Fighters, and I am thankful for the carefulness and way and manner in which they treat the anti-Fascist resistance fighters here." About the Germans and German identity, she described her sentiments, "Actually, disrespect, abhorrence, loathing about what they tolerated, if they weren't all criminals themselves."

When we asked her to describe her own complex relation to politics and Jewish selfhood, she said, "I've always said that I am a Jew. I've never been silenced about that, but this conscious Jewishness, that's something the Holocaust made me." Asked to explicate this "something," she replied, "First, I am a Jew. I feel myself a citizen of the German Democratic Republic. I am a GDR Jew." Much like Herr Berger, she has taken on a GDR identity, a state identity that emphasizes Staatsbürger, formal

---

2. I am undoubtedly giving Marx here a one-sidedly favorable reading. For a more critical reading, see Sander Gilman's careful reading of this essay along with Marx's later rewriting in *The Holy Family*. Gilman argues that Marx's hatred for what he called the "Sabbath Jew" and the "finance Jew," along with his virulent attacks on Lasalle, were the result of "his antithetical self-image: thus his confusion and the vehemence of his own rhetoric when confronted by the contradictory aspects of that "Jew" which he sees within himself" (1986, 208).

citizenship, over membership in any ethnonational identity. But, unlike Herr Berger, she has resisted any integration into the German Kulturnation, instead emphasizing her own cultural identity as a Jew. Her own relations to America and the United States from her period of exile are omitted entirely. Though she remembers these experiences fondly, and stated that she would love to visit her relatives and friends in the United States once again, she did not indicate any personal bitterness or animosity for being denied an opportunity to reconnect with this part of her past. For Frau Eisler, identity is necessarily discontinuous. Her identification with culture, Jewishness, is set alongside her citizenship, GDR—but she is a national nowhere. Moreover, though Jewish by birth and fate, she insists on keeping this cultural identity separate from categories of race and religion. Her citizenship, by contrast, is the one thing she has chosen, based on a shared ideology.

We had several more interviews and letter exchanges with Frau Eisler following the opening of the Wall. During this tumultuous period, she was alternately withdrawn or active in representing her life and that of her husband in the public sphere. In a letter dated April 7, 1991, she referred us to an interview she had given in March 1990 to Manfred Engelhardt, which he edited and published in *Deutsche Lebensläufe: Gespräche* (Berlin: Aufbau Verlag, 1991, 27–48). In this interview, she lays the blame for the collapse of the GDR on the scandalous leadership of the *nomenklatura,* "What I am so appalled by is that the leaders in the Party isolate themselves. [They] have no idea what is happening among the people. They have forgotten everything, although they themselves suffered under fascism." She laments the fact "that our chance was wasted and that we now must live through such a decline, that the people don't want to hear from us anymore."

On April 30, 1991, Jeff Peck went back to Frau Eisler with our film director, Martin Patek, for a filmed interview. The following excerpts are from an interview that took place, then, a full seven months after formal unification of the two Germanies. This translation, edited and shortened, is mine.

Jeff: How do you feel about all these events [since 1989]?
Frau Eisler: Very divided. Naturally, I am happy that the Wall has fallen, for I have always had my reservations about how long one can imprison a people. That is very positive. But there are also many negatives. [Among these negatives, she lists a "general insecurity" about the future, unemployment, and rising criminality. She also mentions the singular and virulent anti-Semitism that had "broken out" in Germany, which she also finds threatening.]

Jeff: After the war you came back to the GDR. Now you are sitting in the Federal Republic, a country that you never really wanted [to be a citizen of]. How do you feel about that?

Frau Eisler: I must be honest [with you], it doesn't really matter whether I am now a citizen of the Federal Republic, or was a citizen of the GDR. It's simply, it doesn't concern me.

Jeff: Do you have a stronger feeling about being Jewish now than you did before?

Frau Eisler: I don't feel any more Jewish now than before. I understood myself to be Jewish before; that is my identity in the first instance. It was always important to me and it will remain important.

Since our first interview, Frau Eisler has changed significantly the way she portrays her identity. The unification of Germany has not resulted in a more unified identity for Frau Eisler, but in more discontinuities in her life course. No longer able to reference the GDR as part of her identity, she now has only her Jewishness, for she is living in a state with which she has shared an oppositional history. She mourns the loss of parts of her identity tied to the GDR: resistance fighter, anti-Fascist, Socialist. After commenting on her disappointment about the "perversions" of East German socialism and her disappointment with this "great fiasco," the failure to realize socialism in the GDR, Jeff asks her if she is sad. She replies, "Of course I am sad that it has come to this. We had once imagined [we would] build a democratic, better, actually more just, humanistic Germany. That was the reason the people returned, that was the great hope of the people who came out of the KZ, who were persecuted as anti-Fascists. Naturally, it's a great defeat, a defeat we have suffered. We have to live with that."

5. Conclusion

This paper has examined how the identities of German-Jews who returned from exile following World War II to live in a divided Germany have been marked by discontinuities between categories of culture, nationality, and citizenship. Rather than begin with the necessarily reductionist categories of the state, the census taker, the doctor, the rabbi, or the psychologist, I went directly to German-Jewish returnees and to their personal histories. These histories reveal emergent and changing subject positions, variously willed by individuals, determined by outside authorities, or negotiated between the two, with regard to states, nations, religions, ethnicities, and, most strikingly, with regard to the Cold War. These positions should not be

confused with "opinions" or "values," idealist artifacts with which the
cultural is often confused; rather, subject positions directly index the
material conditions in which people actually live.

Formerly exiled German-Jews offer privileged insights into the relations between identity, exile, and politics because they are an extreme and
exceptional case. As Carl Schmitt has argued, politics is made by who
decides on the exception, and the Jews have often served as the exception
in German, if not in European, history.[3] This "decision" has not been just
a German or Jewish one, but one of world-historical dimensions, part of a
"global ecumene" (Hannerz 1992) in which a transnational flow of images
and interactions has contested the meaning of "German-Jew." I have
argued that the German-Jew is a living presence in a space where they
were consigned to death and memory. The fact that non-Jewish Germans
tend to project onto them qualities and meanings that they had no part in
generating should not lead us to privilege these projections in our studies
(see R. Gay 1992: 467–84). Today these often philosemitic meanings, not
restricted to the German-Jew but often extended to the European Jew,
include guardians of memory, the conscience (and origin) of the West,
and a litmus test for German democracy. In this highly emotional and
political field, the specificity of the German-Jewish subject, particularly
those who returned to Germany, has been blurred and confused, if not
effaced.

It is commonplace in the popular media to assume that Germanness
and Jewishness are radical alterities that entail mutually exclusive identities, to stress the cultural autonomy and timelessness of Jewish culture as
distinct from the same aspects of German culture, and to think of the
"Jewish community" as a homogeneous, distinct group that never
changes. We have inherited this conceptualization of culture from German romanticism and nineteenth-century debates on cultural nationalism, and anthropologists have been perhaps the major carriers of this
basically Herderian tradition. It is, however, extremely misleading to
assume that culture is thinglike, a set of essences distinct from other

---

3. Schmitt's discussion of the shifting nature of the political, and his criticism of
liberalism's dangerous tendency to depoliticize and negate what is essentially political, are
extremely important insights. I disagree with Schmitt, however, with regard to where the
authority to decide on the exception should reside. Although Schmitt questions the reduc-
tion of politics to state doctrine, and thereby questions the sovereignty of the state, he also
argues that the state should be the ultimate arbiter. However, by "state" he does not mean
the liberal idea of state as opposed to society, which he criticizes for simply reversing the
Hegelian idea of state as "a realm of morality and objective reason" (1976, 77). Rather, he
defines the state as founded in a historically determined and contested "political." It
follows from this empirically valid claim that states are one of many instances of authority
in a competition over definitions. For me, then, the state has no a priori grounds to justify
its claim to ultimate moral authority (see Borneman 1992, 1–36; 74–118).

essences that endure over time, passed on by generational transmission (see Moore 1994; and Clifford 1988). The German-Jew has a historical and syncretic identity, fundamentally shaped in interaction with the experience of diaspora and political division, and in a hybrid space provided by two cultural traditions.

With this in mind, one does no justice to German-Jewish identity by considering the Jews as always external to the Germans, by assuming that the Jews have always had to choose between cultural autonomy or assimilation into an unchanging Germanness, or, conversely, that the Germans have to fear being Jewified, recalling the Nazi notion of a "zersetzende Geist" (a decomposing, perverting spirit). Indeed, the very idea that the Jews could so easily pervert the Germans indicates a basic Nazi insecurity, even admission of an inferiority complex, that German spirit was itself incomplete and thus open to influence by a projected "outside" that was already "in."

This kind of thinking is reinforced by the idea of a homogeneous nation, written into the West German Basic Law of 1949, or Constitution, that Germanness is inherited by blood, that a German is necessarily limited to a single citizenship and hence must choose to which culture s/he belongs. As is well known, this ethnocultural ideal of German nationality has never been historically realized. At least since the Middle Ages, Germans have been divided into many competing principalities, each with distinct tribal identities. In the last several centuries, millions of ethnic Germans have been living outside any German state along with millions of non-Germans (primarily Slavs and Jews) living within the different German states. It is further reinforced by an assimilationist model of the "Volk" that has traditionally assumed the Jews, alone with the Gypsies of all the peoples in Europe, to be nonassimilable to the major "nationalities" on the continent. The inspiration for this idea is the nineteenth-century Mazzini formula, that a culture, nation, and state are isomorphically related, a program on which the Zionist movement also modeled itself (see Brubaker 1992; Hobsbawm 1990). This model of an ethnocultural nation-state continues to inspire the leaders of the vast majority of the 190 states in existence as of this writing, despite the fact that only a handful have anything approaching a homogeneous nation.

German-Jews do not fit neatly into this either/or question, for clearly they could be either, neither, or both German and/or Jew. In their lives, culture, nation, and state are more often than not disjunctively instead of continuously related. In this sense they are a "third" with respect to the binary German/Jew or native/foreigner in that they resist easy categorization and thus pass back and forth between them, between German and Jew, between native and foreigner. Moreover, during their periods of exile, many had obtained another citizenship

(Soviet, American, British) and become fluent in another language, further complicating the program of a continuous national history and bounded cultural identity expressed in a single language that realizes itself in a state. By migrating back to Germany, these German-Jews have challenged and destabilized the assertion of the binary opposition German and Jew. In passing between cultures, nationalities, and citizenships, they continue to make anxious those who want to assert a more stable opposition between categories of Germanness and its radical other. Being "in-between," however, has neither been easy nor a constant state. Indeed, both German states and other interested actors and organizations have continually pressured people to choose, for example, between East and West, Jew and German, Israel and one of the German states. In various ways, German-Jewish returnees have resisted these choices.

The Jews in this study returned from three different experiences of exile—the Soviet Union, the United States, and England, the nations of the "morally correct"—following World War II. They returned from this position within the morally correct to the land where the genocide took place. For those in the East, as I've already mentioned, the return was justified in antifascist terms. They claim they returned to eliminate fascism; they remained on the side of morality. For those in the West, the reasons for return vary tremendously. Few have anything to do with morality; most returnees claim that they just got stuck in Germany and then made the best of it. But, to the extent that some justified the return to Germany in moral terms, it was to build a democratic Germany. This difference between the condensed symbols of "antifascism" and "democracy" has been a major theme of debate in the unified Germany. And since the unified Germany is being redone according to the West German model of democracy, and since the "morally correct" Soviet Union has dissolved, the antifascist subject position of people in the East, Jews included, has been criticized and severely undermined.[4] Moreover, the unification of Germany was never a major goal, or reason for return, of the Jews in this study. Those who returned because Germany was divided, and because they thought that this division was right, suddenly find themselves to be displaced peoples in a country not of their choosing.

---

4. For example, a major exhibition of "Jewish Lifeworlds" opened in January 1992 in Martin Gropius Bau in Berlin. At issue for some of our East Berlin Jewish friends was the fact that only the learned, textualist, and religious traditions were represented, and that the exhibit ignored Jewish "antifascist resistance." One of our interview partners even sent us a letter with a clipping of a critique of the exhibit. This person understood the exhibit as part of an effort to delegitimate Communist and political contributions of Jewish culture.

The point I want to make is that both exile and place of return, East or West, provided different positions of German-Jews with regard to the Holocaust, the division of Germany, and now unification. First, the Holocaust affected this group directly, but, unlike those who survived the war in one of the camps or in hiding in Germany, they survived in exile, and exile is remembered as life not death. Second, memory of the Holocaust has been shaped by return, by being positioned as German citizens living in German culture. Memory is shaped by direct confrontation with the site of Holocaust culture—place, sounds, sights—that other Jews remember from afar. Thus, return has entailed a different living out of the Holocaust trauma, a kind of working-through condemned by most of the Jews in America and Israel. But this working-through differs for those who returned to the East instead of the West. Devoting one's life to eliminating fascism, even if considered a failed project by some of the participants themselves, is not the same kind of working-through as dedication to building a free press or fostering democratization.

What a successful anti-Fascist working-through entails remains highly disputed. However, it would be oversimplistic to claim that the East German anti-Fascist policy was totally ineffectual, or even, as some claim, counterproductive. An opinion survey done between October 1 and October 15, 1990, indicated that West Germans were much more anti-Semitic than were East Germans. In response to the question of whether Israel was a state like any other, to which Germany had no special obligation, 57 percent of the West Germans responded positively, only 40 percent of the East Germans. In response to the question of whether the Jews instrumentalize the Holocaust, 45 percent of the West Germans said yes, compared to 20 percent of the East Germans. In response to the question of whether Jews have too much influence over world politics, 44 percent of the West Germans said yes, while 20 percent of the East Germans said no (cited in Benz 1991, 21). To be sure, the opinions indicated in surveys are hardly reliable reflections of what people actually do, since they usually reflect back the opinions of the questioner. In this case, the questioner was the American Jewish Committee, which I presume had no interest in showing West Germans to be more anti-Semitic than East Germans. The only conclusion I want to draw is that the anti-Fascist policies of the GDR, and reeducation more generally, should not be dismissed so lightly since such efforts had some influence on opinion and behavior (see Borneman 1996). How deep and how significant these changes are is a matter for further research.

Lastly, given the end of the Cold War, is the Jewish returnee to Germany again repositioned? Certainly the dissolution of the Soviet Union coupled with the unification of Germany has dramatically changed the configuration of power as to who can determine morality. And with the elimination of the GDR Jews in the East have been directly challenged to reexamine their postwar lives. With the United States and the United Nations seemingly unable to assert moral leadership on a world scale, it appears as if the issue of right is increasingly being decided at a national level. Even if this trend does not continue, Jews in Germany no longer occupy the singular space they did during the Cold War. Nor are they likely to reoccupy the phantasmic space they did in the nineteenth century (see P. Gay 1978; Gilman 1991; and Gilman 1986). Moreover, the increase in xenophobia and antiforeign actions in Germany has not been paralleled by a similar increase in anti-Semitism. German-Jews appear to have lost their iconic status, though they are not yet merely a sign in the forest of symbols. This forest is now being reassembled, and we have much to learn from the experiences of German-Jews. "If their success was largely illusory in immediate terms," writes the German-Jewish, American historian George Mosse, "in the long run they presented an attractive definition of Jewishness beyond religion and nationalism" (1985, 20). At a time when ethno-nationalism in discrete, sovereign states is being posited as the only viable form of group identity, German-Jewish struggles to move beyond this form are indeed an alternative that deserves our attention.

References

Beigel, Greta. 1953. *Recent Events in Eastern Germany* 1–18. New York: Institute of Jewish Affairs.

Benz, Wolfgang. 1991. "Der Schwierige Status der jüdischen Minderheit in Deutschland nach 1945." In *Zwischen Antisemitismus und Philosemitismus: Juden in de Bundesrepublic,* ed. W. Benz, 9–23. Berlin: Metropol Verlag.

Bodemann, Y. Michael. 1993. Jews in West Germany. Speech delivered at Cornell University.

———. 1983. "Opfer zu Komplizen gemacht? Der jüdisch-deutsche Bruch und die verlorene Identität Anmerkungen zu einer Rückkehr in die Bundesrepublik." *Die Zeit* 1 (December 30): 28.

Borneman, John. 1996. "Education after the Cold War: Remembrance, Repetition, and Rightwing Violence." In *Cultural Authority in Contemporary Germany: Intellectual Responsibility between State Security Surveillance and Media Society,* ed. Michael Geyer and Robert von Hallberg, Chicago: University of Chicago Press.

———. 1992. *Belonging in the Two Berlins: Kin, State, Nation.* Cambridge: Cambridge University Press.

Borneman, John, and Jeffrey Peck. 1995. *Sojourners: the Return of German Jews and the Question of Identity.* Lincoln: University of Nebraska Press.

Brubaker, Rogers. 1992. *Citizenship and Nationhood in France and Germany.* Cambridge: Cambridge University Press.

Clifford, James. 1988. *The Predicament of Culture: Twentieth Century Ethnography, Literature, and Art.* Cambridge, Mass.: Harvard University Press.

Diner, Dan. 1986. "Negative Symbiose: Deutsche und Juden nach Auschwitz." *Babylon* 1:9–20.

Gay, Peter. 1978. *Freud, Jews, and Other Germans: Masters and Victims in Modernist Culture.* New York: Oxford University Press.

Gay, Ruth. 1992. "What I Learned About German Jews." *American Scholar* 54:467–84.

Gilman, Sander. 1991. *The Jew's Body.* New York: Routledge.

———. 1986. *Jewish Self-Hatred: Anti-Semitism and the Hidden Language of the Jews.* Baltimore: John Hopkins University Press.

Hammer, Manfried, and Julius Schoeps, eds. 1988. *Juden in Berlin, 1671–1945: Ein Lesebuch.* Berlin: Nicolai.

Hannerz, Ulf. 1992. *Cultural Complexity: Studies in the Social Organization of Meaning.* New York: Columbia University Press.

Hobsbawm, E. J. 1990. *Nations and Nationalism Since 1780: Programme, Myth, Reality.* Cambridge: Cambridge University Press.

Jacobmeyer, Wolfgang. 1983. "Jüdische Überlebende als 'Displaced Persons.' " *Geschichte und Gesellschaft* 9:421–52.

Kirchner, Peter. 1991. "Die jüdische Minderheit in der Bundesrepublik." In Wolfgang Benz, 1991, *Zwischen Antisemitismus und Philosemitismus: Juden in de Bundesrepublik.* Berlin: Metropol Verlag. 29–38.

Luize, Wilhelm, and Richard Höpfner. 1965. *Berlin ABC.* Berlin: Presse- und Informationsamtes des Landes Berlin.

Moore, Sally Falk. 1994. "The Ethnography of the Present and the Analysis of the Process." In *Assessing Cultural Anthropology,* ed. Robert Borofsky, 362–75. New York: McGraw Hill.

Mosse, George. 1985. *German Jews Beyond Judaism.* Bloomington: Indiana University Press.

Ostow, Robin. 1990. "The Shaping of Jewish Identity in the German Democratic Republic, 1949–1989." *Critical Sociology* 17 (3):47–59.

———. 1989. *Jews in Contemporary East Germany: The Children of Moses in the Land of Marx.* New York: St. Martin's.

Peck, Abraham J. 1991. "Zero Hour and the Development of Jewish Life in Germany After 1945." In *A Pariah People?* Jewish New York: American Jewish Archives.

Richarz, Monika. 1988. "Juden in der BRD und DDR seit 1945." In *Jüdisches Leben in Deutschland seit 1945,* ed. Micha Brumlik, Doron Kiesel, Cilly Kugelmann, and Julius Schoeps, Frankfurt am Main: Athenäum.

Schmitt, Carl. 1976. *The Concept of the Political,* trans. George Schwab. New Brunswick: Rutgers University Press.

Yahil, Chaim. 1971. "Berlin: Contemporary Period." In *Encyclopedia Judaica,* vol. 4. New York: Macmillan.

4

Reordering Memories: Jewish and German Images about the Other

The Cultural Operations
of Germans and Jews as Reflected
in Recent German Fiction

Jack Zipes

Prologue

In 1893, Oskar Panizza wrote a fascinating and highly disturbing story entitled "The Operated Jew." It concerns Itzig Faitel Stern, a small, squat young man, with a protruding chicken breast, prominent nose, thick eyelashes, fleshy lips, black hair, and bow legs. Itzig speaks German with a strong Yiddish accent and uses his arms and legs to gesticulate whenever he makes a point. When he decides to attend the University of Heidelberg, he comes under the influence of a German, the narrator of the story, evidently a gentile of high quality. This friend persuades Itzig to get rid of all his obvious "Jewish" features, and given the great wealth the Stern family possesses Itzig is able to procure enough money to undergo several torturous operations to have his body straightened and to take lessons in rhetoric and elocution. Eventually he can pass for an Aryan in the best of German upper-class societies, and he successfully courts a blonde-haired beauty named Othilia. However, at their wedding reception, Itzig drinks too much and decomposes in front of the horrified eyes of all the guests, his friend, and the famous doctor Klotz who had performed the operation on Itzig. "Klotz's work of art lay before him crumpled and quivering, a convoluted Asiatic image in wedding dress, a counterfeit of human flesh, Itzig Faitel Stern."[1]

In 1922, Mynona (pseudonym for Salomo Friedlaender) published "The Operated Goy" as a direct parody of Panizza's "The Operated

---

1. Oskar Panizza, "The Operated German," in *The Operated Jew: Two Tales of Anti-Semitism*, trans., with commentary, by Jack Zipes (New York: Routledge, 1991), 74.

Jew." It concerns the young Count Kreuzwendedich Rehsok, who comes from one of the leading anti-Semitic families in Germany. He has soft, wavy, almost silvery, blonde hair, a pronounced white forehead, a straight nose, thin lips, a Prussian chin, proud neck, a wonderful posture, and long elegant legs with pangermanic feet. His parents send him to Bonn to study, and, since they are aware that he may come into contact with rich, female, Jewish students, who are dangerously seductive, they give him a gigantic servant named Odin and two ravens to protect him, to fend off the luring Jews, and to keep him pure Aryan. His family hopes that he will marry an Aryan woman named Frigga and have children to be called Balder, Bragam, Hermod, Thor, and Tyr. However, when Rebecca Gold-Isaac hears about all these precautions and plans, she becomes enraged and decides to captivate him, and perhaps even marry him, out of revenge. Since she is both cunning and beautiful, she manages to charm Count Rehsok with the result that he is willing to do anything for her and ardently desires to marry her. However, her father, a millionaire, will not let Rehsok marry her unless he is circumcised. Rebecca is even more demanding: the count must undergo several operations at the hands of the famous Dr. Friedlaender to become squat, bow-legged, and dark, and he must also study the Torah and learn to speak Hebrew and Yiddish. Eventually he changes his name to Moishe Kosher (Rehsok spelled backward), and, though all the aristocratic Borussians near Bonn storm the marriage reception and try to ruin the celebration, they are defeated by the gigantic Odin (now paid by Rebecca's father) and the police.

> Now Mr. and Mrs. Moishe Kosher are living today as committed Zionists in a country villa near Jerusalem. To be sure their offspring are not called Balder, Brage, Hermod, Tor and Tyr. Instead, they have more melodic and honest names: Shlaume, Shmul, Feigelche, Pressel and Yankef.—The Rehsok clan has vainly sought to the present day to change its name and must consequently put up with the fact that when, something is not completely kosher, people in their circles say that it is not completely "rehsok."[2]

Panizza, a doctor, who also wrote an anticlerical play, *Das Liebeskonzil* (1984), and had to spend one year (1895–96) in prison for his outspoken criticism of Catholicism, felt drastically persecuted by the German state. Eventually, in 1905, he succumbed to paranoia and was

---

2. Mynona [Salomo Friedlander], "The Operated Goy" in Zipes, *The Operated Jew,* 85. Friedlaender's story originally appeared as "Der operierte Goj: Ein Seitenstück zu Panizza's operirtem Jud," in *Trappistenstreik und andere Grotesken* (Freiburg: Walter Heinrich, 1922).

committed to an asylum near Bayreuth, where he spent the next sixteen years of his life, never really comprehending the events of the world around him. He died on September 28, 1921.[3] Salomo Friedlaender received a Ph.D. in 1902 with a concentration in philosophy. He became a free-lance writer in Berlin and an important figure in expressionist circles. In 1933, he fled the Nazis and managed to survive World War II in France, but only under difficult conditions. He died penniless in Paris on September 1, 1946.[4]

Another Friedländer, Saul, born in 1932 in Prague, describes in his autobiography *When Memory Comes* the "operations" performed on him in France during the 1940s that transformed him into a Catholic so that he could escape the Nazis. His parents were less fortunate, for they were caught trying to escape to Switzerland and sent to a concentration camp to be annihilated. A historian, Saul Friedländer is perhaps better known for his most recent work, *Reflections of Nazism: An Essay on Kitsch and Death*.[5] Friedländer seeks to discover the structures of the imagination past and present that lead to representing Nazism in a new discourse that couples kitsch with a fascination with death so that the horror and pain of nazism is no longer re-evoked; rather reverie and the attraction of spectacle shift our focus, distract us into complacency.

In the course of his book, Friedländer deals with Rainer Werner Fassbinder's film *Lili Marleen* and discusses how Fassbinder conceives a myth about Germans and Jews in the Barthean sense of the term. Fassbinder's ideological myth has ordinary people at the mercy of

> Jewish capitalists on the one hand, embodied by the patriarch of Zürich; Nazism on the other, symbolized by this vivid light, Adolf Hitler. And thus the real struggle is not between the Nazis and their enemies, but between the forces of evil (Jewish capitalism and Nazism) on the one hand, and the good people (Wickie and her song, that devil of a good pianist, and the millions of anonymous soldiers) on the other: those who are going to die.[6]

Indeed, Fassbinder projects his own view of how "good" common Germans are operated on by sinister forces of immense power associated with Jews and Nazis. As Friedländer remarks,

3. Cf. Peter D. G. Brown, *Oskar Panizza: His Life and Works* (New York: Peter Lang, 1983); and Michael Bauer, *Oskar Panizza: Ein literarisches Porträt* (Munich: Carl Hanser, 1984).

4. Cf. my essay "Salomo Friedlaender: The Anonymous Jew as Laughing Philosopher," in *The Operated Jew*, 110–37.

5. Translated by Thomas Weyr (New York: Harper & Row, 1984).

6. Ibid., 48.

in *Lili Marleen,* everything is kitsch and at the same time everything breathes uplift and edification. . . . Everything in it has the rhythm of legend, of the sacred. Good and evil are recognized. Beneath the melodramatic aspect of the story (a sweet, loving, poor girl is abandoned by a rich young man), one sees the mark of the great tragedies. It is also the mythic annulment of time that reveals to us that the story recounted here is not a simple episode but the expression of eternal verities represented by stereotypes rather than by specific characters.[7]

Friedländer, the Jewish historian, is uneasy about how Fassbinder, the German playwright, operates with history, about how he conceives a myth about Germans and Jews that apparently reiterates some of the mythic notions of Nazism itself. This is the same Fassbinder who wrote the play *Garbage, the City and Death,* which was produced in Frankfurt in 1985, three years after his death, and created a national scandal.[8] If we recall, on opening night the real play was never performed. Instead a planned spectacle occurred, with German Jews in the audience taking the stage while over a thousand people outside the theater protested the production of the alleged anti-Semitic play. Charges and countercharges followed, with Günter Rühle, the play's director, supposedly asserting that "no hunting season for Jews was over" in West Germany. Or, in other words, they could once again become targets of criticism, even if it meant contributing to anti-Semitic stereotypes.

Fassbinder's pathetic play reeks with abstract, mythic stereotypes. The plot, if there is one, concerns the Rich Jew, who seeks revenge on Müller, a transvestite, whom he suspects of having murdered his parents during the Nazi period. Müller's wife, who is in a wheelchair, had beaten their daughter, and he himself had raped his daughter. This daughter, named Roma, is a prostitute who enjoys the Rich Jew's patronage. Eventually, however, the Rich Jew murders her at her request and escapes prosecution because he is good friends with Müller II, the corrupt police chief, who appears to be at the beck and call of the Rich Jew. In fact, the Rich Jew is a "mythic" super Jew, whose effect in Germany is described rather straightforwardly and seriously in the play by Hans von Gluck.

---

7. Ibid., 49.
8. See Andrei S. Markovits, Seyla Benhabib, and Moishe Postone, Rainer Werner Fassbinder's *Garbage, the City and Death*: Renewed Antagonisms in the Complex Relationship Between Jews and Germans in the Federal Republic of Germany," *New German Critique* 38 (Spring/Summer 1986): 3–27; and Johann N. Schmitt's inaugural Paul Lecture, published as *"Those Unfortunate Years": Nazism in the Public Debate of Post-War Germany* (Bloomington: Jewish Studies Program, Indiana University, 1987).

He's sucking us dry, the Jew. Drinking our blood and blaming everything on us because he's a Jew and we're guilty. I rack my brains and I brood. I tear at my nerves. I'm going under. I wake up nights, my throat like it's a noose, death stalking me in person. My reason tells me they're just images, myths from the pre-history of our fathers. I feel a sharp pain on my left side. My heart, I ask myself? Or the gallbladder? And it's the Jew's fault. Just being there he makes us guilty. If he stayed where he came from or if they gassed him I'd be able to sleep better. They forgot to gas him. This is no joking matter. And I rub my hands together as I imagine him breathing his last in the gas chamber. I rub my hands together again and I moan and I rub and I say "I'm Rumpelstiltskin: ah how fine that no one knows this name is mine." He's always one step ahead and all he leaves us is charity. Garbage, worthless objects.[9]

As in *Lili Marleen*, there is a grand collusion between the forces of evil, the corrupt police chief, and the Rich Jew, against the basically good and victimized common Germans—the Müllers. Of course, the play differs from *Lili Marleen* in a major chilling respect. Whereas the film revealed that the Nazis and the powerful rich Jews were in a certain sense equals, the play implies that the Rich Jew is basically in control of the police and the city. In other words, a Jew is determining the destiny of Frankfurt, if not Germany, depending on how you want to read the play. As Gertrud Koch has perceptively commented in regard to Fassbinder's portrayal of Jews in his films and plays, his

> aesthetics are based on allegoric constructions in which the German-Jewish symbiosis that has been conjured up many times is given a special place. Whether one agrees or disagrees with Gershom Scholem's notion that the German-Jewish symbiosis never existed and its idea was carried on in Auschwitz ad absurdum, its adjuration keeps returning as a ghost in the imaginary—as a love relationship or friendship with fatal results.[10]

We have come a long way since Panizza's "The Operated Jew," in which a Jew essentially annihilates himself out of self-hate. Panizza's

---

9. Rainer Werner Fassbinder, *Plays*, ed. and trans. Denis Calandra New York: PAJ Publications, 1985), 180.

10. Gertrud Koch, "Todesnähe und Todeswünsche: Geschichtsprozesse mit töd-lichem Ausgang: Zu einigen jüdischen Figuren im deutschen Nachkriegsfilm," in *Jüdisches Leben in Deutschland seit 1945*, ed. Micha Brumlik, Doron Kiesel, Cilly Kugelmann, and Julius Schoeps (Frankfurt am Main: Athenäum, 1986), 272–73.

story is rich in meaning because of its ambivalent ending: Itzig fails to become a straight-arrow German Aryan either because his Jewish condition prevents him from fully assimilating and abandoning his roots or because he is unworthy and decrepit in the eyes of Germans and can never be a "true" German. Whatever the case may be, Itzig is punished; his "identity" is determined in relation to Germans, just as the Germans determine who they are by distancing themselves from Jews. Panizza depicts the impossibility and undesirability of assimilation.

Mynona, or Salomo Friedlaender, takes a different view some twenty-five years later. World War I has ended. The Weimar Republic has been founded. The assimilated German Jews have many more liberties than they have ever had before. Writing in a light vein, Friedlaender spoofs the ridiculous nature of anti-Semitism and plays with stereotypes. In his story, the operation of the anti-Semitic count is a success. The Germans and Jews do not annihilate themselves. A German aristocrat can become a Jew. Anti-Semitism can indeed be overcome. Of course, Rebecca and the count do leave Germany and emigrate to Palestine, but at least they marry and have children, and Mynona/Friedlaender asserts at the end of his tale that anti-Semitism has abated and Professor Friedlaender, who had performed the operation on the count, has a booming business. It appears that Jews can define their own identities, compel anti-Semites to respect Jewish identity, and foster assimilation.

Some sixty years later, when Panizza's prognosis of what might happen to Jews if they try to become German has tragically proven to be true, Mynona/Salomo Friedlaender's optimism has become another Friedländer's uneasiness, especially when he reads Fassbinder projecting the triumph of the Jew in Germany. Mysteriously, behind the scenes, in the subconscious of the common and even aristocratic German, the Jew lurks and determines German identity and destiny. Like Panizza before him, Fassbinder unveils the dark side of contemporary German society (as well as his own dark fantasies), and his play assumes an ambivalent if not paradoxical form: it outrageously presents German and Jewish stereotypes in an outlandish endeavor to critique the stereotyping in the operations between Germans and Jews and the normative standards of West Germans while contributing his own ammunition to the mythic dimensions of anti-Semitism.

The Problem

It is not easy to write about the operations of Germans and Jews in recent postwar German fiction, especially since I feel constantly compelled to refer to the Holocaust as the definitive moral measure of their common operations. Obviously, it is impossible to ignore the role that the Holocaust has played in determining the relationship between Germans and Jews since 1945. However, I want to emphasize that my essay as *essai* is not altogether about the Holocaust's impact on Germans and Jews; it is *not* about Holocaust literature or imagining the Holocaust. There have been some fine books dealing with these topics in the past few years such as Lawrence Langer's *The Holocaust and the Literary Imagination* (1975), Alvin H. Rosenfeld's *A Double Dying: Reflection on Holocaust Literature* (1980), Sidre Ezrahl's *By Words Alone: The Holocaust in Literature* (1980), and Hamida Bosmajian's *Metaphors of Evil: Contemporary German Literature and the Shadow of Nazism* (1979). Consequently, I do not want to repeat or reiterate what they have discussed. Moreover, despite the crucial significance of the Holocaust, I share an *uneasiness* with Friedländer in making the Holocaust the focal point of my study on the relationship between Germans and Jews as represented in recent German fiction: the Holocaust can easily turn into and has been turned into kitsch, spectacle, false exorcism, morbid fascination, and ideological myth.

I prefer to use the concept of "operation" to understand and frame schematically how Germans and Jews have sought to define themselves since 1945 in order to develop their identities, which includes self-images and images of each other, because it can help explain the historical relationship of Jews and Germans before the Holocaust, during Nazism, and in the aftermath. As I have already indicated in my discussion of Panizza, Friedländer, and Fassbinder, Germans and Jews cultivated unique ways of operating on one another, of operating with one another—not cooperating. These cultural operations are crucial to grasp if we want to understand what constitutes ethnic and national identity. In a recent book, *The Unmasterable Past,* Charles Maier maintains that

> any meaningful concept of a national identity must posit a subsisting component, which requires description in terms of nonhistorical variables. We need to know history, therefore, to understand identity; but history will not suffice. If it did, countries would move in worn grooves, and trajectories of development would be predictable. German history, above all, teaches that national behavior has scope for unexpected veerings and craziness, atrocious (and corrective) possibilities beyond what historical knowledge can prepare us for.[11]

---

11. Charles Maier, *The Unmasterable Past: History, Holocaust, and German National Identity* (Cambridge: Harvard University Press, 1988), 151.

In the case of Germans and Jews, it is nearly impossible to produce a definitive concept of identity. However, I believe that the history of the cultural operations of Germans and Jews since 1945, with the aid of sociopsychology and literary criticism, can reveal how meaningful Germans and Jews are for each other in the formation of their identities. That is, I believe that no matter how tragic and atrocious their symbiotic relationship—whether a positive or negative symbiosis—has been in the past, I believe that their operations on and with one another since 1945 have compelled Germans and Jews to raise issues about anti-Semitism, racism, tolerance, responsibility, guilt, and democracy that have led to a crucial redefinition of their identities that could prove a turning point for the future of the Federal Republic's image and self-image—and possibly for the image and self-image of Jews in Germany.

Whether on a national or personal level, identity is a process, and within the process the category of "operation" is one I want to develop. I have already shown how this category can by used to characterize the interactions of Germans and Jews, to grasp literary projections in relation to the manner in which Germans and Jews seek to identify themselves, and to reflect upon the problematic issues of anti-Semitism, assimilation, self-hate, and mythic ideology. The category as metaphor implies that there is a "wound," that something is wrong, tarnished, nonfunctioning, failing. An operation is necessary to heal the wound, to fix it, to sew it up, and to make sure that it will not cause difficulties again. The operation is based on a diagnosis that there is a model to be emulated so that our bodies can function in as near a perfect manner as possible. We are conditioned to accept the model and to want an operation if we do not feel or look a certain way. Hence, the evolution of plastic surgery, the plastic body, the body as machine, the machine as body. The norm is dependent on operations. The civilizing process of any nation-state makes full use of socio-psychological and even physical operations to maintain a normative behavior. The normative model can only be imagined or grasped if there is an other, the other, or others. This other is the negative opposed to the positive. This other is, psychologically speaking, a fearful figure, an awe-inspiring figure, a figure that is used to create bonding among the like-minded, a figure that is to create disgust and repulsion, a figure that needs to be operated on.

In the case of the Jews, it is interesting to note that they became extremely important as the other in German societies during the eighteenth and nineteenth centuries as the Germans moved toward the formation of the nation-state and toward forging a sense of German identity. It was easy to stigmatize the Jews as the other in the eighteenth and early nineteenth centuries because of their distinct garb, religious customs, and their ghetto dwellings. However, as Jews became more assimilated and the Prussian edict of emancipation was promulgated in 1812, new ways had to be found to keep designating Jews as the other. In his remarkable study *Der Name als Stigma,* Dietz Bering demonstrates how, among many other apparent operations, something as "trivial" as names became crucial in stigmatizing Jews as the other.[12] Though the Prussian Edict declared Jews citizens, it also compelled them to do away with the traditional genealogical system of bestowing names according to the father's first name. For instance, Moses ben Mendel (Moses the son of Mendel) had to changed to Mendelsohn or other names had to be selected according to Prussian law. Basically Jews became free to choose their own names unless they were already bearing declared family names. Despite protests by the orthodox Jews, who wanted to maintain traditional Jewish custom, the Jews were supposed to assimilate, or supposed to want to assimilate, and they were to assimilate on Prussian terms. Bering remarks that the state sought to obligate the despised minority to dissolve itself in the respected majority. Nobody thought about changing their views and making a respected minority out of the despised one.[13]

The "difficulty" with Jewish emancipation for many Germans was that it would prevent Jews from being recognized if they stopped wearing distinctive clothing and beards, spoke in German, and had the same names as Germans. After hundreds of years of associating Jews with the Antichrist and the Devil, most Germans were not ready for religious tolerance. The result was that the nineteenth century witnessed a gradual erosion of the freedom given to Jews to choose their own names. The majority of Germans wanted to keep all Jews distinctive, even those who converted or who simply wanted to assimilate and were possibly agnostic. For instance, as early as 1816, a law was issued that prohibited Jews from changing their names "arbitrarily" and from giving their children Christian baptismal names, and the laws that followed up to 1848 kept limiting the choices of Jews, so that they were prevented from choosing Christian first names, and compelled them to choose from lists of names that were common among Jews. Despite the fact that it was practically impossible to designate what exactly a "Jewish" first name or surname was, since Jews in the diaspora had generally assumed names common to the country in which they lived and had a great variety of first names and surnames, the Germans began arbitrarily categorizing certain names as

---

12. Dietz Bering, *Der Name als Stigma: Antisemitismus im deutschen Alltag, 1812–1933* (Stuttgart: Klett-Cotta, 1987).

13. Ibid., 47.

Jewish, and these became accepted because they helped the Germans mark Jews and stigmatize them.

It was due to this stigmatization that those Jews who wanted to be fully assimilated in German society sought to change their names, and Bering's study of hundreds of petitions by Jews (and in some cases by Christians) to have their first names or surnames changed to make them "less Jewish," anonymous, or assimilated reveals the psychological and social pressures that Jews felt because of the manner in which they were singled out by their names in a discriminatory way. By 1870, with the shift in anti-Semitism from religious discrimination to racist prejudice, the laws stipulating how and whether Jews could change their names became increasingly stricter. For instance, in 1894, an order was issued by the minister of the interior that Jews would not be allowed to change their names if they wanted to make their lives easier with regard to anti-Semitic movements. In 1898, the arbitrary change of Jewish first names was prohibited. In 1900, the spelling of an apparent Jewish name could not be changed. Finally, in 1900, the minister of the interior was given exclusive power to decide whether people of the Jewish religion or Jewish ancestry could change their family names, and in 1903 the right of Jews to change their names upon conversion to the Christian religion was denied.

Of course, there were reforms, and more frequently permission was granted to Jews to change their names during and after World War I, up to 1933. However, the damage had been done. By the turn of the century, the laws set by the Wilhelminian Reich, the actions of the civil servants, and the attitudes and behavior of the German people had established a network of discrimination through names that stereotyped and stigmatized Jews and made them into objects of mockery and degradation—the dangerous other, the insidious anti-Christian, the greedy capitalist, the subversive political force that sought to undermine the "goodness" and "purity" of the German national character.

Stigmatization, name calling, is a form of operation that causes psychological harm and leads to physical abuse, marking the other as the ambivalent other: the absence of something crucial within oneself, the desired other, and the threat to one's essential identity, the oppressive other. In each case, the other appears to be superhuman and to have a hold on the self, a mark to be eradicated or a mark to be absorbed. For the Jews, the German as other is often a model to be desired and emulated, or a figure of destruction. The other arouses feelings of awe or of paranoia and self-doubt, for the German appears to have a hold on the Jew's identity, and it appears safer and perhaps more ideal to abandon one's Jewishness than to live in self-doubt.

Recent Fiction

The cultural operations of Germans and Jews during the past twenty years reflect a desire on the part of Germans and Jews to redefine the images and self-images each group has of one another, images and self-images that contend with traditional stereotypes in the hope of forging a new understanding between Germans and Jews. Recorded in texts, marked down in texts, the cultural operations often take the form of antithetical stereotypes or mental representations that can help us learn to what extent and if Germans and Jews have come to identify themselves through the other in nonpathological ways. As Sander Gilman has argued in his book *Difference and Pathology,*

> stereotypes are a crude set of mental representations of the world. They are palimpsests on which the initial bipolar representations are still vaguely legible. They perpetuate a needed sense of difference between the "self" and the "object" which becomes the "Other." Because there is no real line between self and the Other, an imaginary line must be drawn; and so that the illusion of an absolute difference between self and Other is never troubled, this line is as dynamic in its ability to alter itself as is the self. This can be observed in the shifting relationship of antithetical stereotypes that parallels the existence of "bad" and "good" representations of self and Other.[14]

Just a superficial glance at the manner in which Germans and Jews have been depicted in novels, films, art, stories, dramas, autobiographies, and other texts during the last fifteen years indicates that there have been major shifts in the metaphorical paradigms used by Germans and Jews to understand the self and the other. I have already referred briefly to Friedländer's *Reflections of Nazism* (1982) and Fassbinder's *Garbage, the City and Death* (1981), and here I would like to focus on three novels, which may be considered paradigmatic of three different ways that writers have endeavored to deal with the question of cultural operations, stereotypes, and anti-Semitism. The novels are Edgar Hilsenrath's *Der Nazi & der Friseur* (1977), Peter Härtling's *Felix Guttmann* (1985), and Jurek Becker's *Bronsteins Kinder* (1986).[15] Hilsenrath is a Jew who has lived in Israel and New York and now

---

14. Sander Gilman, *Difference and Pathology: Stereotypes of Sexuality, Race, and Madness* (Ithaca: Cornell University Press, 1985), 18.
15. Edgar Hilsenrath, *Der Nazi & der Friseur* (Cologne: Literarischer Verlag Braun, 1977); Peter Härtling, *Felix Guttmann* (Darmstadt: Luchterhand, 1985); and Jurek Becker, *Bronsteins Kinder* (Frankfurt am Main: Suhrkamp, 1986).

makes Berlin his "home." Härtling, one of the foremost contemporary West German writers, has also written an autobiographical work, *Nachgetragene Liebe* (1980), which tries to recall his father from the Nazi years. Becker, one of the foremost contemporary East German writers, has repeatedly dealt with the theme of Germans and Jews in such works as *Jakob der Lügner* (1969) and *Der Boxer* (1976). Each writer can be considered representative of a particular critical viewpoint of stereotypes, a viewpoint broadly developed by the cultural and social group to which he adheres. Each author writes predominantly in the first person, employing a masque or fictitious narrator to work through problems concerned with German-Jewish identity, national identity, and self-image. Insofar as they highlight current steretotypes, they reflect shifting attitudes that have a bearing on the tendentious ways that Germans and Jews operate with and on each other.

Hilsenrath's *Der Nazi & der Friseur* is a picaresque novel similar in some ways to Günter Grass's *Die Blechtrommel* because of its grotesque images and macabre sense of humor. It also picks up some of the themes and motifs that Panizza and Friedlaender developed in "The Operated Jew" and "The Operated Goy." The antihero or picaro of this novel is Max Schulz, alias Itzig Finkelstein. Born a bastard on May 23, 1907, in the small city of Wieshalle, Schulz, frog-eyed, short, and dark, grows up in Anton Slavitski's barbershop where he is often beaten and subjected to the sight of beastly lovemaking between his mother Minna and Anton. One of his best friends is Itzig Finkelstein, blonde, blue-eyed and tall, whose father Chaim owns the best barbershop in Wieshalle, called Der Herr von Welt, which is opposite Slavitski's shop. Schulz's dream is to own a shop like Chaim's one day, but in the meantime he must tolerate the crude conditions in Slavitski's shop. When the Hitler regime begins, he becomes a member of the SS and eventually a guard at the concentration camp Laubwalde, where 200,000 Jews are murdered, among them Chaim and Itzig Finkelstein, whom he personally kills. Pursued as a mass murderer when the war comes to an end, Schulz switches his identity in Berlin and becomes Itzig Finkelstein. He has a concentration camp number tatooed on his arm and lets himself be circumcised. He reads books about Jewish religion and history, and the officials declare him to be Itzig Finkelstein. After working as a dealer on the black market for a few years, Schulz decides that the future as a Jew looks better in Israel. So he leaves on the ship *Exitis*. During the voyage he carries on such imaginary discussions with Itzig Finkelstein as

> Dear Itzig. They say that one hates what one wants to deny. I, Itzig Finkelstein, at one time Max Schulz, always looked like a Jew . . .

even though that's not true. But they said it. Yes, they said it: he looks like a Jew!

Think about it, Itzig. Just for this reason I should have hated you. In order to deny something that's not me . . . merely because I was afraid that I could be it. Or, because they believed that I was it even though I knew that I wasn't it. Do you understand that?

You see then. You understand it. Me, too. In spite of it all I've never hated you. Strange . . . huh? But it's true. I, Itzig Finkelstein, at one time Max Schulz, never hated the Jews. Why didn't I hate you? I don't know. I only know: I, Itzig Finkelstein, at one time Max Schulz, didn't hate Jews.[16]

After arriving in Israel, Schulz finds a job in Schmuel Schmulevitch's barbershop in a small town outside Tel Aviv. Aside from fighting with an Israeli terrorist group against the British forces and with the Haganah, Schulz becomes a respected Zionist and barber. In fact, he becomes such a perfect Jew that, toward the end of his life, after he finally has his own barbershop, he cannot convince a retired judge that he really was the mass murderer Max Schulz. He dies of a heart attack in 1968 even though, or because, the doctors try a transplant operation with the heart of a rabbi.

Hilsenrath's novel is a fascinating exploration of the stereotypes that Germans and Jews have of one another. What appears to be a perfect Jew is a mass murderer, an operated German, who cannot shed his Jewishness and yet cannot be saved by a Jewish heart. Schulz's ironic autobiography explodes the traditional German and Jewish stereotypes and compels the reader to rethink German-Jewish operations from 1907 to 1968, for nobody is what he or she appears to be in the novel. In fact, the more Schulz becomes the other, the more difficulty he has in regaining a sense of his German identity. It even appears that his punishment, the only just punishment for Germans, is to become "Jewish," or the other. By becoming Jewish, Schulz is no longer a danger to himself or others. He gradually comes to feel and act as the other, thereby breaking down and exploding the stereotypes that drove him to become a murderer.

If Hilsenrath's purpose is to explode stereotypes through humor and by minimizing his own fear of the other, namely, the German, by transforming a killer into a sympathizer, then Härtling's novel *Felix Guttmann* can be considered a completely different, more serious, and traditional approach to the German-Jewish symbiosis. There is absolutely no humor in Härtling's work; it is the somber recollection of Felix Guttmann. Born

---

16. Hilsenrath, *Der Nazi & der Friseur*, 222.

in Breslau in 1906, Guttmann has a rich and difficult life before he dies in 1977 in Frankfurt due to an accident. The re-collector of Guttmann's fate is ostensibly Härtling, who had lost his father in 1945 and regains a father in Guttmann (the good man) when Guttmann rents out part of his house outside Frankfurt to the author and his family. It is after Guttmann's death that the Härtling narrator endeavors to reconstruct Guttmann's life, and as the narrator unravels Guttmann's history, he makes comments on the problematic aspect of biographical writing, especially since he is reconstructing a Jewish identity.

Guttmann's life is the stereotypical (perhaps prototypical) one of an assimilated Jew. The only son of a middle-class Jewish garment dealer, Guttmann forms a strong friendship with Casper Liebstock in Breslau through their love for literature and deep interest in Socialist politics. When Guttmann moves to Berlin, he studies law and mixes in left-wing circles, but, unlike Casper, who joins the Communist party, Guttmann prefers to keep his distance from political parties. However, as a lawyer, he defends political victims and helps his friends when the Nazis assume power. During the 1930s, he works for a Zionist organization until he himself is endangered in 1939 when he makes his way to Palestine. In 1948, Guttmann returns to Germany and recommences his profession as a lawyer in Frankfurt, ostensibly never making much of his Jewishness. He marries a woman from Berlin in 1956, about which we learn very little. In fact, the postwar years are almost a blank. There are only the indications and the implications of the narrator: Guttmann, a modest humane man, simply reassimilated in Germany, never pointing a finger, picking up where he left off in 1938, practicing law, the just lawyer.

Härtling's novel could be considered an answer to Fassbinder's play, for it was written during the scandal caused by *Garbage, the City and Death.* Instead of the superhuman Rich Jew, Härtling depicts the "normal" Jew. That is, there is a normalization of the Jew, who, though he has his own unique history, is the simple good man. The Jew as good and noble, however, is an idealization that comes dangerously close to philosemitism and can lead to a positive stereotype that distorts the other, perhaps to minimize the guilt of the narrator. If the Jews are forgiving and assimilate so well into postwar German society, then perhaps Germans should not concern themselves with the past so much but get on with the future. The positive Jew thus represents the yearning for a return to normality on the part of the author and of many Germans as well. Therefore, the author's recollection undermines his moral intention: the yearning is for a normality that never existed.

This yearning is also reflected in Jurek Becker's novel *Bronsteins Kinder.* However, here neither Jews nor Germans are normalized. The narrator, Hans Bronstein, eighteen years old, lives in East Berlin and recalls the traumatic year of 1973, which also happens to be the year that Ulbricht died and the year that the Weltfestspiele were held in the GDR. Interweaving the past with the present, Bronstein, another East German version of Holden Caulfield, who impresses us with his honesty and sensitive reactions to the world around him, tells us how and why he has experienced an emotional breakdown. It all began with an accidental discovery: his father owned a small cottage just outside Berlin where Hans began having rendezvous with his girlfriend Martha. One time Hans comes upon his father and two Jewish friends who are interrogating a former Nazi guard of a concentration camp. This man is tied to a bed and kept prisoner under harsh conditions. Shocked, Hans leaves the cottage and thinks to himself: "I had believed that, after thirty years, they could live like normal human beings, and suddenly this room. —as if they had only waited thirty years for such an opportunity. As if they had only been wearing a mask even when they had been ostensibly behaving in a normal way."[17]

Hans feels that he must share his secret with his sister, Elle, who is in a mental institution because of the abuse she suffered while being hidden by some German farmers during World War II. Although Elle insists that Hans should let his father do what he must and not interfere, Hans is torn; he does not know whether he should report his father and friends to the police or sympathize with their position. He fears that they will kill their prisoner after they finish interrogating him, and on the night that he finally decides to help the prisoner escape he finds his father lying on the bed, dead from a heart attack. Hans frees the prisoner, who eventually leaves East Berlin as a retired person and settles in the West. Hans himself finds no solace or consolation.

More probing and more compelling than Härtling's novel, Becker's work reveals how the normalization of German-Jewish operations cannot work, especially if repression or amnesia are part of this normalization. Hans wants to keep the past out of the present, but so does the former concentration camp guard, who has gone unpunished and leads a "normal" life. The disruption of the norm reveals to what extent the past has not been lived through in a nonpathological manner. At the end of the novel Hans does not know what it means to be a Jew, nor does he know what it means to be an East German citizen.

The recent novels about German and Jewish operations project images of Germans and Jews trying to reorder their images of each other, to create new sterotypes that diminish the fear each group has of each other. In essence, we are dealing with the re-creation of a new German-Jewish symbiosis that is even more evident in the fiction that

---

17. Becker, *Bronsteins Kinder,* 27.

has appeared since Becker's *Bronsteins Kinder* in 1985. In such works as Babara Honigmann's *Roman von einem Kind* (1986), Irene Dische's *Fromme Lügen* (1989), Rafael Seligmann's *Rubinsteins Versteigerung* (1989) and *Die jiddische Mamme* (1990), and Maxim Biller's *Wenn ich einmal reich und tot bin* (1990), the authors respond to the growing need for self-identification by Jews and the outbreak of anti-Semitism and xenophobia that has intensified since the reunification of Germany in 1989. The atmosphere in which the writing about Germans and Jews is being done is one filled with anxiety and tension and one that has also allowed for the repressed stereotypes of Jews and Germans to resurface. The future of both German and Jewish identity will depend a great deal on how the repressed stereotypes are transformed and projected in the operations between Germans and Jews. There can be no return to "normalcy," for there has never been a "normal," or nonpathological, relationship between Germans and Jews. The stereotypes and images of Germans and Jews that are currently being projected in various texts by Germans and Jews are therefore the beginnings of a move toward understanding of the other in a way that will not be destructive or self-destructive.

The norm of German-Jewish operations is still in the process of being formed. The markings of the texts and in the texts result from the cultural operations between Germans and Jews. They are traces not only of the past but of possibilities of re-forming the norm that have resulted from a transformation of the German-Jewish symbiosis in the post-Auschwitz era, marks and traces indicating that one can move beyond atavistic mythic yearnings as reflected in the works of Fassbinder. As Dan Diner has remarked,

> Auschwitz as a phenomenon (and all that belongs to it as a past historical event) appears to have its consciousness raising future still in front of it. As the distance to the event increases, the view of the incomprehensible occurrences is becoming sharper. As the event moves further away, its outlines rise more clearly from the haze caused by the shock of the rupture in civilization that Auschwitz has meant. Sense requires an answer in view of what has really become non-sense. The memory of Auschwitz, the presence of that happening often apostrophied euphemistically as "the past," is taking hold of the volatile consciousness in the direction of the future.[18]

---

18. Dan Diner, "Negative Symbiose—Deutsche und Juden nach Auschwitz," in *Jüdisches Leben in Deutschland seit 1945,* ed. Micha Brumlik, Doron Kiesel, Cilly Kugelmann, and Julius Schoeps (Frankfurt am Main: Athenäum, 1986), 243–44.

Reconstructions of History: From Jewish Memory to Nationalized Commemoration of Kristallnacht in Germany

Y. Michal Bodemann

> Instead of isolating events from their representations, this approach recog-
> nises that literary and historical truths of the Holocaust may not be entirely
> separable. That is, the truths of the Holocaust—both the factual and the
> interpretive—can no longer be said to lie beyond our understanding, but
> must now be seen to inhere in the ways we understand, interpret, and write
> its history. Indeed, since the facts of the Holocaust eventually obtain only in
> their narrative and cultural reconstructions, the interrelated problems of
> literary and historical interpretation might now be seen as conjoining in the
> study of "literary historiography."
>
> —James E. Young (1988, 1)

In early 1992, a visitor to Berlin might have observed an astonishing
series of events. While an initiative led by Leah Rosh, a noted leftist-
liberal television personality, continued to push for a central monument
to the Jewish victims of the Holocaust, at the exclusion of Gypsies,
homosexuals, and political opponents of nazism,[1] others in the German
middle class, from moderate conservatives on to the Left, were commemorating the fiftieth anniversary of the Wannsee Conference, which
was held on 20 January 1942 in a villa at the Wannsee, a lake on the

---

1. Subsequently this memorial was tentatively approved by the Berlin Senate. It was
to be located at the site of Hitler's bunker between the Brandenburg Gate and Potsdamer
Platz. See *die tageszeitung* (hereafter taz), 14 May 1992. Currently, plans in this regard
appear to have been laid on ice.

outskirts of Berlin. As is well known, of course, this conference concerned itself with the implementation of the "Final Solution of the Jewish Question," with Reinhard Heydrich in the chair, Adolf Eichmann recording the minutes, and other administrators of the genocide-to-be, listening, commenting, and making the occasional joke.

In early 1992, now lavishly renovated, this villa was turned into a memorial with a permanent exhibition and pictorial material not unlike that found in the Yad Vashem in Jerusalem—grueling photos of the Shoah and of the steps leading up to it. Today, the villa houses a library, an archive, and study center, and its education department supplies visiting school classes with a variety of educational material. In the previous decades, however, the villa served a variety of interests, most recently as a retreat for high school students from a working-class district of Berlin. In the early postwar years, it was used, among other things, as an officers' club by the American military. From the sixties onward, Josef Wulf, a local historian of the Shoah, supported by a variety of individuals and organizations, pressured the government to turn this villa into a memorial. This request was consistently refused by West German officials and the media: one did not need "another macabre memorial site." A few years ago, however, sentiments changed, and official authorities in Berlin themselves took charge of the planning and financing of this memorial.

Even more lavish support went into another project, a unique exhibit that opened only a week earlier, called Jüdische Lebenswelten ("Jewish Lifeworlds"), a monumental exhibit of Judaica portraying the varieties of Jewish cultural, but mostly religious, life all over the world. This exhibit was neither initiated nor sponsored, as one might surmise, by the Jewish community, but by the local Berlin government instead. Officially the exhibit cost well over 7 million dollars, the most expensive ever mounted in Berlin, with artifacts and donors from Israel and Italy to Australia, the Netherlands, and North and South America. A third exhibit under the aegis of the Berlin Academy of Arts opening shortly thereafter concerned the history of the Kulturbund, the cultural organization that Jews were forced to establish after 1933, and a fourth and a fifth exhibit, on more local issues relating to Jewish life and death, were taking place simultaneously in the city of Berlin alone. It is therefore apparent that there is no dearth of attention to Jewish issues in Germany today and rather generous sponsorship by the official German authorities.

One of the most important and visible poles around which such commemorations began to grow in Germany was that of the anniversary of Kristallnacht; in the meantime, the Shoah and the Jewish topos have evolved into a culture and, indeed, into an industry of remembering in

Germany. In this chapter, I will first briefly point to some characteristics concerning the role of collective memory and will then discuss this by retracing the genealogy of Kristallnacht (Crystal Night) itself.

When we speak of commemoration of historical events and of historical memory, we are obviously not merely concerned with individual acts of remembering but with acts of collective remembrance. Both the prefix in the German verb *gedenken* (Grimm, Grimm, *Wörterbuch*) and the etymology of *memory*, which is traceable to the Indo-European root MER, with the meaning not only of 'recording' but also of 'mourning' and 'martyr' ('witness'), attest to the fundamental social nature of remembrance. It is also associated with death and personal sacrifice and is surrounded by an aura of sanctity—a term which itself is closely related to Latin *sanguis* "blood". The following analysis, then, will address martyrdom: not merely the terror, the degradation, and the annihilation directed by the state and the majority population against a minority but also the witnessing of the event today. I will therefore address Kristallnacht as one historical moment at the onset of the Shoah and the ways in which this moment is being remembered in Germany today.

Theater of Memory

While individual remembering entails the reenactment of events and images in one's mind, collective memory needs a medium shared by two or more individuals. This medium is in essence a stage, a theater (Johnson 1982, 207ff.) in which events are being reenacted. I would argue that acts of remembrance themselves take place first and foremost in theatrical settings: there is an audience, a stage, there are actors, there is a stage set, and the play, the drama itself. What distinguishes the theater is that it is separated from normal everyday practice, outside the stream of history. Akin to the scientific experiment, theater functions outside everyday practice and can therefore be repeated. History, on the other hand, "does not repeat itself" and cannot be repeated on the stage. It can only be provisionally represented through language, bodily movements, and images. It is a space apart from the everyday world in which historical occurrences are being reenacted in particular ways and presented to the audience in order to relive the joys and sufferings read into the event itself. In Nietzschean terms of monumental, antiquarian, and critical history, remembrance is the stage for monumental history. Neither the stage, however, nor the play itself are ever fixed: they are contested terrain fought over by opposing interests and consequently always subject to modification.

The date on which Kristallnacht is being commemorated, 9 November, itself incorporates a history of remembrances. Before 1938, it was celebrated by the Nazi party as a day of heroism and martyrdom. On the night of the 8–9 November 1923, Hitler, emulating Mussolini two years earlier, marched on the Feldherrnhalle in Munich in order to seize power in Bavaria. The date of this putsch was set with care: on 9 November 1918, the Kaiser had abdicated and the Republic was proclaimed. This putsch, of course, failed miserably. From 1928 onward, the Nazi party ritually reenacted this event on an annual basis; in particular, it was also used as the day on which the new recruits to the SS were sworn in (Adam 1988, 75; Scholtz 1967, 297). In Nazi historiography, this appeared later on as the "bloodbath at Feldherrnhalle."

When I speak of a culture, an industry, or even an epidemic of commemorating in Germany today, this pertains especially to the fiftieth anniversary of Kristallnacht, which I experienced in Berlin in November 1988. On the occasion of this day, I estimate that approximately ten thousand individual acts of commemoration took place all over West Germany. Such acts included numerous, perhaps hundreds, of programs on local and national television and radio, including late-night TV talk shows; special exhibits relating to Jewish themes and the Shoah, down to small rural communities; programs sponsored by the churches, special invitations to former Jewish citizens to visit their home town or city, free of charge, for a week; lectures on Kristallnacht and the Shoah, from semester-long programs in the universities to individual lectures by Jewish citizens in local high schools; concerts of Jewish music, art exhibits on Jewish themes and by Jewish artists, books, special articles, and dossiers in newspapers, vigils, and more.

The evening of this 9 November in Berlin, as in some other big West German cities, was filled with frenzied activity and tension. A local initiative, for example, the Geschichtswerkstatt (history workshop), had mounted a street exhibit on Berlin's main boulevard, the Kurfürstendamm, with large, tablet-type posters in front of what in 1933 were Jewish-owned buildings or buildings inhabited by Jews, outlining the history of the building and its inhabitants, and especially what happened to them on Kristallnacht—also the history of the Aryanization of its formerly Jewish businesses and the fate experienced by former Jewish tenants, listed by name, in the Nazi period. There were local vigils (including a twenty-four-hour vigil by one man on the sidewalk with many candles and support from friends) and ceremonial speeches and remembrances that included virtually the entire political elite from the president and the chancellor on down.

The most dramatic event, however, took place in the Bundestag on 10 November, in relation to the address by its Speaker, Philipp Jenninger, at the official and most solemn commemorative ceremony. This ceremony, which included a poem on the Shoah by the Jewish writer Paul Celan, recited by the Jewish emigré actress Ida Ehre, was intended to be, as Elisabeth Domansky has put it, one of the highlights of Jenninger's career; it became his downfall instead.

> Not only was he interrupted by angry invectives from a representative of the Greens from the very beginning, but he had to watch as most of the Greens, some Social Democrats and even some Liberals rose and left the Bundestag under protest. . . . What Jenninger saw was a sea of stony faces intermingled with parliamentarians who buried their faces in their hands. Those who stayed in their seats seemed to do so involuntarily, as under a spell. . . . The stress of the situation had its impact, however. He grew more and more confused, seemed unable to read his manuscript, began to stumble over words, mispronouncing them, his South German accent becoming progressively more and more noticeable. When it was over, everybody who had listened to his speech . . . seemed to concur that there was but one solution: Philipp Jenninger had to resign. (Domansky 1991: 66)

The most astonishing point about the event was that no one could pinpoint what really was so objectionable about his speech. In this address, Jenninger took his audience back to the thirties and the way ordinary Germans thought about Germany and the Jews at that time. Jenninger also described in detail some particularly horrendous crimes committed by the Nazis, and he quoted from an often cited speech by Himmler. As Domansky put it,

> Jenninger . . . had to resign not so much because he had said something wrong, as because he had "sounded" wrong and because he had said what he had to say on the wrong occasion. His downfall was a consequence of his poor performance . . . (ibid., 68–69)

There was more to it, however. Domansky points out correctly that Jenninger delivered his speech from the persecutors' perspective and that, unintentionally, by conjuring up the Nazi "Volksgemeinschaft" he referred to an earlier form of German national identity from which most Germans have been trying to get away; the speech, moreover, reiterated the chasm between Jews and Germans that Germany today is attempting to cover up (see Bodemann 1983).

After 9 November 1989—the collapse of the Berlin Wall—some,

especially German-Jewish, commentators argued that things would never be the same, that with the commemoration of its fiftieth anniversary, the memory of Kristallnacht would finally be buried by the Germans and drowned out by a new national holiday to remember not the state pogrom but the liberation of the East German people (see, e.g., Diner 1990, 101). This prediction, however, was at best only partially correct, and I will sketch below the course of Kristallnacht commemorations in recent years.

The rise of interest in Jewish issues in a wider West German public, especially the question of commemorating the Shoah and the anniversary of Kristallnacht, has been noticeable since about 1978. Indeed, on the fortieth anniversary of Kristallnacht, in 1978, the editor of *Aufbau*, the German emigré paper in New York, commented as follows.

> It is quite apparent that after years of neglect and years of silence, the world public has become "holocaust" conscious; a development that already began several months ago. . . . The course taken by public consciousness and by peoples' conscience are often opaque: here we have a case before us that with the instruments of logic we cannot fully explain. . . . With bitter and painful satisfaction are we taking cognizance of this mass explosion of sympathetic remembrance. (*Aufbau*, 3 November 1978)

The Pogrom: Postwar Silences and Remembrance

The questions that I would like to raise are therefore these: why this epidemic of remembrance now, why the previous silence, and especially why, of all the events with which to remember the Shoah in Germany, has Kristallnacht become the central focus of remembrance? The editor of *Aufbau* spoke correctly of the years of neglect. That neglect, as well as the more recently developing industry of commemoration, can be documented in West German newspapers. Take, for example, *Die Zeit*, one of Germany's most prestigious weekly papers. *Die Zeit* has not a word on Kristallnacht on the tenth anniversary in 1948. Up to 9 November 1958, *Die Zeit* printed a front-page editorial in relation to 9 November 1918, the fortieth anniversary of the abdication of the Kaiser, and then, however, on page 2, seemingly unaware of the anniversary, the detailed history and especially the destruction of a well-known Jewish clothing store in Hamburg. On the thirtieth anniversary, in 1968, there was another brief comment, on page 1, on the abdication of the Kaiser, and no reference at all to Kristallnacht. This comment—we are, of course, in the midst of the student movement—reads as follows.

Fifty years of counterrevolution—with this slogan symbol addicted [symbolsüchtige] members of the Berlin APO [extraparliamentary opposition] wanted to commemorate the day on which in Germany the Kaiser was thrown off the throne. . . . The descendants of Rosa Luxemburg in 1968, who could deny it, are seized by the same idealistic fire. (*Die Zeit*, 8 November 1968)

In other words, neither the established powers nor the Left at the time found that Kristallnacht was of much relevance. This changes radically, however, in 1978, a few months before the airing of the television series "Holocaust." Now *Die Zeit* publishes several pages of a well-researched "dossier" on the events in November 1938 and in the following issue a long essay by a prominent Jewish critic and professor of literature, Hans Mayer, entitled "The Burnt Synagogue." In other West German publications, the situation is quite similar. Neither the Berlin *Tagesspiegel* nor the *Frankfurter Allgemeine Zeitung* write much, if they write anything, on Kristallnacht in the early years; at best, we hear about commemorative ceremonies organized by the Jewish communities. Only in 1978 do we find a significant change.

It is now my thesis that this memorial day is being newly invented in West Germany and was usurped by the German public and its state(s) beginning in the mid-sixties, with the help of the Jews as a presumed collectivity. This invention really begins with the date itself, and here I should briefly speak about "what really happened" around 9 November 1938 in Germany.

For a long time, the popularly accepted version of events might be sketched as follows.[2] On 7 November, Herschel Grynszpan, a seventeen-year-old Polish Jew, shot more or less by accident Ernst vom Rath, a German diplomat in Paris in place of the German ambassador, in desperation over the fact that he and his family did not receive travel visas or in order to draw world attention to the mass deportation of Polish Jews from Germany. After the diplomat's death on 9 November, the Nazi leadership organized the pogroms that were watched with horror—or tolerated somehow—by a powerless population in Germany and Austria.

A historically more accurate version would be about as follows: the anti-Jewish activities, including vandalizing synagogues and shops, began as early as in the spring of 1933. They increased in 1935, decreased in 1936, and then began to reappear beginning in 1937. In

---

2. This presentation follows, grosso modo, the Kristallnacht narrative as presented by Döscher (1988, 72ff.) for the early years. See also Adam (1988, 81) despite some imprecisions.

Vienna, so-called Aktionen, in which Jews were rounded up, began in early October 1938. Various attacks on Jewish pedestrians and on synagogues and businesses occurred between the seventh and the sixteenth of October and then again on the twenty-first and twenty-fifth of October. These were quite likely "trial runs" intended to test the waters for a more carefully planned pogrom sometime in the future.

Following the Paris shooting—which occurred probably not for family or political motives but because of an intimate relationship between Grynszpan and vom Rath[3]—the opportunity for such a pogrom had arisen. In order to emphasize the importance of the case, vom Rath was promoted from Legationsrat to Botschaftsrat by Hitler the next day; he died in the late afternoon of 9 November. On that day, Hitler, the party leaders, and the Alte Kämpfer Nazis of the first hour, met, as each year, at 20:00 for the annual commemoration of the "beer hall putsch" in Munich. At about 21:00, during dinner, Hitler hears the news about vom Rath's death. He has an "intense discussion with Goebbels" and leaves the dinner without addressing the gathering. Shortly after 22:00 hours, Goebbels informs the gathering about the death of vom Rath and says that in reaction to hostile manifestations against Jews in some areas the party should not prepare or organize any anti-Jewish manifestations. But if they would occur spontaneously they should not be opposed. At 22:30, orders are given by the Gauleiter present to their subordinates to start actions against Jews, and a secret telex by Heinrich Müller, Eichmann's boss, is sent to local Gestapo offices at 23:55.

It must be stressed that, following the shooting, the first pogrom-type activities had begun immediately, on the seventh and the eighth of November, but the ninth was remarkably quiet—the quiet before the storm. The pogroms thus came into full swing only in the early morning hours of the tenth. The SS was given specific orders only at 4:00 to blow up synagogues, and, while the Graz synagogue had already been blown up at 0:30, all major fires and the destruction of synagogues started in Vienna at 9:15 and continued until about 13:30.[4] Near Munich a castle belonging to Baron Hirsch went up in flames before midnight, but by and large there were few fires before 2:00 or 4:00 on the morning of the tenth, and most of the destruction of businesses and synagogues took place during the day on the tenth of November, long after orders had been issued from Berlin to stop the attacks.[5]

---

3. This is argued persuasively in Döscher 1988, 60ff., 174.

4. This account of events in Vienna is based on the detailed study of archival sources provided by Rosenkranz (n.d.)

5. For a careful and concise account, see Graml 1988, 1–37.

The Date and the Name

We find, in short, and contrary to, for example, Adam (1988, 81), that the attacks were spread over a long period of time; they culminated on 10 November but had started in some areas, such as Vienna but also in Hesse, Magdeburg-Anhalt, and elsewhere, on the seventh.[6] They also continued in various localities such as Breslau days after 10 November.[7] It makes sense, therefore, that in November 1938 *Aufbau* speaks broadly of "these days," "this hour," and "these days in November." Similarly, a declaration of the Central Committee of the then illegal Communist party of Germany talks about the "shame of the Judenpogrome," suggesting a series of attacks without indicating any particular date.[8] In similar terms, the Mitteilungsblatt der *Hitachdut Olej Germania* talks about the "events of the last weeks"; it also publishes, however, an anonymous eyewitness report about what happened on the tenth of November in Berlin and elsewhere.

One year later, *Aufbau* publishes a commentary entitled "10 November." This, as we have seen, is the correct date, if there is any specific date, because not only the preponderance of the arrests but also the bulk

---

6. Especially in Hesse, significant pogrom activities occurred on 7 and 8 November in numerous towns. In a letter to Rabbi Wilhelm Weinberg, in 1949, Herbert Piontek, a young gentile physician in Frankfurt, speaks of Kristallnacht as the "*dies ater* of 8 November" (Weinberg papers, unpublished). Lenhardt (1988, 12) reports attacks against Jews on the evening of 8 November in small towns and villages such as Kirchhain, Niederklein, Schweizberg, and Neustadt, no activities on the ninth or the tenth but arrests and deportations on the eleventh. Frequently, however, historians and surviving eyewitnesses who claim to remember many details place the events on 9 or 10 November. Jewish sources have succumbed to the same errors. Valentin Senger, for example, a journalist and writer who survived with his family in Frankfurt, originally claimed that he saw a burning synagogue on the morning of the ninth; only in later editions of his book did he change the date to the tenth. In a letter to the *Allgemeine Jüdische Wochenzeitung* (6 January 1989) a reader pointed out that the Kassel synagogue was not destroyed on 10 November, as reported in the *Allgemeine* edition of 4 November 1988. Rather, the synagogue was destroyed in the late evening hours of 7 November; the photo therefore had to have been taken on 8 November. Numerous memorial plaques claiming the destruction of a particular synagogue on 9 November are therefore usually incorrect. More recent plaques tend to show an inscription of "9/10 November." Loyalty to the date of the ninth is difficult to break.

7. This is reported, for example, by Ernst Stein, a Berlin rabbi who lived in Breslau at the time (Ernst Stein, personal communication.)

8. "Gegen die Schande der Judenpogrome—Erklärung des Zentralkomitees der KPD," originally in *Die Internationale*, 1938, 11/12 p. 67–8; republished in Siegbert Kahn, "Dokumente des Kampfes der revolutionären deutschen Arbeiterbewegung gegen Antisemitismus und Judenverfolgung," in: *Beiträge zur Geschichte der Deutschen Arbeiterbewegung*, 1960 (2), pp. 555–557.

of the destruction and burnings only began in the early morning hours of 10 November and lasted until the early evening. The Nazis themselves must have recognized this as the correct date, because that same year, 1939, in the Lodz Ghetto, synagogues were set on fire on 10 November as well.[9]

A few years later, however, memory concerning that date has become blurred. In *Der Weg*, for example, the Jewish community paper for Greater Berlin after the war, its various contributors cannot agree on a single date. While there is no question that, particularly in Berlin, all pogrom-related activities occurred on 10 November, *Der Weg*, in its edition of 8 November 1946, believes the pogrom to have occurred "on the 9th and the 10th [of] November"; the edition of 7 November 1947 mentions both the ninth and the "Night of terror of the 8th to the 9th of November." Only the *Jüdisches Gemeindeblatt*, published in Düsseldorf—the precursor of the *Allgemeine*—publishes an editorial on the pogroms on 9 November 1946 entitled, "9 November 1938!" by the minister of North Rhine Westphalia, H. Renner, who—significantly—is a German not a Jew. In short, the later consensus to move the date back one day to the ninth has an obvious motive: both the abdication of the Kaiser and Hitler's Munich beer hall putsch occurred on the ninth of November, and this is a German, not a Jewish, calendar of remembrances.

The motive for moving the historical event onto the previous day is apparent, for example, in a longer article in the Berlin daily *Der Tagesspiegel*. Here we find a reflection on 9 November 1958 entitled: "Three times the 9th of November." And for all three events—this is still the Cold War—the Left is held responsible. The article argues Marxist ideology in the Social Democratic party is making it difficult to win over the entire working class to the side of the state. The democracy of Weimar lost its bearings because it could never free itself from the threat from the Left, and indeed social democracy as a whole bears partial responsibility for Hitler's putsch in 1923, which was also encouraged by the Communist insurgency in central Germany. All this, the article concludes, led to 9 November 1938, when "a shocked population learns that the people's rage has just been unleashed [entladen]."[10]

---

9. From 9 to 11 November 1939, the Nazi actions in Lodz followed the pattern of the events in 1938: on 9 November, the day on which vom Rath died, the first execution takes place in the ghetto. Synagogues are set on fire on the tenth, and Judenräte are arrested on 11 November, some of whom are tortured and shot. See Loewy and Schoenberner 1990, 18.

10. The connection between these dates was pointed out on previous occasions, however. The Berlin Jewish weekly *Der Weg*, in an editorial of 7 November 1947, spoke of the rise of anti-Semitism and the search for a scapegoat following the collapse of the

As with the date, there is also uncertainty about the name of these events. The Nazis themselves at the time do not have a succinct name for it. At 24:00 on 10 November, it was announced over the radio that the Aktion was completed (Adam 1988, 80). Other Nazi sources such as the *Völkische Beobachter* speak of the "Judenaktion." The Communist underground publication, as if in direct response to this, spoke, as we have seen, of the "Judenpogrome." The New York *Aufbau* conveys something of the incomprehensibility and the speechlessness that many German Jews must have felt. In the edition of *Aufbau* following the pogroms, they are described as the "disgustingly joyful feast of a Sicilian Vesper," an "orgy," an "excess," of the "undignified attack of the strong against the weak," of the "ransacking and murdering mob," of an "outrageous (event) that defied virtually any classification." The *Mitteilungsblatt der Hitachdut*, no less perturbed than *Aufbau*, nevertheless exercises self-control: "we are too proud to express our feelings in this situation. The Jewry of Germany is mute." The Jewish evaluation of Kristallnacht in its own time is therefore much closer to that of the current analysis by some younger historians such as Hans-Jürgen Döscher, who wrote,

> In contrast to earlier views, the pogroms of 1938 appear less as an incisive moment [Zäsur] and rather as a new, radical approach on the path toward the existential annihilation of the Jews in the German Reich. Large sections of the population welcomed or tolerated these policies. (Döscher 1988, 174)

The term *Reichskristallnacht*, or simply *Kristallnacht*, is, according to some, a creation of the Berlin vox populi, according to others an invention by Goebbels's propaganda ministry. However, I have never found any reference to this term in official Nazi sources, and I am inclined to subscribe to the hypothesis that this term was indeed a popular invention, which began to be used in written sources by 1946. This term expresses a singular ambiguity: if it was the creation of the sharp tongues of the Berliners, does it allude to Jewish wealth and deny the violence, including that against persons? Or does it poke fun at the Nazis by associating the pogrom with a wild orgy and denying the Nazis' political intent (they, as we have seen, called it an Aktion arising from the "people's rage")? Be that as it may, the signifier of shattered glass or

---

Kaiserreich. The opponents of democracy were becoming ever stronger and a "straight path leads from 9 November 1918 via 9 November 1923 to 30 January 1933 and to 9 November 1938. And this path appears to be continuing straight beyond 8 May 1945 . . ." The differences are obvious, however: an attack against antidemocratic, anti-Semitic forces in *Der Weg* and an attack against the SPD and the Communists in the *Tagesspiegel*.

shards was clearly central to the reading of the event early on. The 5-million-reichsmark levy imposed on Berlin Jewry, for example, was termed the "Scherbenfond."[11]

Sources from 1946 onward often understood this term as a Nazi euphemism. Renner, the minister of North Rhine Westfalia, in the article in the *Jüdische Gemeindeblatt* quoted above, for example, considers this term to be tainted and associated with *Nazism*. He speaks in an inverse equation of " 'the heroes of Kristallnacht,' the henchmen of Hitler." *Aufbau* in 1939, which may have been the first publication to call for turning 10 November into a day of remembrance, was entirely unfamiliar with the term. Neither did the *Mitteilungsblatt* in Palestine use this term in 1945. One year later, however, most papers began using it, Jewish and non-Jewish alike, with the difference that normally Jewish papers placed it in quotation marks, thus indicating their disapproval or ambivalence, and the German papers usually without quotation marks, thus taking the term for granted. Moreover, Jewish sources vary this term more often with terms such as *Novemberpogrom, Pogromnacht*, and the like, and the term *Kristallnacht* itself is tabooed in the German papers beginning in about 1978. It was then replaced, by and large, with the term *Reichspogromnacht*,[12] a term whose weakness lies in the fact that it represents a misunderstanding of the euphemistic-sarcastic term *Reichskristallnacht*.

To sum up, it is important to see that the date became fixed on the ninth by the mid-1950's, on the initiative of German, not Jewish debates and that later on the term *Kristallnacht*, always viewed with unease by Jews and anti-Fascists, became tabood. The German public therefore dissociated itself from a vivid yet ambiguous term that earlier the Germans themselves had created.

Amnesia and Communal Remembrance

How did the Jews remember Kristallnacht in West Germany in the following years? Clearly, Jews would never forget the events of November 1938; they were in bitter memory, and yet their remembrance was embedded within the general societal atmosphere of postwar Germany. I have analyzed five editions each for the weeks before and after

---

11. The term was coined by Hans-Erich Fabian in *Der Weg* on 8 November 1946. The 1946 editorial in the *Jüdische Gemeindeblatt* cited above also speaks of *Scherben* (shards, bits) and *Bruchstücke* (fragments) of Jewish households that were thrown onto the street.

12. It also occurs in such book titles as Brumlik and Kunik's *Reichspogromnacht* (1988).

Kristallnacht in the years of 1958, 1968, and 1978 of the *Allgemeine Wochenzeitung der Juden in Deutschland*, later the *Allgemeine Jüdische Wochenzeitung*, the principal German-Jewish weekly founded shortly after the war. In the 1958 editions, 5.65 percent (4.5 of 76 pages) deal with the pogroms, and in the 1968 editions the figure rises slightly to 6.91 percent (6.5 of 94 pages); in 1978, however, the proportion dedicated to Kristallnacht suddenly jumps to 29.6 percent (19 out of 64 pages), or roughly one-third of the entire content of the five issues analyzed. The attention paid to this event there increases still further by 1988. It must be stressed, however, that the developments in the *Allgemeine*—the increase in commemorative content in its articles and reports beginning in 1978—are not out of line with similar developments in non-Jewish papers or with the extraordinary increase in public commemorations in the larger society. The weekly *Die Zeit*, for example, increases its volume of commemorative material quite proportionately to that of the *Allgemeine*.

Nevertheless, the "victims of fascism" of the early postwar era, particularly the Jews, formed a community distinctly separate from the surrounding society in West Germany and to some degree in the East as well. Its commemorations of the war and of the Holocaust, large in number, bore a decidedly communal rather than public character. Examples are 1 September, the onset of World War II; the second Sunday in September, the international day of the "victims of fascism" (OdF day) which did not refer to any particular historical event in order not to favor any particular group of victims; and 8 May, the day of the defeat of nazism. These often smallish, one-event type commemorations were quite distinct from the large public, state-sponsored commemorations that evolved fully in the seventies. At first, at least, until the Cold War finally succeeded in dividing them, they were commemorative events that included all victims, Jewish and non-Jewish alike. The Berlin Jewish community paper *Der Weg* writes of this occasion in its issue of 13 September 1946 rather sternly.

> The Jewish community will participate [in the commemorative cere-mony, YMB] in its entirety. . . . It will be expected that everyone whose health permits it will take part in this joint ceremony. (*Der Weg*, 13 September 1946)

Even three years later, with the Cold War in full swing, *Der Weg* features the OdF day prominently. In a lead column on the front page, the paper reviews the "hell of nazism" for the Jewish people and at the same time points to those who "together with us opposed the flood and plague of fascism and risked their lives for the ideals of humanity, freedom and peace . . . we have many true friends whose numbers are growing steadily" (*Der Weg*, 9 September 1949).

As the quote indicates, and despite its weaknesses, which I will deal with below, OdF day had the advantage of carrying a universalistic message within which the Jewish community could organize on behalf of its own interests. Thus, in the 9 September issue of *Der Weg*, a memorial service "in the context of the Memorial Day for the Victims of Fascism" is advertised, which appeals to both the western and the eastern constituencies but nevertheless signals the internal division: the first part of this memorial service in the Weissensee Jewish cemetery is covered by addresses by the (American-born) rabbi Steven Schwarzschild and by Heinz Galinski, while the second part of this service featured the transfer of the remains of Herbert Baum, a (Communist) Jewish resistance fighter executed by the Nazis. This second part of the service featured Julius Meyer, both an orthodox Jew and a Communist, and a rabbinical assistant (Prediger), Klein, also Communist oriented. This joint service, with other western and eastern representatives, was considered nothing less than "sensational" (*Der Weg*, 16 September 1949).

Most importantly, then, the early commemorations were events sponsored and conducted by the antifascist/Jewish spectrum, commemorations of a small, and often closed, community,[13] and it was this community that invited outsiders, albeit in the second row. This is evident, for example, in a letter by Frankfurt lord mayor Walther Kolb, responding to an invitation to participate in the reopening ceremony of the Westend Synagogue on 24 August 1950.

> I confirm at the same time that I shall be glad to accept this invitation, and, if you wish, I shall in a speech and in a particularly solemn manner place this house of God into the protection of the City of Frankfurt. However, may the request be expressed that, on the grounds of the dignity of the office which I occupy, that the Lord Mayor of the City of Frankfurt would not appear in last place in the line up of speakers . . . (quoted in Kugelmann 1988, 15)

It is apparent from the articles in *Allgemeine* and other Jewish papers that Jews living in Germany in the postwar decade found that the pogroms and the Shoah had been largely forgotten in West German society. A

---

13. See, e.g., Heinz Galinski's statement concerning Kristallnacht commemorations in 1958: "Usually a sad, dark day toward the end of the civic calendar year. A day of depressiveness and of quiet closure in an inner world which no one can take from us. A real day of remembrance . . ." (*Allgemeine*, 7 November 1958).

resolution to Rosh Hashana by the newly founded Zentralrat (Central Council of Jews in Germany) in 1950 states, for example, "the veil of forgetfulness is being spread ever more firmly and impenetrably over the evil deeds [Untaten]." A few months later, *Der Weg* in Berlin conducted its own survey regarding news coverage concerning the commemoration of Crystal Night. The results were found to be "disgraceful."

> While, during the past years, a number of larger papers have still commemorated "Kristallnacht" and while in past years some German radio stations devoted at least ten or fifteen minutes to the memory of this gruesome day, it was rather calm on these days in the year 1950. On 9 and 10 November, we have read over 100 papers for each day and came to the surprising—or, according to the German mentality, normal—result that exactly four papers commemorated the twelfth anniversary of the destruction of Jewish houses of worship, of Jewish homes and of the beginning of the liquidation of Jewry. (*Der Weg*, 17 November 1950)

Nevertheless, the distance from the horrors of November 1938 is being experienced by postwar Jewry itself. On the occasion of the tenth anniversary of the pogroms, the lay leader of the Jewish community in Berlin, Hans-Erich Fabian, wrote an article entitled "Ten Years."

> Is it really only ten years ago when the "boiling soul of the people" [kochende Volksseele] was ordered to be unleashed against the Jews? Was it really only ten years ago when in the night of the eighth to the ninth [*sic*] of November synagogues in all of Germany were burning? . . . Sometimes it seems to us as if not merely ten years have passed since that time, as if it happened long before that. In the life of nations, ten years are not a very long time, but in the life of the individual it is a long time, when the events precipitate each other, when it is a time of suffering. (*Der Weg*, 5 November 1948)

There is no question that many Jews at the time, and particularly Zionists, also attempted to suppress the memory of this trauma and humiliation. Numerous reports by travelers to Palestine/Israel express the feeling that the "cruel burden of the past suddenly fell from my shoulders, and the misfortune was put behind me like a bad dream" (Aron Saurymper, in *Der Weg*, 9 September 1949). Much earlier still, on the occasion of Crystal Night 1946, *Der Weg* published a poem by Ilse Blumenthal-Weiss entitled *Ausblick* (outlook), which expresses these sentiments.

We will have children who do not know
that somewhere dark in the realms of shadow
figures cower and creep past us
crawling like beggars after strangers' crumbs

We will have children not tormented
by chains and hateful diatribes in alien lands,
who only give their homeland love and closeness
as echo of their youthful steps.

We will have children who in faithfulness
took on severity and shackles of their soil
who walk upright and renew the covenant
people [Geschlecht] of the future! Proud, free Jews!

(*Der Weg*, 15 November 1946)

Still, nine years later, in 1957, Ernst Gottfried Lowenthal, a historian and writer on German Jewry, echoes the sentiments of amnesia. He observed that the Stauffenberg attempt on Hitler's life on 20 July 1944 is "regularly and rightly" being commemorated but the big papers are silent about the "so-called Kristallnacht" (*Mitteilungsblatt der Hitachdut*, 10 November 1957). The "muteness" of German Jewry of which the *Mitteilungsblatt* in Palestine spoke in 1938 had obviously taken hold.

Compare to these silences in 1948 the following statement in the form of a "vow," in November 1978, of the German-Israeli Society, which consists predominantly of non-Jewish West Germans.

We still hear the crashing and splintering of the inventory of Jewish stores. We [*sic*] are still pursued by the hostile fire of burning synagogues. Full of shame do we remember the ninth of November 1938, the day on which the annihilation of Jewish people began in Europe. These crimes could happen because at the time millions of Germans kept silent . . . (*Allgemeine*, 10 November 1978)

Here, then, the events are moved into the present—as if the pogrom had taken place in the very recent past. It must be asked, then, why the night of the pogroms has returned so close to home? Why this strange epidemic of commemoration with an untold number of separate commemorative events? Moreover, it must be a historically unique phenomenon that a people has decided to commemorate its own crimes. There is no parallel in either Japan or Italy, nor do citizens of the United States, for example, commemorate American atrocities in Vietnam or other places. Why, furthermore, this day out of many commemorable days? Is it not odd that the Germans have been unable to mourn the destruction of Dresden as the destruction of Hiroshima is being mourned, or the brutal expulsion of 12 million Germans from the Eastern territories—an event that concerns Germans far more directly than does Kristallnacht? Indeed, one perceptive German rabbi asked sarcastically in 1958,[14] when, in the midst of the economic miracle, the West Germans could not commemorate the horrors of the war, of German refugees, and of the bombings, how can one expect them to remember the Jews?

Why, when West Germany did not remember the Jews in 1948, 1958, or 1968, did they begin to do so in 1978, at a time when the same politicians who on one hand solemnly commemorated with kippot and in synagogues at the same time opposed the continued prosecution of Nazi crimes beyond the statute of limitations? And why were there commemorations combined with so much forgetfulness? Note, for example, how chancellor Helmut Schmidt, at the commemorative ceremony in the Cologne synagogue put his own symptomatic case of amnesia in 1978:

> The truth is also that many Germans disapproved of the crimes and the misdemeanours; also, that very many others at the time *knew nothing or almost nothing.* The truth is that, *nevertheless, all this took place before the eyes of a large number of German fellow citizens* . . . It is not to us to appeal to the Jews in the world for reconciliation. But we may ask for reconciliation nevertheless . . . (*Allgemeine*, 10 November 1978; my italics)[15]

In a recent debate in the West German magazine *Konkret* and some other contributions (e.g., Maser 1991; Groehler 1992; Kuczynski, Gossweiler, Pätzold 1992) the GDR has been castigated for its anti-Semitism, camouflaged as anti-Zionism, and for the hypocrisy or indifference in its memory of the Jewish victims. These contributions fail to point out, however, the astonishing parallels to West German commemorations. West German politicians, for example stand at the graves of SS troops in Bitburg only a few years after the Cologne

---

14. Robert Raphael Geis, in *Allgemeine*, 10 November 1978 (the article was published posthumously).

15. Ten years later, again, the events are far more clearly—and incorrectly—remembered by another leader of the SPD who was considerably younger at the time.

I myself will never forget how as a twelve-year-old together with my classmates I saw from the schoolyard the neighboring synagogue go up in flames. . . . What happened on 9 [*sic*] November 1938 did not happen in concealment. It happened before everyone's eyes. Any adult could see that the state and its institutions did not protect the victims and that it helped those instead who broke the law—the law that was in force at that time as well. (Hans Jochen Vogel, in *Die Zeit*, 30 December 1988)

Synagogue commemoration and ride roughshod over other Jewish sensitivities and concerns. They ignore Jewish protests against the destruction of the remains of the Frankfurt Jewish Ghetto, in 1987/88; they refuse to recognize the Shoah in the new preamble to the German constitution. I would argue therefore that the new Kristallnacht commemorations have little to do with real-existing Jews. They are, most of all, an important element in German-identity politics (Yuval-Davis, 1992). Commemorations construct identity, and national commemorations construct national identity; Kristallnacht today therefore is a crucial component in the reconstruction of German national identity as articulated particularly clearly for example by Richard von Weizsäcker. These commemorations moreover have to do with fantasies about Jews and with the problems of loss and of guilt. They need Jewish actors; not lead actors, however, but extras.

In the GDR: Nationalized Commemoration and Benign Indifference

In the postwar period in most German towns and cities, very little attention was paid to the victims of Nazism and war, least of all to its Jewish victims. In some of the major cities, but especially Berlin, this situation was somewhat different. Berlin was the battleground in East/West confrontations, with large Social Democrat and communist-antifascist constituencies, and the largest postwar Jewish community outside the DP camps. Also, even though the large and prominent pre-war Jewish community had disappeared, its shadows still seemed present and exerted influence. Until at least 1949, the new Jewish community attempted to constitute a neutral ground between the contending political camps and parties and in its commemorations, it assumed an integrative political role; its leaders represented all major political parties including the SED.

More by convention, the second Sunday in September was chosen as "OdF Day," as the "Day of the Victims of Fascism," which in the late forties began to be commemorated in other parts of East and, for a short time at least, even West Germany. In 1947, as already in 1946 for example, the Berlin Jewish community called upon its members to attend the OdF rally in the Lustgarten square, and join it in a distinct formation. This rally was addressed, among others, by Louise Schröder, the Vice Mayor of Greater Berlin, a Social Democrat. Significantly, on a day without exclusively Jewish meaning, and on a secular occasion as well, memorial services were held "in all synagogues"?[16]

---

16. *Der Weg*, 23 September 1947.

The ninth of November, on the other hand, was coordinated jointly by the OdF office and the Jewish community, with representatives of both groups addressing the gathering. Nevertheless, in the competition between OdF Day and 9 November, OdF day was at a disadvantage in the long run: it was an artificial date without memory and therefore lacked the "drama" of Crystal Night.[17] Crystal Night, on the other hand, excluded other victims and was thus not very popular with the SED and a broader spectrum of antifascists. Since it is fashionable at the present time to discredit the German Communists, their attempt to create a community of both (non-Jewish) antifascists and victims of fascism, particularly Jewish ones, should be recognised, however contradictory their imagination of such a community might have been. While we see, in the late forties and early fifties, progressively more space being devoted to Kristallnacht in the Berlin Jewish paper *Der Weg* and the Jewish papers in the West, the OdF events nevertheless continue to be announced prominently, and they receive equal billing with others. As the Cold War escalated and as Communists were eliminated from other organizations and positions in the West, the OdF memorial day also atrophied in West Germany. In the East, however, OdF day continued strong for much of the existence of the GDR. With the split in the Berlin Jewish community in 1953, and the disappearance of OdF day in the West, it turned into a specifically East German day of remembrance.

There can be no doubt that the Slansky trials and Stalin's anti-Semitic campaign had an incisive impact on the future role of the Jewish community in the GDR. Many Jews and Jewish Communists, including the leaders of all major communities, the organic intellectuals of East German Jewry, had fled the East by early 1953, and for much of the following twenty-five or thirty years of its existence the community was turned into an appendage of the party. Especially in the anti-Semitic environment of Stalin's last years, the SED had little use for its Jews as either a religious or an ethno-national group. They were seen, increasingly over the years, as an instrument of foreign policy and, inside the GDR, if of any use at all, as an element of the "antifascist basic order." On the other hand, Jews were still seen by many in the upper echelons of the party as comrades in arms and friends (Eschwege 1991, 154); they were an important, albeit sometimes obstreperous, element in the anti-Fascist catechism and could not simply be ignored. Two examples may illustrate the ambivalent position of the GDR vis-à-vis its Jews.

On the occasion of the tenth anniversary of Kristallnacht, on 10

---

17. For a perceptive analysis of the commemorative culture in the GDR, see Combe 1990.

November 1948, the party paper *Neues Deutschland* (ND) published an article entitled "The Background of Kristallnacht" in which its author, Paul Merker—a member of what was to become the SED's polit-bureau—pointed to anti-Semitism and the terror against the Jews as the major political principles of nazism. This position was not in conformity with the party, which saw in nazism simply as an extreme form of capitalism and found its anti-Semitism to be epiphenomenal.[18] On the previous day, on the other hand, in what reflected the ambivalence of the SED, the ND had published an announcement concerning the Jewish community's memorial services on the tenth anniversary of Kristallnacht. The announcement was located in a minuscule six-line statement, tucked away between other short news such as the availability of dry potatoes, the arrival of flour and potato seedlings for distribution, and the discovery of "47 cases of [smuggled] cocoa"—Jews at the time were held to be the prime culprits for all black market activity. On the same day, the ND published several pages on the thirty-first anniversary of the October Revolution in Russia and on the thirtieth anniversary of the "November Revolution" in Germany.

In the following years, and in contrast to West German papers, the ND dealt with Crystal Night on a frequent if not a regular basis, usually on 10 November because the 9 November editions prioritized both the Russian October and the German November revolutions. In 1956, for example, the Committee of Anti-Fascist Resistance Fighters and the Jewish Community of [East] Berlin published in both its 9 and 10 November editions a call for participation in a Sunday morning rally in Friedrichstadt-Palast. In its Monday edition (12 November), the paper reported on its front page the speeches given there. In 1968, reports on the commemorations appeared on 9, 10, and 11 November, and in 1978 the paper devoted a sizable amount of space to Kristallnacht from the ninth to the eleventh of November, including a letter by Erich Honecker to Helmut Aris—then president of the Association of Jewish Communities in the GDR—delicately counterpoised with a report on Jewish settlements built by Israel in the occupied territories.

In these reports over the years we find the following basic themes: first, the leadership of the anti-Fascist resistance fighters—the Communists—over the Jews; second, anti-Semitism as an epiphenomenon of German monopoly capitalism; third, the protection (*Geborgenheit*) given to Jews in the GDR; and, in contrast, fourth, the survival of anti-Semitism and Nazism in West Germany. The first theme,

---

18. In one of the purges, in 1952, on the eve of the Slansky trials, Paul Merker, a non-Jew, was put on trial as a stooge of Zionism and the U.S. financial oligarchy.

jointly with the fourth, are illustrated, for example, in the following juxtaposition in a 1956 report on Kristallnacht commemorations by the ND: Rabbi Riesenburger had reported to the rally that in recent days Fascist bandits had daubed a West Berlin synagogue with swastikas and Nazi slogans. According to the report—we are in the time after the Hungarian uprising—the rabbi

> addressed this question to all of humanity: "Have you forgotten what happened? Have you forgotten the millions of dead of the fascist mass annihilation and of the second world war?" The member of the International Auschwitz Committee, comrade Bruno Baum, answered him: No, the working class has not forgotten. It will, as in Hungary, in the fraternal alliance with the heroic fighters of the Soviet Union, firmly oppose any fascist development. . . . [The working class] will not allow a repetition of Crystal Night nor of the horrible crimes of Hitler and Horthy fascism. . . . (ND, 21 November 1956)

We see here, then, an inversion of the conventional leadership role: the rabbi asks questions instead of answering questions, and the Communist comrade provides the answers. This theme of the Communist leadership and the big-brother role is reenacted likewise at the same rally in the speech by writer Peter Edel, a (Jewish) survivor of several camps. Edel recounts his sufferings and the suffering of his family and, in all his deep despair in the concentration camp, he meets Werner Seelenbinder, a Communist and national hero in the GDR, who shortly before his own execution gives Edel encouragement.

Themes 3 and 4 are pervasive until at least the early eighties and typically appear in conjunction with each other. In 1968, for example, otherwise a meager year in reporting on commemorations, one year after the Six Day War, the president of the Jewish communities "expressed his deep disquiet over the neofascist development in West Germany," but in the GDR, the "citizens of the Jewish faith have found their true home . . ." In 1978, likewise, Erich Honecker, in his message to the Jewish communities, emphasizes that the GDR is a secure homestead (Heimstatt) of humanism; the state secretary for church affairs stresses that imperialism and fascism, the roots of racism and anti-Semitism, have been eradicated "once and for all"; and the leader of East German Jewry responds with thanks for the attention and care given to the Jewish communities by the GDR. In the GDR, he says, "we feel social and human security" (ND, 9–12 November 1978).

From the early fifties onward, after Paul Merker–type heterodoxy concerning the pogroms has been eliminated, the commemorations lapse into a petrified and ritualized cult of addresses and wreath layings. Instead of vivid stories of individuals' experiences during Kristallnacht, Jewish and non-Jewish accounts alike provide little more than the statistics and the overall setting, as in the Jewish communities' "Appeal to the Jews in the World and all People of Good Will," on the occasion of the twenty-fifth anniversary in 1963.

> Twenty five years ago, flames blazed out of 177 houses of worship to the sky. On that ninth of November, 7,500 businesses of Jewish citizens fell victim to destruction and looting. Human dignity was pushed into the mud. Kristallnacht was the first major phase of the Nazis' infamous "Final Solution of the Jewish Question" in the course of which six million Jewish men, women and children suffered a horrible death.

The scholarly treatments of Crystal Night are pressed, similarly, into a rigid doctrinal corset. One of the first historical analyses of Kristallnacht appeared in the ND on 9 November 1968, written by Werner Müller, a historian at the paper. His article sketches the basic points of the "witches sabbath" unleashed by the Nazis, a pretext for the expropriation of the Jews, and most of all as a "psychological preparation of the population" for World War II. Müller again cites a November 1938 article in the underground KPD's paper *Rote Fahne* (and of the paper *Die Internationale*) entitled "Against the Shame of the Jewish Pogroms."[19] This article blames German capital for anti-Semitism and describes the "struggle against the pogroms" as an "inseparable part of the German fight against Nazi dictatorship and for freedom and peace." In West Germany, Müller concludes, those who unleashed Kristallnacht are once again in power.

On the fortieth anniversary, the ND publishes an article by historian Kurt Pätzold, which again recounts the basic events of Crystal Night and blames I.G. Farben and German monopoly capital for this "satanic deed." With the pogroms, Pätzold argues, Germans were to become accustomed and indifferent—and would even welcome—"the fate of all those who were described to them as 'un-German,' 'anti-German,' as 'enemies of the people' or 'enemies of the race,' as 'communists' or 'Jews.' " The article, then, makes one feel almost sorry for the Germans who had to endure Nazi indignities, and here, as elsewhere, Jews are victims among others; Communists were the first and the principal vic-

---

19. See footnote 8.

tims and in their martyrdom still managed to provide leadership to the Jews. Before the Jews arrived in the concentration camps, Pätzold writes, they often, due to their bourgeois upbringing, tended to see the Communists as their opponents. When they arrived in the camps, they found the Communists already there. Now many "Jewish Germans" began to recognize that the "revolutionary-humanist program" of these "forces of the German working class included the extinction of anti-Semitism and of all racism"; for many Jews, this encounter was an "important experience."

A second long article in the same paper praised the reconstruction of the Rykestrasse synagogue with funds made available by the government of the GDR. Between an article by a well-known GDR historian and a report on the government's efforts on behalf of its Jewish community, we find a discernibly greater amount of attention paid to Jewish issues—in the very same year when, albeit on a much greater scale, we have seen the same development in the West. Both the West and the East, I would argue, reacted to grass roots movements, particularly in the churches in their respective states, and indeed to the ever greater attention that could be detected in much of the western world. This became apparent ten years later, in 1988, when the ND commemorated the "fascist Kristallnacht fifty years ago" on most of its first six pages, now with the seventieth anniversary of 9 November 1918 relegated to back pages, beginning on page 5. On page 2, the paper listed twenty Jewish individuals, most of them citizens of the GDR, who were awarded various orders. Additional articles on Crystal Night were published the following day.

I would contend that the role of GDR Jewry in its commemorations of Crystal Night fits the historical role assigned by the state to Kristallnacht. This involved, first of all, the hegemony of state and party over the Jewish community, and the nationalization of its commemorations; on the other hand, the Jewish community was indeed of service to the state in that it supplied ideological labor especially in helping to underpin the anti-Fascist conception of the GDR and—not unlike in West Germany—their very existence as a living proof that here nazism had been extirpated. The *Nachrichtenblatt der Jüdischen Gemeinde*, bulletin of the East Berlin Jewish community, put it as follows in December 1954.

We have not only attempted to shape a dignified religious life, but have also observed the societal developments of the past months and have become involved wherever it was necessary for the Jewish community to step forward. Be it working for unity of our native

city [Vaterstadt] or of our fatherland, for maintaining peace or culti-
vating amicable relations with our neighboring peoples, especially
the Soviet Union. We have also not neglected the memorial days.
On these days, we looked back and reflected on whether we had
done everything necessary so that the madness of fascism and of
anti-Semitism will not be repeated. [This was a reference to the
"new dangerous developments for Jews in West Germany" YMB].

In Berlin—the communities elsewhere in the GDR had soon become minuscule—the pattern of commemorations at first glance appeared to continue along the lines of what it had been before the division
of the city and the secession of the West Berlin Jewish community in
1953. Nevertheless, the Jewish community, after the escape of its leadership to the West in 1953, turned ever more into a secondary, but necessary, player in the OdF commemorations in September, and its new
leadership, beholden to the party or appointed by the state,[20] abandoned its "monopoly" over the Kristallnacht commemorations. On OdF
Day in 1954, for example, the Eastern community called its members to
the large national demonstration in the morning but also to its own
memorial service in the afternoon at the Weissensee Jewish cemetery,
which included speeches by a member of the executive and by the rabbi.
For Crystal Night commemorations, probably on Sunday, the precise
date is not mentioned. The community was evidently "engaged" to participate with the Communist-led VVN (Association of Nazi Persecutees)
of West Berlin to lay a wreath and commemorate Kristallnacht at
Bahnhof Grunewald—one of the deportation points to the camps. The
Grunewald memorial meetings, attended by relatively small groups of
people, at least after 1953, were to be the community's contribution to
demonstrate the "unity of progressive forces" in East and West. On
Saturday night, however, at 18:00, the community "in the presence of
many hundred people" held its own memorial service, a chance to meet
old friends also beyond political lines.

In the years following 1958, and through most of the sixties and
seventies, full-fledged Kristallnacht commemorations became ever more
sporadic and lacked the previous commitment from within the community, whereas OdF day continued to be celebrated, usually with large
national commemorations in the morning and small Jewish memorial
services in the afternoon. The increasing neglect or at best perfunctory
character of the commemorations reflected not only the quality of Jewish leadership in the communities but also the fundamental change in

20. Concerning the change in leadership, see Eschwege 1991, 156.

the leadership of the Committee of Anti-Fascist Resistance Fighters.[21] While in the early years of the GDR the Kommitee consisted to a large degree of Jewish Communists, who did indeed have an understanding of the significance of the pogroms, they were gradually supplanted by members of the Nationalkommitee Freies Deutschland—mostly Wehrmacht soldiers who had been reeducated by the Soviets and certainly anything but resistance fighters. In the early sixties, especially on the twenty-fifth anniversary in 1963, and after the building of the Wall, Kristallnacht and OdF commemorations tend to become centralized in particular sites such as Dresden, and they are being consolidated, with the Jews commemorating "in partnership" with anti-Fascist organizations such as the National Front and the Committee of Anti-Fascists, but now on exclusively Jewish terrain such as the Rykestrasse synagogue and Weissensee cemetery.

It is important to point out that, although anti-Fascism formed part of the basic creed of the GDR, and with the exception of 1988, the top political hierarchy of the GDR was entirely indifferent to these Jewish commemorations. Only on extremely rare occasions did any of the top brass attend the memorial services. These included, in the fifties, Otto Nuschke, a vice-chair of the Council of Ministers, and on two or three occasions a state secretary of church affairs. These commemorations thus resembled an administrative act with little or no participation from the population, the Jewish population included. Typically, the city in which a commemoration was held would send a city councilor to represent it, and a deputy of the state secretariat for church affairs would often be present. The following account of the dedication of the Sachsenhausen Memorial Site is characteristic in this regard: the memorial was dedicated on 23 April 1961 with Walter Ulbricht as keynote speaker, followed by addresses of "resistance fighters from 24 nations, including Israel," and with (East Berlin's) Rabbi Riesenburger as honorary guest (*Mitteilungsblatt*, August 1961).

On the occasion of this dedication, a commemoration was held in the nearby Oranienburg Jewish cemetery, which had also been brought into a "dignified condition" on orders of "the government of the German Democratic Republic." Here, "Rabbi Riesenburger spoke words that came from his heart and that touched everyone, and Kantor Nachama let ring out the ancient Jewish prayers of mourning." On this occasion, although around the corner from the Sachsenhausen camp and

---

21. For this and the following statements, I have relied on information provided by Peter Kirchner, the last president of the East Berlin Jewish community (interview with the author, 11 August 1993).

on the same day, Walter Ulbricht and the GDR politicians were not to be seen. For the Jews, this and similar commemorations were, occasionally at least, intimate communal, almost private, events.

Why the revival of commemorative events in 1978, and especially the commemorative epidemic in 1988? The reason for this, as for the revival of the Jewish communities themselves, to the extent to which they still existed, clearly cannot be separated from the broader international revival of Holocaust memory. Here the role of transitive institutions such as the churches and the foreign diplomatic missions is of particular relevance. Due to their contact with churches in West Germany, the East German Lutherans as well began to address the Holocaust in the sixties, and they began to develop an active Christian-Jewish dialogue, including holding their own Crystal Night commemorations, as early as 1963 in Leipzig. Second, in 1978, foreign ambassadors and the West German permanent representative to the GDR began to attend the commemorative services of the Jewish community. The state, puzzled by this attention, was virtually forced into its own involvement, leading eventually to the commemorations of 1988, prior to which, in many towns and cities in the GDR, Jewish cemeteries and other Jewish sites were suddenly rediscovered and hastily restored just in time for the laying of wreaths.[22]

What, in sum, does the culture of commemoration in the GDR tell us about the role of the Jewish community there—a community that lost its genuine leadership in the purges in and before 1953 and that for most of the existence of the GDR lacked all internal democracy? First, internally, the anti-Fascist commemorations, one of its major annual activities, although treated with benign indifference by the state, helped keep the traces of Jewish identity alive. Moreover, the theme of Kristallnacht, its ideological vicissitudes notwithstanding, could serve as an integrative element for East German Jewry, religious believers and nonbelievers, supporters of the regime, and those at some distance. Apart from the self-aggrandizement of some of the Jewish functionaries, this may be part of the reason why Kristallnacht continued to be observed through much of the years of the GDR.

Second, vis-à-vis state and party, Jewish leaders provided a unique service. With their monopoly on Kristallnacht, they buttressed the "anti-fascist basic order" of GDR state and society and, occasionally at least, served as an instrument of foreign policy—most apparently so in the last

---

22. In the Mecklenburg city of Güstrow, for example, a stonemason was ordered to produce a memorial stone, to be placed in what was left of the Jewish cemetery, nine days before the Crystal Night commemoration there.

years of the republic. They were not without independent will and did have maneuvering space, which, like other institutions in the GDR, they did not fully use. On a number of occasions they resisted manipulation by the state, such as in 1967 when the leadership was to sign a declaration condemning Israel (Eschwege 1991, 156) or later when the Berlin leadership under Peter Kirchner, for example, objected to harsh anti-Israeli attacks in the media.

Despite their politically and socially useful role, however, and despite material and social privileges which they enjoyed, they did remain politically second class.[23] In terms of GDR mythology, they were victims but not fighters against fascism (Groehler 1992), and in the GDR itself, as first a religious and second a separate ethno-national group of dubious status, they were in an anachronistic or contradictory political position: their near-invisibility was rewarded with benign indifference. In this sense, the situation of Jews in the East represented, as in a warped mirror, the situation of Jews in West Germany.

Myth, Dramaturgy, and Ideological Labor

Why, then, invoke 9 November to remember the victims of fascism? In the West as well, other options existed, especially in the postwar years, such as the September dates mentioned earlier. Indeed, Kugelmann (1988, 14) suggested that Kristallnacht may have turned into a day of remembrance more by chance. To deal with its genealogy, we have to continue to review the early commemorations. I argued that in those years commemoration constituted remembrance of *all* victims. Propst Grüber, a Protestant opponent of the Nazis who helped Jews in trouble, after 1945 a cochair of the VVN speaks on the occasion of 9 November not only of the pogroms against Jews but also of the butchery of thousands of Soviet prisoners of war in Sachsenhausen concentration camp.[24] Heinz Galinski, soon to become president of the Berlin Jewish community, also plays, until 1949, a key role in the VVN. In

---

23. The Konkret debate in particular raised the issue of anti-Semitism in the GDR without providing a clear answer. I would argue that anti-Semitism was present in the GDR as well but that it played a minor role as far as individual Jews were concerned. The government must nevertheless be faulted for its unwillingness to seriously address German crimes against the Jews. In light of the Shoah, this indifference to the Jews should indeed be described as an anti-Jewish policy. Some of the indifference of the leadership may well have had to do with the indifference of a considerable number of prominent politicians of Jewish origin in the GDR, according to the maxim that minister A, a Jew, feels just as we do about a given Jewish issue.

24. Propst Heinrich Grüber, "Unsere Schuld—Unsere Verantwortung," in Vereinigung der Verfolgten des Naziregimes 1948, 3–5.

short, the definition of who is a victim was broader at the time and
included, especially, the Communist and Socialist anti-Nazi resistance.
In the West, only the extraordinary influence of the churches after the
war, a political yet heavily religiously tinted discourse articulated in the
early Adenauer era, and the Cold War period of anticommunism and
antisocialism elevated the West German Jews, as "fellow citizens of the
Jewish faith," above other categories of persecutees and often turned
them into the only legitimate victims. The ironic parallel to that in the
East was the dissolution of the (Eastern) VVN and the scurrilous separation of "anti-Fascist resistance fighters" from a lower category of
(Jewish) "victims of fascism," which attempted to deny the particularity
of Jewish suffering (Maser 1991, 406).

This definition of the victim is one explanation for the elevation of 9
November above other possible commemorative days, in the West at
least. There are, however, other roots in its overall genealogy. The
pogrom occurred on 10 November. No one has pointed so far to the
proximity to 11 November, St. Martin's Day in the Catholic calendar.
Indeed, some witnesses of the pogrom, in Düsseldorf, for example,
remember the Martinszüge, or processions of children, on the evening
of 10 November 1938.[25] An equivalent of Halloween, this is the beginning of the carnival season in central Europe. On St. Martin's Day, as on
Halloween, children go from door to door and ask for gifts, but it is also
a day when in some areas particular persons or families were harassed or
even terrorized.[26] In many areas, "Saint Martin's fires" would be lit, and
these fires play a central role in the folklore of many areas of Germany
(Handwörterbuch 1932–33, vol. 5, 1707ff). Carnival is also the time
when the legal order and the order of property relations is temporarily
suspended and turned upside-down. This historical genealogy has also
been identified by Ernst Bloch, who writes,

> ancient terrains of utopia are thus being occupied by St. Vitus danc-
> ers [Veitstänzer], the Germanic romanticism of blood has arrived at
> the petty bourgeois, and has piped up an entire army of Feme
> murderers and guardians of the crown. (Bloch 1962, 62)

This inherent conflict between bourgeois order and a witches' sabbath is reflected in the conflict between Nazi propaganda minister Josef

---

25. *Allgemeine Jüdische Wochenzeitung*, 4 November 1988.

26. Clara Gallini (1992) points to a parallel of this in her discussion of the *caccia ai
marocchini*, a racist attack by a juvenile gang on Shrove Tuesday 1990 in Florence. For a
French account of carnival, see Ladurie 1979; for the long and often submerged traditions
of it, see Ginzburg 1989.

Goebbels and Reichsmarschall Hermann Göring, responsible for the economy and the military. The German economy was in poor shape at the time. Göring was interested in extracting capital from the Jews, not in destroying it, and also in maintaining harmonious economic relations with the outside world. The organized pogrom, however, was Goebbels and Hitler's initiative: As Göring put it to Goebbels in a meeting on 12 November, "I would have preferred it if you had killed two hundred Jews instead of destroying such value . . ."[27] We see here, then, a carnival extended into the diabolical, a revolt inside nazism against the Nazi state.

Carnival and the Saint Martin's fires and processions, moreover, are not only a motif in German popular culture that in a submerged form suggested the pogroms in the first place; they also have an emblematic quality, which has become inscribed in the later remembrances of Kristallnacht. The photographic material that has been used to represent Kristallnacht essentially falls into three categories: first, burning synagogues;[28] second, destroyed storefronts; and, third, Jewish men, flanked by SA or SS, marching through the cities or towns to collection points on their way to concentration camps. It is this third element that not only reiterated the pattern of the Martinszüge during the pogroms but is also present in its representations later. It is not pictorial representation alone, however. The marches—or chases—of Jewish men are being repeated in demonstrations and silent marches today, as on 8 November 1988 in Berlin and elsewhere. In the city of Oldenburg, for example, a Judengang, or Jew's walk, has been practiced for some years now: on the ninth of November (note that these arrests took place, for the most part, on the tenth and many on the eleventh or twelfth) some citizens march to the courthouse jail from which Jews were sent to the concentration camps (*Frankfurter Rundschau*, 9 November 1990).

Yet another connotation of Kristallnacht, however, lies in a certain emblematic affinity with Christmas and is at the same time its negation: the crystal, or the snow; the candlelight, or the fire; and the peacefulness, or the ominous silence of darkness and night. In 1946, Julius Meyer, then one of the leaders of the Berlin Jewish community put it like this:

---

27. Protocol of a discussion between Göring, Goebbels, Heydrich, and others on 12 November 1938, reprinted in *Der Prozess gegen die Hauptkriegsverbrecher vor dem Internationalen Militärgerichtshof* (Nürnberg 1948), 28: 499–540 (Document PS 1,816). It is quoted in Döscher 1988, 131.

28. These include altered photographs such as the one that came to represent the burning synagogue on Oranienburger Strasse. On the history of this synagogue during nazism, its rescue by a local chief of police, and the touched-up photo showing a fire that never occurred, see Knobloch 1990, 156–58.

It was on a cold winter evening, the snowflakes fell gently onto the ground, the streets were brightly lit, because the fiery torch of the mighty peoples' struggle [gewaltigen Völkerringens] did not yet move through the world. It turned silent, and a night as so many nights arrived. Then, in certain places of this city and in all cities of this country sinister forces came together with a fixed target! And when darkness came, they moved through the streets and destroyed the stores that had previously been marked as Jewish, they robbed and they fell upon us. When the stars in the sky wanted to light up the night, they were pushed aside, because red, red like blood, did missiles of fire shoot up into the air. Our sanctuaries, our synagogues, Houses of God, reared themselves up in the glow of fire and then collapsed in dust and ashes.[29]

Yet even the most fundamental imagery of the night in Kristallnacht is only very marginally borne out by the facts. While some of the synagogues were indeed set afire during the night, most of them burned in the early morning, and the overwhelming number of synagogues were seen burning during the day. Moreover, as indicated above, most of the destruction took place not during the night but in broad daylight. The emblem of night, however, is suggested by allusions to the "night of the long knives," the Röhm-Putsch of 1934, which in turn refers to the night of Bartholomew in Reformation France (Graml 1988, 27).

Still another event makes this a suitable day in the German commemorative calendar. Jews in many places, and especially in Israel, see the Yom Hashoah as the principal day to commemorate the Shoah. This day is set aside in remembrance of the Warsaw Ghetto uprising (Kugelmann 1988, 13ff.; Funkenstein 1989). But for Germans this day is unsuitable.[30] The uprising is an event in a foreign land, involving

---

29. *Der Weg*, 15 November 1946 (an address delivered in the Berlin Funkhaus on 9 November 1946). Sections of this speech appear verbatim in an address by Rabbi Riesenburger in 1958 (published in *Der Weg* in 1959) and in a different version by Riesenburger in the December 1978 edition. It is unclear who borrowed from whom, but the mythical depiction of the events also expresses its suspension from lived history.

30. Conversely, it was recognized early on in Palestine that Kristallnacht as a day of remembrance was no match for Yom Hashoah. The German-language paper *Yedioth* observed in 1945:

The day of remembrance of 10 November, the day of the *burning of synagogues in Germany* is, in the Yishuv of Palestine, not as popular as that other date of annihilation that is associated with the invasion of the Germans into Poland, the day of the Polish Jews. This is understandable if one considers that with the invasion of Poland, mass annihilation began. The tenth of November 1938, on the other hand, did not

non-German Jews—Jews, moreover, who were seen as participating in active resistance or even as Zionists. But Kristallnacht commemorations depict Jews who are not active but passive: they are nonheroes and essentially ahistorical figures. The pogroms, then, are a historical event that is fundamentally assimilable: it is linked to Germany, to *German* Jews, that is, to a group of people who have been assimilated into Germany as "good citizens."

Precisely this representation of Jews as silently suffering victims— here we can see the theater of memory at work— is a distinct feature of this commemoration in Germany. This commemoration, it must be stressed, however, is fully accepted by the Jewish participants. This can also be viewed in yet another way, however: the commemorations of Jewish suffering celebrate a distinctly female stereotype—like women, Jews are helpless and suffer silently[31]—as against that of the "bad boys," the cult of male bonding in nazism in general and in Kristallnacht in particular: "the guys' night out".[32] They are not only German Jews, but in the theater of the collective memory they also become good Bürger, good citizens. It is not the dirty Jew in rags, with peyes, kaftan, or streimel, who is being led away but respectable citizens whose fine furniture is being thrown onto the street, whose businesses are being destroyed, whose store windows are being smashed, and whose houses of prayer are set on fire. This is a version of events with which the churches and the average German citizen can identify, and here today's Germany is taking sides with the law-abiding Göring against the diabolical Goebbels.

Finally, the plot, the who dunit: Goebbels's lie to the world that this

---

yet bring about an annihilation of tens of thousands and hundreds of thousands; it represents a high point of a different type in the history of that mass madness that we call nazism. It was perhaps the ideological high point of the entire epoch. On this day . . . the synagogues went up in flames, and the frolicsome lords over these lands thought they could annihilate with it the word of the living God . . . (*Yedioth*, 9 November 1945; emphasis in the original)

Here, too, we see how remembrance is identity politics and how it creates racialized discourses: a day signaling mass annihilation is associated with Polish Jewry; the day of the annihilation of the spirit, on the other hand, is linked to German Jewry. The question of the German-Jewish spirit is addressed at the end of this article where the author expresses some resignation regarding the question of the "remaining value of centuries of Jewish history in central Europe" and its contribution to the emerging Jewish state.

31. Silent suffering is a recurring theme in the *Mitteilungsblatt der Hitachduth* in November 1938.

32. The female stereotype of the Jew was also inherent in Nazi ideology, of course: Jews as cowardly, chatty, shallow, and weak, in stark contrast to the male Aryan ideal, both physically and in terms of character traits.

Aktion was the spontaneous eruption of the *kochende Volksseele*, of the people's rage boiling over. It is being stressed over and over in German postwar articles that this was a lie, which in turn fails to come to grips with the fact that the state-sponsored pogrom was being tolerated, more or less sympathetically, by the population. The population certainly did not hesitate in areas such as Berlin, for example, to loot the Jewish stores. Moreover, Kristallnacht has the necessary dramaturgical and theatrical quality. It is drama because it portrays the very onset of the Holocaust; it is emblematic, with vivid imagery; it is a play of good guys and bad guys involving violence.[33] Rita Thalmann (Thalmann and Feinerman 1988, 7) has recognized this point. She observed that "nothing is missing in this classical tragedy, not even the poetic-cynical designation Kristallnacht." It is therefore more suitable for the stage of memory than are the perpetualized torture and degradation, the routines of the production of disease and death, and the silence of the smoke that later rises from the crematoria of Auschwitz.

What role do the West German Jews play in this culture of commemoration? From 1945 down to the sixties, we find two directions in the forms of remembrance. On one hand, as pointed out above, there is quiet, private, Jewish commemoration, which is expressed, for example, in the message of the Central Council of Jews on the twentieth anniversary of the pogroms. Here, the pogroms are set in the framework of attacks against family, friends, and community, and therefore, the commemoration as well should be focused on family and the inner Jewish environment.

> On the ninth of November, it will be the twentieth return of the day on which Jewish houses of prayer went up in flames. In all German cities the windows of Jewish shops crashed onto the streets. A stream of looters forced its way in. Jews were attacked in their homes and some shot before the eyes of their relatives. Many thousands of Jews set out on their way to the concentration camps. . . . In these days of November, commemorate your family members who perished, your friends and neighbors, the millions of Jewish victims. . . . Forgetting would here be wrong. (*Allgemeine Jüdische Wochenzeitung*, 7 November 1958)

At the same time Jews living in Germany needed a legitimation for returning there or moving there in the first place. In the earlier years, at

---

33. Georges Sorel has stressed the importance of violence in myth; Carl Schmitt, however, took the more decisive step of linking it to national consciousness (Schmitt 1988 [1923]).

least, this turns into a resigned and exculpatory view of the crimes. The message cited above continues:

> A new beginning was made, and we were guided by the idea that it cannot be useful to humanity to draw artificial curtains made of prejudice and hatred. The reestablishment of Jewish houses of prayer and communities is a witness to the invincibility of the spirit and of the eternal "and yet" of Jewish history. We address ourselves today to our German environment not in an accusatory or admonitory or lecturing tone, also not with demands for restitution. . . . It has been shown that the wave of destruction, once set into motion, could no longer be stopped . . . (Ibid.)

In short, then, the commemoration of the Shoah moves from a private stage of remembrance by a broad spectrum of victims of nazism in the immediate postwar period toward a commemoration that assumes religious overtones. It is a stage that is initially, and partly, usurped by the churches, pushing out of its way the Communists and Social Democrats as early co-sponsors with the Jews (Gypsies and gays being on the sidelines from the beginning), and later on receives greater participation of local politicians such as mayors. Only when the bulk of the first postwar generation of politicians had begun to leave the political arena with their retirement (politicians who built their careers under Hitler, who were implicated in nazism and continued under Adenauer, who were at least thirty years old in 1945), only when they began to withdraw from the political scene in the mid-seventies, could the commemoration take on a broader political frame of reference and become an act of state, most visibly first in the Cologne synagogue ceremony in 1978 with Chancellor Schmidt and President Scheel.

Previously, the Jews, together with other persecutees, were in control of their ceremonies of remembrance; subsequently, however, the state began to take the lead and be in charge, just as the state today is in control of the various memorials and exhibits pointed out above. In the early years, the commemorations were initiated and administered by Jews; Jews were, after all, mourning their own families and friends. Later on, however, Jews could even be barred from active participation in these new German/state commemorations. For example, Heinz Galinski's indirect but strongly voiced request to speak before the Bundestag was turned down in 1988 by the speaker, Philipp Jenninger, who wanted his own speech to be at the centre of the official commemoration (*Frankfurter Allgemeine Zeitung*, 29 October 1988; *Der Tagesspiegel*, 7 November 1988). On this occasion, the only Jewish person involved in the ceremony was the octogenarian actress Ida Ehre, reciting a poem by Paul Celan. An autonomous Jewish voice was therefore absent.

At the point where these commemorations had turned into national commemorations, Jews were needed, the dead Jews and live bodies of Jews; they furnished the state with what I have called ideological labor (Bodemann 1988, 1990), as actors in the annual atonement ritual, as witnesses to the international world, and they were also needed to position Germans in the place of the Jews in order to deal with the historical guilt. This was especially apparent in 1988 when the ceremonies took place on the theme of a saying by the Baal Shem Tov in his longing for Zion: "Remembering is the secret of deliverance, and forgetting prolongs the exile." I would therefore argue that, just as the Jews through remembrance were longing to be delivered from exile, so the Germans are longing for their Zion, for a land unpolluted by blood and ashes, a land free from guilt. In order to accomplish this, they had to become, in their own consciousness, Jews themselves.[34]

The Eclipse of Memory and Negative Celebration

This analysis so far has stopped at 1988, the fiftieth anniversary of Kristallnacht, and with good reason. With the opening of the Berlin Wall on 9 November 1989 and the euphoria associated with it, Kristallnacht moved into the background of national attention; for some time, the very survival of its commemoration seemed to be in question. Even political leaders such as the Social Democrat Hans-Jochen Vogel, who in 1988 had still given a fine address commemorating Kristallnacht (Vogel 1988), now saw no problem in his proposal to have the ninth of November proclaimed as an all-German National Day. That Kristallnacht would now be forgotten was the firm conviction of several Jewish leaders and intellectuals at the time, and it was at least a concern of others, expressed in a range of articles and comments.[35] There are probably several reasons why in the

---

34. An ever increasing number of cases illustrate this intense identification of Germans with Jews. One such case is that of Peter Handke. In his autobiographical *Kindergeschichte*, Handke speaks of his descent from an Unvolk ("un-people," "mis-people"). He sees his wishes fulfilled when his daughter is admitted to a Jewish school in Paris. "It [Jewry] was the only real people to which the adult had ever wanted to belong" (1981, 204). For a more recent case, not perhaps of seeking a Jewish identity but of being suspected of being Jewish by visiting American tourists and attaining an affinity with Jews by identifying with Jewish concerns and issues, is an anecdote told by the German Marxist philosopher Wolf Fritz Haug (1992, 408).

35. For one of many examples, see the feature on the writer Valentin Senger who expressed his "fear that the ninth of November could some day be turned . . . into a memorial day for bringing the two German states together" (*Süddeutsche Zeitung* [SZ] 9 November 1992).

end this day did not emerge as the official national unity day. First, the objections of Jewish leaders—and the fear of embarrassing criticism from the outside world—had an effect on public debates. Second, the euphoria about unification in the population, both East and West, in the Left and in parts of the Right, began to wane within months after the opening of the Wall and probably dampened the enthusiasm for this day as well. The Left in East Germany, especially the PDS, saw in all commemorations of unity nothing less than a re-emerging German nationalism. Last, and most importantly, it seems plausible that the Kohl government preferred to have the fruit of its own political achievement of unity recognized in the formal administrative day of unification rather than acknowledging the grass roots movement in the East—a chaotic, carnivalesque, yet demo-cratic upheaval with the collapse of the Wall. In what follows, I will attempt to sketch some of these developments.

With unification, there have been some remarkable transforma-tions in Kristallnacht commemorations, which came to evolve most clearly in Germany's new capital, Berlin. Evidently because of the great success of 9 November rallies in previous years, especially in 1991 in Berlin, Cologne, and other large cities, some top politicians decided to put themselves at the helm of a similar demonstration in 1992. This rally, dubbed the Grossdemonstration, under the patronage of German president Richard von Weizsäcker, was placed under the theme of article 1 of Germany's constitution—"The dignity of man/woman is untouchable." The official call to participate in this rally stressed that "Our history to us is a reminder and an obligation"; it addressed incidents of attacks against asylum seekers and other "for-eigners" as well as against Jewish memorial sites. It appealed to citi-zens to individually oppose hatred and violence on the anniversary of "the night in which what began with burning synagogues, ended with extermination camps and a world war." In short, Crystal Night was used as an analogy of possible new developments and thus as a politi-cal weapon; it was not, however, an occasion to remember this event per se.[36] This appeal, "across all party lines and differences of opinion,"

---

36. In von Weizsäcker's speech itself, the ninth of November had become an anal-ogy of German history, a "date of national destiny" (ein deutsches Schicksalsdatum): "Within two hours, it will get dark. . . . Then, according to the rules of the old testament [*sic*], the new day begins. It is the ninth of November, a German day of fate. Several times in our history, it turned into a signal for a violent loss of our freedom . . . when the Jews were being robbed, chased in the streets and when their synagogues were burned. Then, three years ago, came the day of freedom. With the unshakable courage of nonviolence, Germans turned swords into ploughshares. They stood against their oppressors, but with their hearts, not with violence. And they prevailed" (quoted in SZ, 10 November 1992).

however, also carried, more subtly, the theme of unification. It argued that "If East and West shall grow together, we have to search for a social balance and life prospects for all people." And finally, in a remarkable form of asymmetry, president von Weizsäcker's sponsorship and speech, as a man from the West, was juxtaposed with the "testimony of [antiracist] personal courage [Zivilcourage]" of a woman from the eastern Quedlinburg, also to be heard at the rally.

In previous years, a number of public commemorative events—events sponsored or cosponsored by the Western Jewish community—often included a march to a Holocaust site such as Jannowitz Brücke or the Grunewald train station—two places from which Jews were transported to the East. At these sites, commemorations with speeches or brief addresses were usually held. In November 1992, this element of the march was continued—except that neither the starting points nor the point of reunion had any significant association with the Shoah. (It is not inconceivable that the death of Heinz Galinski some months earlier had something to do with this omission, for he in all probability would have insisted on including "Jewish" *lieux de memoire*, and with his authority he might well have succeeded.)

This was clearly no accident and did not depend simply on the presence or absence of particular political actors. From the viewpoint of the actors and the president as the scheduled speaker, Crystal Night had become a faint backdrop, one date in the common historical experience for all Germans. The rally, however, also contained an element of a concealed commemoration/celebration of German unity. The rally had two initial assembly points. In the West, it was West Berlin's Wittenbergplatz and Gedächtniskirche (memorial church), which has been preserved as a ruin and as a reminder of the war, a symbolic locus and focal point for West Berlin as a whole and at least since 1968 a rallying point for leftist demonstrations. At the Wittenbergplatz, a simple board lists the "places that we must never forget," with the names of major concentration camps. In the East, on the other hand, the assembly point was the Gethsemane church, which has been a principal center of the dissident movement with its significant links to the Protestant church.

It is my contention that the East German conception provided elements of the framework for the commemorations in all of Germany. National pride, patriotism, even the conception of Germany itself have been tainted by nazism and were rejected in the official creed of the GDR; in contrast to other countries, they cannot be positively evaluated. In recording neonazism and German nationalism on the background of Kristallnacht, the GDR's "anti-Fascist tradition" has been brought into unified Germany: this day represents the merger of the distinctly Western tradition of Holocaust commemoration with a key element of GDR identity, its anti-Fascist foundation. Some of this can be illustrated by the commemorative practices in the East in recent years. On the first anniversary of the opening of the Wall, candles were lit inside Gethsemane church, an event of communal reflection rather than joyous celebration. While this event recognized the opening of the Wall, it also mourned the failure of the dissident movement's effort to establish a democratic GDR, and it also expressed its apprehension about—allegedly Western-inspired—racism and new German nationalism.

These two rallies, which were to constitute the Grossdemonstration in November 1992, from the East and from the West respectively, united at Lustgarten Square in the historic center of Berlin: the Neues Museum to the north, the Berlin Imperial Dome to the east, the Palast der Republik—the building housing the GDR parliament and the site of the old Stadtschloss (castle)—to the south, and the Museum of German History (Zeughaus) to the west. A *Tagesspiegel* editorialist described the scene on the "eve of the ninth of November" as "ghostlike."

> the situation meanwhile is serious enough and hardly a day represents better the disunity of the only just united nation as the ninth of November. In 1938, with the "Reichspogromnacht," the Nazis pushed open the gates of Auschwitz, in 1989 the Wall fell, and in 1992 we might possibly be facing another turning point . . . (*Der Tagesspiegel* [TSP], 9 November 1992)

The two assembly points in East and West, as two places representing distinct Eastern and Western political practices, thus were to find their symbolic suspension in this central square of Berlin, for well over a century a place of public manifestations. It was a merger/suspension of Eastern anti-Fascism and antichauvinism together with the Western religiously inspired tradition of Kristallnacht commemorations and anti-racist initiatives.

However, the appropriation of this middle-class grass roots movement, just like the earlier—largely successful—appropriation of Kristallnacht commemorations by the mainstream political establishment, turned into a fiasco. For the CDU, SPD, and FDP politicians, putting themselves at the helm of a mass rally of this sort, with over 300,000 participants, was to have been a convenient and effective advertisement to the international community—but also to German right-wing forces—that the representatives of Germany were concerned about Hoyerswerda and Rostock, just as they were previously concerned about Dachau and

Auschwitz. A substantial element in this demonstration interpreted this as insincere political propaganda, however, and the pervasive cries of "hypocrite" reflected the feeling of large segments of the demonstrators. The violence and egg throwing by little more than a hundred radical youth was merely a more extreme expression of opposition against the usurpation of this event by the political class, and instead of demonstrating to the world the antiracist commitment of the political parties the demonstration merely intensified the debate, and opposition, to legislation against closing the borders to asylum seekers. In this vein, *die tageszeitung* editorialist Jürgen Gottschlich wrote, "the CDU's hoped for rally in support of the government's foreign policy did not at all take place. The crowds had long redefined the event into a manifestation, lastly, for maintaining the constitution's right to asylum"(taz, 10 November 1992), and the *Süddeutsche Zeitung* concluded that the "instrument of the demonstration is not suitable for democratic politics" (SZ, 9 November 1992). The rally was therefore a contested terrain between the political class and the mass of the demonstrators. As one person present at the demonstration put it, "while we step forward in order to shield our constitution, the politicians come from behind and steal from us our paragraph 16 [the constitution's asylum section]" (*Frankfurter Rundschau* [FR], 9 November 1992).

Leading German papers as well represented the Berlin rally and other events around the ninth of November in a similar vein. Kristallnacht itself, in earlier years the subject of lengthy historical analyses and dossiers, especially concerned with the local events that supposedly occurred on that day in 1938, had been moved to the background; at the most, it was being used as an analogy in "admonishing memory" (Rita Süssmuth, in FR, 10 November 1992). Indicative of this relegation of the pogroms to the background, defining it once again as an event of the past perfect, was the layout, the graphic presentation, in a number of papers. SZ, FR, and FAZ, all on 10 November, on inside pages, summarized the Kristallnacht events in a boxed-in format; the overwhelming majority of the articles and reports, however, did not address the pogroms at all. Characteristically, the Berlin demonstration was portrayed as a "Sunday stroll," a Volksfest, a popular festival that included "dancing and singing," even jokes and clowns. The new carnival atmosphere at another large rally, in Cologne, attended by over one hundred thousand people, with the theme of "Rock gegen Rechts" (Rock against the Right), was described as follows.

They wanted to sing out loud their fear and their anger, to give a public signal. . . . Subsequently, on the fifty-fourth anniversary of the Reichspogromnacht, the group hammered out [the song[37]] Kristallnaach . . . and there was no one who did not feel he or she was not addressed. . . . Already two days before the start of carnival, the people of Cologne demonstrated that one could lock elbows even with total strangers and start first attempts at Schunkeln [linking arms and swaying from side to side]. (TSP, 11 November 1992)

Clearly events with a festival atmosphere to them, though perhaps a reasonably effective tool with which to oppose racism, could not possibly fit the act of mourning such horrible crimes as the pogroms. These 1992 events themselves, and also their representations in German media reports,[38] have very little to do with Kristallnacht. They are acts of negative celebration and, albeit largely unarticulated and with an antinational discourse, are an underground celebration of German unity; the opposition to racism and xenophobia serves as a common denominator agreeable to both the Western and Eastern middle classes. These antiracist rallies with the legitimatory backdrop of Kristallnacht were distinct also from a range of smaller memorial services of a more exclusively communal-Jewish nature held in a number of communities, services reminiscent of the commemorations of the early fifties. The volatility of the commemorations in 1992 has shown to what extent Germany is still in flux, in search of a new equilibrium.

It is my contention that the combination of German unification, the rise of the ultra right, and the increase in racist violence have brought significant changes to the Jewish role in Germany. At the Berlin rally, Ignatz Bubis, the leader of German Jewry, was present, but he was not an official speaker. However, as widely reported, he addressed the rally after it had been disrupted and officially declared to be closed. The day after, the Berlin *Tagesspiegel* quoted him as having said "I am ashamed for what happened here; we are not in the year 1938, but in 1992." According to the *Frankfurter Allgemeine Zeitung*, moreover, Bubis added, "A comparison [Gleichsetzung] is an insult to the victims [of Nazism, YMB]." Bubis therefore as well—while by no means discounting the importance of Kristallnacht commemorations—placed Kristallnacht in the past perfect. On this day, then, Jews found themselves standing alongside Germans in order to condemn "antiforeigner" violence; they were no longer the

---

37. Here in the local Cologne dialect.

38. Foreign reporting tended to stress the association with Kristallnacht to a far greater degree. *Le Monde*, the *New York Times*, the *International Herald Tribune*, the *Toronto Globe and Mail*, and the *Toronto Star*, for example, tended to move the Kristallnacht theme to the center of their reports and even saw these rallies as Kristallnacht commemorations.

principal victims, as they had been in West Germany, and not even second-class victims, as they had been in the East. The Jewish writer Ralph Giordano conveyed a sense of this when he remarked that he "counted on a broad alliance [Bundesgenossenschaft] in the fight against xenophobia and the political Right." Clearly, the Jews had lost their unique status in German society. They are now part of an alliance, or Bundesgenossenschaft—a particularly positive term assigned, after all, to members of the group that perpetrated the Holocaust—signifying far more than a mere alliance. Indeed, in some of his public pronouncements, Giordano vacillated between close association with Germany—calling it even his "fatherland," unheard of for a postwar German Jew—and, in contradiction thereto, revitalizing the social relevance of the Jews by placing them alongside the foreigners as fellow victims.

Indeed, this and other statements suggest genuine fear of neonazism but also an uneasiness about no longer being the central victim and the point that Jews, too, have to fear neonazism—certainly a correct statement given that a considerable part of neonazi activity is addressed against the Jews. The actress Ester Bejarano, for example, says that "she, too, is afraid" (FR, 9 November, 1992), and, as we have seen, another survivor, the journalist Valentin Senger, remarks that "in the last couple of weeks, I have this entirely new fear."[39] No longer being the center of attention, as victims, is being addressed again, by equating the forces leading to nazism with racist forces today. Micha Brumlik, for example, compares the attacks against Jews in Berlin's Scheunenviertel, a Jewish ghetto in Berlin before 1933, with xenophobic violence today and finds that in both cases attacks were being ignored by police (FR, 9 November, 1992). Another key representative of the Frankfurt Jewish community, Michel Friedman, complains that Germany still has no official memorial day (FR, 10 November 1992)—an issue that could only be seriously raised at the point at which the ninth of November had lost its quasi-official function.

It is important, moreover, to look carefully at the *language* of racist violence, which can take quite diverse forms as we know from other societies. In Germany, there is little evidence of burning crosses on front lawns or murderous, racially motivated violence between street gangs as in the United States. These and similar forms of violence suggest primarily a will to oppress the other group or force them into cultural conformity, as in the debate around wearing the *chador* in France or using the turban for Sikh members of the police force in Canada. In Germany, the language of violence expresses a wish to exterminate, not simply to oppress, as indicated in the persistent pattern of fire bombing immi-

---

39. SZ, 9 November 1992; see also footnote 35.

grants' homes and places of worship. There is a significant parallel here to the type of violence against the Jews that occurred under nazism, expressed so decisively during the 1938 pogroms.

As racist violence increases and as the social position of immigrants in Germany—"foreigners" so-called even when they have lived in Germany for several generations—is made more visible, the marginalization of the Jewish victim increases at the same pace. After the fire bombing and subsequent riots in Solingen, Turks for the first time were presented as commentators after the news on national television, and speakers for the Turkish immigrant group received, for the first time, some significant visibility in the media. They have therefore begun to assume the role of the generalized "other" represented by the Jews so far. Indeed, German victimology in relation to Jews now furnishes the pattern for the "foreigner" as victim. An official state memorial service, for example, was held for the Solingen victims in the mosque of Cologne; as mentioned above, the synagogue of Cologne was the site of the first state sponsored commemoration of Kristallnacht in 1978.

In sum, the Jewish fear that Crystal Night would be eclipsed by a new national day celebrating German unification clearly has not been borne out by developments. The Kohl government—in some part certainly also worried about Jewish concerns and fears and especially Jewish reactions abroad—decided against this date. The ninth of November 1989 would have glorified (and partly misinterpreted) popular movements and, moreover, would even have glorified a carnivalesque, chaotic atmosphere leading eventually to unity. The Kohl government did not wish this and evidently preferred a commemoration of the administrative-political unification achieved on 3 November 1990. This emphasizes the government's own merits in accomplishing the absorption of the GDR into the Federal Republic.

The ninth of November has thus turned, ostensibly as a festival against racism, into a negative celebration, into the tacit day of German unity, embodying diverse and partly contradictory elements that are shared by *all* Germans, not just those of the West or the East: 1918, 1923, 1938, and 1989. In this negative celebration, the days of the pogrom in early November 1938 have been turned into a mere "date and name," a backdrop used to combat racism and neonazism today. As such, this new negative celebration must be welcomed, even though it eclipses memories of suffering and of extinction of an alien minority in Germany over two generations ago.

The columnist William Pfaff has recently observed,

The West European problem remains, at its vital core, the German problem, and to an important extent this is the all-European problem as well. Germany is still not comfortable with itself, nor confident of its future, and this insecurity fuels an anxiousness about Germany elsewhere, above all in countries to the East. (*International Herald Tribune*, 12–13 June 1993)

Just how uncomfortable Germans are with themselves will continue to be apparent in the way they deal with their Jews, the past, and with memory.

Bibliography

Adam, Uwe Dietrich. 1988. "Wie spontan war der Pogrom?" In Pehle 1988, 74–93.

Bergmann, Werner, and Rainer Erb. 1990. *Antisemitismus in der politischen Kultur nach 1945*. Opladen, Westdeutscher Verlag.

Billstein, Aurel. 1978. *Der große Pogrom, die "Kristallnacht" in Krefeld*. Krefeld, AStA Kollektiv Druck.

Bloch, Ernst. 1962. *Erbschaft dieser Zeit*. Frankfurt, Suhrkamp.

Bodemann, Y. Michal. 1991a. "Die Endzeit der Märtyrer-Gründer: An einer Epochenwende jüdischer Existenz in Deutschland." *Babylon* 8:7–14.

Bodemann, Y. Michal. 1991b. "Gedächtnistheater. Zu den Grussadressen für Rosh Haschana." *Babylon* 8:100–115.

Bodemann, Y. Michal. 1990a. *Staat und Minorität. Antisemitismus und die gesellschaftliche Rolle der Juden in der Nachkriegszeit."* In Bergmann and Erb 1990, 320–331.

Bodemann, Y. Michal. 1990b. "The State in the Construction of Ethnicity and Ideological Labour: The Case of German Jewry." *Critical Sociology* 17, 3: 35–46

Bodemann, Y. Michal. 1989/1990/1991/1992. "Federal Republic of Germany." Reports in the *American Jewish Yearbooks*. New York, The American Jewish Committee.

Bodemann, Y. Michal. 1988a. "Staat und Ethnizität. Der Wiederaufbau der Jüdischen Gemeinden im Kalten Krieg." In Brumlik (1986), pp. 49–69

Bodemann, Y. Michal. 1988b. "Was hat der Gedenktag überhaupt mit den Juden zu tun? Nachbetrachtungen zu der 'Reichspogromnacht' und dem Umgang der Deutschen mit ihrer Geschichte." *Frankfurter Rundschau*, 29 November 1988.

Bodemann, Y. Michal. 1983. "Opfer zu Komplizen gemacht? Der jüdisch-deutsche Bruch und die verlorene Identität. Anmerkungen zu einer Rückkehr in die Bundesrepublik." *Die Zeit*, 30 December.

Brumlik, Micha, et al., eds. 1986. *Jüdisches Leben in Deutschland nach 1945*. Frankfurt, Athenäum.

Brumlik, Micha, and Petra Kunik. 1988. *Reichspogromnacht. Vergangenheitsbewältigung aus jüdischer Sicht*. Frankfurt, Brandes und Appel.

Combe, Sonia. 1990. "Des commémorations pour surmonter le passé Nazi." In

Alain Brossat, Sonia Combe, Jean-Yves Potel, and Jean-Charles Zsurek, eds., *A'l Est, la mémoire retrouvée*, 269–94. Paris, Editions La Découverte.

Diner, Dan. 1990. "Deutschland, die Juden und Europa." *Babylon* 7:96–104.

Domansky, Elisabeth. 1991. " 'Kristallnacht,' the Holocaust and German Unity. The Meaning of November 9 as an Anniversary in Germany." *History and Memory* 4, 1:60–94.

Döscher, Hans-Jürgen. 1988. *Reichskristallnacht. Die Novemberpogrome 1938.* Frankfurt, Ullstein.

Eschwege, Helmut. 1991. *Fremd unter meinesgleichen. Erinnerungen eines Dresdner Juden.* Berlin, Ch. Links Verlag.

Funkenstein, Amos. 1989. "Collective Memory and Historical Consciousness." *History and Memory* 1, 1:3–21.

Gallini, Clara. 1992. "Gefährliche Spiele—Symbolisch praktizierter Rassismus in der Alltagskultur." In Kalpaka and Räthzel 1992, 359–72.

Ginzburg, Carlo. 1990. *Ecstasies: Deciphering the Witches' Sabbath.* London, Hutchinson Radius.

Grimm, Jacob, and Wilhelm Grimm. 1854–1971. *Deutsches Wörterbuch.* 16 vols. Leipzig, S. Hirzel.

Groehler, Olaf. 1993. "Juden erkennen wir nicht an." *Konkret* 3:50–54.

Groehler, Olaf. 1992. "Aber sie haben nicht gekämpft." *Konkret* 5:38–44.

Graml, Hermann. 1988. *Reichskristallnacht. Antisemitismus und Judenverfolgung im Dritten Reich.* München, Deutscher Taschenbuch Verlag.

Handke, Peter. 1981. *Kindergeschichte.* Frankfurt am Main, Suhrkamp.

Handwörterbuch des Deutschen Aberglaubens. 1932–33. 5 vols. Berlin, de Gruyter.

Haug, Wolfgang Fritz. 1992. "Zur Dialektik des Anti-Rassismus." In Kalpaka and Räthzel 1992, 407–30.

Johnson, Richard, et al., eds. 1982. *Making History: Studies in History Writing and Politics.* London, Centre for Contemporary Cultural Studies and Hutchinson.

Kahn, Siegbert. 1960. "Dokumente des Kapfes der revolutionären deutschen Arbeiterbewegung gegen Antisemitismus und Judenverfolgung." *Beiträge zur Geschichte der deutschen Arbeiterbewegung.* 2:552–57.

Kalpaka, Annita, and Nora Räthzel, eds. 1992. *Rassismus und Migration in Europa.* Hamburg, Institut für Migrations- und Rassismusforschung e.V., Argument Verlag.

Knobloch, Heinz. 1990. *Der beherzte Reviervorsteher.* Berlin, Morgenbuch Verlag.

Kropat, Wolf-Arno. 1988. *Kristallnacht in Hessen. Der Judenpogrom vom November 1938, Eine Dokumentation.* Wiesbaden, Kommission für die Geschichte der Juden in Hessen.

Kuczynski, Jürgen. Kurt Gossweiler, and Kurt Pätzold. 1992. "Material fürs Sieger-Tribunal?" *Konkret* 8:44–58.

Kugelmann, Cilly. 1988. "Die gespaltene Erinnerung: Zur Genese von Gedenktagen an den Holocaust." In Brumlik and Kunik 1988, 11–20.

LeRoy Ladurie, Emanuel. 1979. *Carnival in Romans.* New York, G. Braziller.

Lenhardt, Gero. 1988. *Judenverfolgung und Bürgersinn: Das Beispiel Kirchhain.* Berlin, Max Planck Institut für Bildungsforschung. Mimeo.

Loewenberg, Peter. 1987. "The Kristallnacht as a Public Degradation Ritual." Vol. 32. Leo Baeck Yearbook. 309–323.

Loewy, Hanno, and Gerhard Schoenberner, eds. 1990. *Unser einziger Weg ist Arbeit: Das Ghetto in Lodz, 1940–1944.* Frankfurt and Vienna, Jüdisches Museum and Löscher Verlag.

Maser, Peter. 1991. "Juden und Jüdische Gemeinden in der DDR bis in das Jahr 1988." *Tel Aviver Jahrbuch für Deutsche Geschichte* 20:393–426.

Pehle, Walter H. 1988. *Der Judenpogrom, 1938: Von der Reichskristallnacht zum Judenmord.* Frankfurt, Fischer Taschenbuch Verlag.

Rosenkranz, Herbert. n.d. *Der Novemberpogrom 1938 in Wien.* Wien, Historisches Museum der Stadt Wien.

Schmitt, Carl. 1988 [1923]. "Die Politische Theorie des Mythos." In Carl Schmitt, *Positionen und Begriffe: Im Kampf mit Weimar-Genf-Versailles, 1923–1939,* Berlin, Duncker und Humblot.

Scholtz, Harald. 1967. "Die 'NS-Ordensburgen.' " *Vierteljahreshefte für Zeitgeschichte,* 15, 3:269–98.

Thalmann, Rita, and Emanuel Feinerman. 1988. *Die Kristallnacht.* Frankfurt, Athenäum Verlag.

Trapp, Frithjof. 1988. "Der Novemberpogrom: Gibt es in der Exilliteratur keine Darstellung der Judenpogrome?" *Exil* 2:5–10.

Vereinigung der Verfolgten des Naziregimes, Landesvorstand Niedersachsen, ed. 1948. *Schuld und Verantwortung: 10 Jahre nach der Kristallnacht, 9 November 1938.* Hannover, VVN.

Vogel, Hans-Jochen. 1988. "Station auf dem Weg zur Hölle: Ein Nachwort zum 9 November." *Die Zeit,* 30 December.

Young, James E. 1988. *Writing and Rewriting the Holocaust: Narrative and the Consequences of Interpretation.* Bloomington and Indianapolis, Indiana University Press.

Yuval-Davis, Nira. 1994. "Identity Politics and Women's Ethnicity." In V. Moghadam, ed., *Identity Politics and Women.* Boulder, Westview Press. 408–24.

Newspapers Consulted, with Abbreviations

AJW   *Allgemeine Jüdische Wochenzeitung.* Formerly *Allgemeine Wochenzeitung der Juden in Deutschland,* and Jüdisches Gemeindeblatt für die Nord-Rheinprovinz und Westfalen.

TSP   *Der Tagesspiegel*
       Der Weg

taz   *die tageszeitung*
       Die Zeit

FAZ   *Frankfurter Allgemeine Zeitung*

FR   *Frankfurter Rundschau*
        Mitteilungsblatt der Hitachdut Olej Germania
        Nachrichtenblatt der Jüdischen Gemeinde von Gross-Berlin und des
        Verbandes der Jüdischen Gemeinden in der DDR
ND   *Neues Deutschland*
SZ   *Süddeutsche Zeitung*
        Yedioth

5

From Cold-War Europe
to the New European Order

Imperialist Agents, Anti-Fascist Monuments, Eastern Refugees, Property Claims: Jews as Incorporations of East German Social Trauma, 1945–94

Robin Ostow

For many years there was little information available and seemingly little interest in Jewish life in the German Democratic Republic. Then, in 1988, two books on East German Jews were published in West Germany.[1] And, since the late 1980s, articles, documentary films, and books, appearing regularly in what have become the Federal Republic's "old" and "new" states have supplied abundant interviews and vignettes of Jews in the "anti-Fascist" Germany. This literature often constructs East German Jews as representatives of an exotic "alternative" GDR life-style. Some articles debate whether the GDR government was anti-Semitic, and, if so, at which levels and in what way.[2] Other authors address the role of the Jews and Jewish communities in supporting the relations with their government, which many Jews experienced as oppressive.[3]

Given that, by the mid-1980s, Jews in the GDR constituted a group of four hundred in a population of sixteen million, we are left with the question: has so much ever been written about so few? More important, what meaning are we to assign to the at times dramatic history of the Jews of the German Democratic Republic? And, finally, now that the

---

1. See S. Arndt et al. 1988; and Ostow 1989b. This book appeared in West Germany in 1988 under the title *Jüdisches Leben in der DDR* (Frankfurt am Main: Athenäum).
2. See Groehler 1992, 1993a, 1993b.
3. See Groehler 1992, 1993a, 1993b; and Burgauer 1993.

"anti-Fascist" state—which most GDR Jews considered their "home"—has disappeared, what kind of future can the Jews of the former GDR look forward to in the unified, post–Cold War Germany?

This essay will argue that, for most of the four decades of the German Democratic Republic, Jewish life barely existed, even for the Jews themselves. The political issues associated with a Jewish collectivity in a socialist Germany became dramatized for the public, and East German Jews lived intensively as Jews in the early years in which the GDR took shape and at the time immediately preceding its collapse. The first incisive moment of Jewish history in the GDR can be seen in the measures against Jews—who were constructed as "imperialist agents"—in winter 1952–53. These actions took place in the context of purges in many sectors of East German society[4] and led to the structuring of the GDR as a product of the Cold War.

The second incisive moment was November 1988 when virtually the entire population of the GDR was mobilized by the Honecker government to observe the fiftieth anniversary of Kristallnacht (the "Night of Broken Glass") the first major pogrom of the Nazis against German Jews. For this occasion, Jews were publicly constructed as monuments to the GDR government's claimed anti-Fascism. Jews as eastern refugees and claimants to property became powerful subsidiary images held by East Germans largely in the years before 1952 and after the dissolution of the GDR in 1989.

The Jewish Population of the GDR: Jews as Eastern Refugees and Claims to Property, 1945–52

For Jews, as for other inhabitants of Eastern Germany, the four decades of the German Democratic Republic began in the chaos of the postwar years. First and foremost was the geographic displacement of people. Altogether sixty million Europeans were uprooted as a result of the war and particularly the policies of the German and Soviet governments.[5] Through the early postwar years, millions of "displaced persons"—including fourteen million German refugees from what had been Germany's eastern territories—were moving through Europe. Most were going from east to west, but some also from west to east.

Among the Jewish population, for obvious reasons, this situation was even more extreme. Of the million Jews who survived the war in Europe, a mere seven thousand remained in the Soviet Occupied

---

4. See Harman 1983, 52.
5. See Botting 1985, 149.

Zone.[6] Some of these Jews were locals who survived the war and stayed on.[7] A few Polish Jewish survivors settled in what became the GDR: they gravitated to its eight Jewish communities. Jews relocating from west to east tended to be members of the German socialist elite. Many of these people became creators and administrators of GDR culture. But they made their careers with the SED (Socialist Unity Party). Their commitment and identity were primarily Socialist, and they kept their distance from the Jewish communities.[8] In other words, pre-GDR migratory currents generated by the Holocaust and the Cold War set the parameters of the composition and cleavages within the Jewish population as they did for the larger East German society.[9]

Within the Jewish communities, at the level of the membership as well as in the ranks of the functionaries, there was a complete rupture with the past. By 1943, all the prewar Jewish communities in Germany had been disbanded. Those Jewish leaders who survived the Final Solution— within the Third Reich or abroad—did not return to their former communities. Rather, new people were coming into the old synagogues and administrative structures. Many of them spoke less German than Yiddish. These refugees from the East had been preoccupied with survival at the age when they might otherwise have been attending university.

The early postwar years were also characterized in the eastern as in the western zones of Germany by negotiations between the Jewish communities and the local authorities and Allied military over subsidies for Jewish communal life, as well as social services for Jewish survivors and displaced persons. In the Soviet Occupied Zone, Jews were classified as victims of fascism and resistance fighters, and were compensated as such.[10] Particularly important, though, was the issue of rights to former Jewish property confiscated by the Nazis.

---

6. Thompson, (1978, 317) reported that, in 1946, 3,480 persons were registered in the GDR Jewish communities (3,000 in 1952). I am assuming that an equal number of Jews lived in the GDR but did not join the Jewish communities. The category of those "racially persecuted" under Nazism, which usually presupposes some "Jewish blood," contains several thousand individuals.

7. Helmut Eschwege, "Die jüdische Bevölkerung der Jahre nach der Kapitulation Hitlerdeutschlands auf dem Gebiet der DDR bis zum Jahre 1953," in Arndt et al. 1988. Eschwege claims that most of these people left Germany or turned away from Judaism. Few of them joined the Jewish communities.

8. See Richarz 1985.

9. See Niethammer 1992.

10. Thompson (1978, 85) claims that this pension was "far less comprehensive and generous than comparable legislation passed at the same time by the West German allied authorities."

Apartments, small factories and shops, and personal belongings still remained private property: however, when the Jewish survivors claimed them, they were violently opposed by . . . those who had become accustomed to think of former Jewish possessions as their own and of the Jewish survivors as intruders. . . . This group was so large that the Communists and other parties that were still legal defended it against the Jewish claims. . . . This struggle over restitution became accompanied by open or covert anti-Semitic agitation.

An even more formidable opponent of restitution was the Communist bureaucracy, which looked on all confiscated possessions as property of the nation. To the bureaucracy, the Jews who requested restitutions were looters of national property who were attempting to subvert the socialist economy by restoring capitalism. (Thompson 1978, 102–3)

The Cold-War Crisis: Jews as Imperialist Agents, 1952–53

The struggles of settling down and creating a new existence—demographically, institutionally, and socially—reached a climax with the anti-Jewish purges of late 1952 and early 1953. This persecution, which permanently altered the demography and structure of the East German Jewish communities, represented a reaction to the conditions outlined above but, even more important, to events originating outside the GDR. The Slansky trial in Czechoslovakia, the so-called Doctors' plot in the Soviet Union, and demands for restitution payments by the new state of Israel (which signed a Reparation Treaty with West Germany in 1952), as well as the larger progress of the Cold War, fueled the crisis.

The anti-Jewish line started in the DDR in mid-December 1952, when the Central Committee of the SED issued a sixty-page circular dealing with the lessons of the Slansky trial. The circular pointed out the importance of Zionism and international Jewish organizations, such as "Joint,"[11] as "agencies of American imperialism," which misused the sympathy of working peoples for Jewish victims of fascist persecution in order to organize espionage and sabotage in the peoples' democracies. (Thompson 1967, 63)

This circular was followed by accusations against Jews in the party press, the purging of many Jews from positions of power in the state

---

11. "Joint" here refers to the American Joint Distribution Committee.

and party bureaucracies, and increased supervision of Jews in the GDR. The leaders of all the East German Jewish communities were interrogated and asked to sign statements that equated Zionism with fascism, denounced the American Joint Distribution Committee—which had been providing care packages and support to Jews through-out Germany—as an agent of American imperialism, and condemned the campaign for restitution payments as exploitation of the German people.[12]

Over the winter, the homes of almost all Jews were raided, iden-tity cards were seized, and victims were ordered to stay close to home. The largely Jewish VVN (the union of those persecuted by the Nazis) was dissolved and replaced by the Committee of Anti-Fascist Resis-tance Fighters, which had a much less Jewish character, and the purges of Jews from prominent positions were extended even to those Jews who supported the government's anti-Zionist, anti-American, and anti-restitution positions. The Berlin Jewish community split in two, and all Jewish institutions in the GDR, except the cemeteries, were closed down.

By the time the crisis subsided—with Stalin's death in March 1953—550 Jews had fled the German Democratic Republic, including the lead-ers of all its Jewish communities.[13] By mid-June 1953, however, there was an abrupt change in policy. Measures against Jews ceased, and the small remnants of the Jewish communities received large government grants to repair and renovate their synagogues. At the same time they were sub-jected to new leaders who were installed by and responsible to the state. Jewish artists and government officials who had lost their jobs were reha-bilitated starting in 1956.

In other words, during this episode, which marked the height of the Cold War, the GDR government publicly constructed Jews as personifi-cations of the external and internal threats to national stability. This purging of "agents" of the capitalist West and of claimants to East Ger-man property and money strengthened the identification of the GDR with socialism and with the other Eastern bloc peoples' republics. And, internally, the destruction of the GDR Jewish communities as grass roots organizations with their own political basis, and the almost complete separation of GDR Jews and Jewish communities from Western organiza-tions and influences, became part of the centralization, or "Sovietiza-tion," of most sectors of public life.

---

12. See Ostow 1989b, chap. 1.

13. Thompson (1978, 317) estimates the membership of the GDR's Jewish communi-ties as three thousand before the purge.

GDR Jews and Jewish Communities in the 1960s and 1970s: Minor Administrative Concerns

After the purges—which affected not only Jewish but also many non-Jewish institutions—the Jewish communities of (East) Berlin, Dresden, Leipzig, Erfurt, Halle, Schwerin, Magdeburg, and Karl-Marx-Stadt were integrated into the German Democratic Republic. This integration was a rather peculiar one from a postwar western perspective. It was carried out from above and with an iron hand. Jews in the GDR were defined as a group that (1) observed certain religious rituals, and (2) was persecuted by the "Fascists." Jewish life in the GDR remained a tense cohabitation of two groups—those with religious and those with political priorities. These groups maintained differing loyalties and experiences of history, and there was little love or trust between them.[14] The crisis of 1952–53 did not overcome this rift but rather deepened it.

Within the Jewish communities, minimal religious services were organized for an overaged and dwindling membership.[15] Bodemann, for example, notes that in these years the observance of Kristallnacht "became ever more sporadic and lacked the previous commitment from within the community."

> On extremely rare occasions did any of the top brass attend the memorial services. . . . These commemorations resembled rather an administrative act with little or no participation from the population, the Jewish population included. Typically, the . . . city in which a commemoration was held would send a city councillor . . . and a deputy of the state secretariat for church affairs would often be present. (Bodemann, "Reconstructions of History," this volume)

All Jewish national claims and all communication and/or identification with the state of Israel were suppressed. And Jewish culture became a rather low-profile, low-energy enterprise. Groehler points out that, as a response to the trial of Adolf Eichmann in Jerusalem in 1961, the first articles and books on the Holocaust were published in the GDR, starting in the mid-1960s. Groehler characterizes the 1970s as a decade when the East German government pursued a dual policy regarding Jews.[16] The Honecker regime actively supported, and at times artificially maintained, its eight Jewish communities.[17] At the same time, anti-Israel

---

14. See Ostow 1991.
15. In some cases this was a nonexistent membership (see Burgauer 1993).
16. Groehler 1992.
17. See Burgauer's view of this policy (1993, 153–56, 208–9).

propaganda was intensified to curry favor with the Arab states. This latter policy represented part of an effort to break the international isolation of the GDR. Behind the scenes, individual Jews and functionaries of the Jewish communities were pressured to endorse the GDR's anti-Israel position.[18]

Interestingly enough, these relatively quiet years—the early 1960s through the early 1980s—may have been some of the best years of the GDR. The economy was expanding and the standard of living was rising. The Socialist dream was proving more complicated than expected, but to many it still seemed attainable. These decades may have been among the best years for many GDR Jews as well. But in the now copious interview material they do not remember living those years *as Jews*. East German Jews recall this period rather as a time of personal and professional development, of more consumer goods, and—for some journalists, simultaneous translators, language teachers, and diplomats, among others—of extensive travel. Some Jews even participated in GDR development projects in Africa and the Arab states. For younger Jewish intellectuals—those born between 1940 and 1955—these years often saw painful confrontations with the state.

In the middle decades, then, the GDR's policies regarding its Jews and Jewish communities were informed by its attempts to gain recognition from the West as an "anti-Fascist" state and from the Arab countries—and the Third World more generally—as an anti-Israel/anti-imperialist state. Internally, most GDR Jews—like many of their non-Jewish neighbors—were busy "building socialism" and enjoying a rising standard of living.

Jews as Anti-Fascist Monuments, 1980–89

This integration of Jews in the GDR, complicated and tense beneath a smooth exterior, held until the mid-1980s. Then it broke down, at first rather slowly. At a time when many non-Jewish GDR citizens were beginning to "discover" and develop "alternate"—Christian, homosexual, Sorb, or punk—identities, three to four hundred Jews from the political/cultural sphere started moving into the religious Jewish institutions.[19] And Jews of both religious and Socialist orientations began to demand permission to visit Israel, with more and more success.[20]

---

18. Groehler (1993b) says they refused.

19. See Ostow 1989a.

20. It began to seem as though almost every Jew in the GDR visited Israel sometime between 1986 and 1990. Several reported watching the collapse of their state on Israeli television (see Ostow 1996, forthcoming).

By the mid 1980s, the Honecker government had begun to negotiate trading ties to western countries—particularly the United States—as part of an effort to revive its moribund economy. International Jewish organizations were perceived in the GDR as channels of communication and potential mobilizers of local Jewish support in western countries for trade with the East. The East German state, then, began to encourage Jewish life within its borders to mediate ties to the West, and also to bolster its political legitimacy as an "anti-Fascist state," in the face of increasing popular impatience with its unwillingness to undertake serious political and economic reform. So, as the GDR went bankrupt, its Jewish communities—and Jewish initiatives outside the established communities as well—were awarded large sums of money to produce Jewish culture.

This policy culminated in November 1988 when literally the entire population of the GDR was mobilized to commemorate the fiftieth anniversary of Kristallnacht. In the presence of invited foreign dignitaries and a battery of international journalists and camera crews, a special session of the Volkskammer (Parliament) was held to honor the Jewish victims of Nazism. Many synagogues and Jewish cemeteries had been restored for the occasion. Tens of thousands of members of the FDJ (the party youth organization) attended a commemorative ceremony at the former concentration camp Ravensbrück. Smaller events were arranged by many organizations throughout the country, and plaques and monuments honoring the Jewish Holocaust victims were unveiled in almost every city. Many special publications were issued, and in the weeks preceding and following November 9, articles with Jewish content appeared in the GDR media almost every day.

Like the crisis of 1952–53, this final GDR drama around its Jewish population acknowledged the ties of Jews to western countries. Representatives of western states and their Jewish communities were invited to attend. But, rather than distancing the GDR from Jewish and western interests, this massive pageant represented an attempted approach to and identification with these groups and their concerns. This East German Kristallnacht spectacle mimicked in particular the mushrooming rituals of Holocaust commemoration that by 1988 had acquired unprecedented dimensions in several countries, especially the United States and the Federal Republic of Germany.

If the purges of 1952–53 and the subsequent restructuring of East German Jewish life became part of the shaping of the GDR as a product of the Cold War, this final public construction of GDR Jews as "anti-Fascist monuments"—tributes to the moral and political integrity of their "homeland"—signified the beginning of the dissolution of the East

German state. Despite these measures, many Jews, as well as non-Jewish East Germans, began to leave the GDR for the West. And a year later, on the fifty-first anniversary of Kristallnacht, the Berlin Wall burst open as a result of uncontainable popular pressure.

The Jews and Jewish communities of the GDR experienced and participated in the "Wende"—the dissolution of the state and the transition to German unification—in many ways. Initially, the East German Jewish communities remained close to the SED. They negotiated with the old and new administrations for diplomatic relations with Israel, for protection against increasingly active neo-Nazi groups, for financial support, and for recognition of GDR Jews as active anti-Fascists.[21] But their reluctance to take a public position on the issues of national, political, and economic reform frustrated many members and supporters who stopped frequenting the Jewish communities and began to work with the new citizens' groups.

In the GDR, many members of the Jewish communities organized their Jewishness as a series of private experiences within the walls of their homes and in community facilities that were often located in courtyards with unobtrusive exteriors, invisible to the non-Jewish population. And in GDR times many relationships invested with value were organized in the private sphere.[22] Most of these people, though, were not producers of culture.

A Jewish cultural tradition from forty years of the GDR evolved in what was actually a prewar German-Jewish institution, the Bildungsbürgertum[23]—the educated classes that produced and maintained a wide variety of intellectual and cultural enterprises. Many older members of this intellectual class have died or severely deteriorated in recent years, but the heritage of this Socialist Jewish cultural elite has, in many cases, passed to the children of the "Jewish Communists," children born between 1940 and 1955.

Before 1989, these younger Jewish intellectuals worked—often free-lance—in a state that generously supported cultural production. Since the collapse of the GDR, they live—as do their neighbors on the Prenzlauer Berg—partly engaged in free-lance projects and partly employed in short-term, publicly financed, make-work positions (the well-known "ABM-Stellen," which often involve low-level social and cultural administration. As children of active Communists, and as individuals

---

21. In previous years GDR Jews had been recognized as "victims of fascism" but not as resistance fighters, a higher status with a larger pension attached to it.

22. For a discussion of GDR society as a Nischengesellschaft, or "niche," society, see Gaus 1983.

23. See Bodemann 1991, 12–13.

who grew up with the socialist utopia, they had identified with the GDR and were bitterly disappointed by its contradictions and failures. And, unlike members of the GDR Jewish communities, whose Jewishness remained a private affair, these intellectuals have produced and continue to produce their experiences of the GDR in the form of novels, biographies, cultural festivals, and new organizations—sometimes but not always with explicitly Jewish content.

From 1989 to 1993, the German Jewish cultural enterprise in the East was moving in three directions simultaneously. Gregor Gysi and Irene Runge continued to work with the old state and party apparatus. But their attempts to be effective in a new political environment led them into a postmodern aesthetic of shifting perspectives and open contradictions. Irene Runge founded a secularly defined Jewish Cultural Association with Israeli travel posters on the wall and a strictly kosher kitchen. Its 1991 Chanuka celebration featured music performed by children of former members of the Central Committee and blessings by an ultraorthodox rabbi. In the same year, as president of the PDS (Party of Democratic Socialism), Gregor Gysi led a delegation from his party on its first visit to Israel in March, and in July he met with Yassir Arafat in Tunis to demonstrate the solidarity of the PDS with the Palestine Liberation Organization.

At the other extreme were those East German Jews who maintained their moral purity by rejecting the GDR altogether. Writers Barbara Honigmann and Hans—more recently Chaim—Noll left East Germany in the mid-1980s. They now pursue intensely Jewish lives in non-German West European countries and write in German as exiles. Living in France and Italy, respectively, relieves them of the discomfort of feeling torn between East German, unified German, and Israeli identities—all rather prickly—but it does not provide them a new home.

Between these extremes one finds East German Jews like Anette Kahane, Wolfgang Herzberg, Jalda Rebling, and Annette Leo. These intellectuals participated in the street demonstrations and the citizens' movement of autumn 1989. They then became involved in cultural projects that examined the careers and experiences of their families—including their own—at the crossroads of Jewish, Socialist, and German history. Their formulations of GDR Jewish culture attempted to exorcise the Stalinist evil and to locate and distill positive elements in the failed utopia, to conserve them for future generations, and to employ them as a standard for observing and judging the unified Germany.

The center of the life courses and thought processes of these East German Jewish intellectuals—regardless of the direction of their Jewish agenda—is the confrontation with the German Communist experiment.

Their Jewish identity is, by comparison, recent, derivative, and, in some cases, rather superficial. These Jews grew up in the villas of Pankow, and not—as did their West German counterparts—in the shadows of Auschwitz. And their cultural production far exceeds their demographic strength.

Jews in the Post-GDR and the New Federal States: Eastern Refugees and Property Claims, 1990–94

The collapse of the German Democratic Republic brought a return of chaos to East Germany, including a renewal of many of the social dynamics and the reopening of major political issues of the late 1940s. Again an east-west migration of considerable dimensions has severely tested the absorptive capacities of eastern Germany. In addition to the Gypsies, the Bosnian refugees, and the asylum seekers from the Third World, thousands and perhaps tens of thousands of Soviet Jews have immigrated to the GDR/Germany since April 1990.[24] Many of them are being settled in eastern Germany where they represent the only hope for the rejuvenation and continuity of tiny Jewish communities that were literally dying.[25] At the same time, the newcomers from the east tax the administrative powers and grate the cultural sensibilities of the handful of overaged East German Jewish leaders who have taken on the responsibility of settling them in. Younger East German Jews who might otherwise provide leadership in this phase of transition are moving to West Germany or are preoccupied with attempting to secure their own existences.

Throughout the interregnum of 1990, multiparty talks took place involving the (West German) Central Council of Jews in Germany, the Conference on Jewish Material Claims against Germany (based in New York), and the governments of Israel and the two Germanies regarding the amounts, scheduling, and recipients of GDR restitution payments. In the end, none were made, but the admission and integration of several thousand Soviet Jews was tacitly accepted as an alternative. Negotiations have also been resumed over rights to former Jewish property in the "five new states." And new agreements were worked out between the Central Council of Jews in Germany and the government in Bonn

---

24. For a detailed account of this, see Ostow, "German Democratic Republic," in *American Jewish Year Book, 1992* (Philadelphia: Jewish Publication Society, 1992), 373–82; and Michal Bodemann and Robin Ostow, "Germany," in *American Jewish Year Book, 1993* (Philadelphia: Jewish Publication Society, 1993), 282–300.

25. In 1989, the seven East German Jewish communities outside East Berlin numbered between 5 and 45 members each. By the end of 1992, they totaled 458. The smallest Jewish community—Halle—had 25 members.

regulating pensions for East German Jewish victims of nazism, who—
unlike Jews in West Germany—were never compensated for lost property. At the same time, the Jewish communities that were formerly
supported by the German Democratic Republic negotiated contracts for
their maintenance with the new federal states.[26]

As in the late 1940s, this renegotiation of the maintenance and status
of Jewish individuals, collectivities, and properties in eastern Germany
has taken place against a background of increasing anti-Semitic incidents.
In 1990, for the first time since the founding of the GDR, the Jewish
communities in the East requested and were assigned police protection.
In 1991, anti-Semitic agitation escalated to stabbing incidents involving
Soviet Jewish victims in Brandenburg, Glauchau, and Rostock. The number of anti-Semitic crimes in Germany soared in 1992 but has since declined.[27] In this case, too, popular anti-Semitism is related to—though
not identical with—competition between Jews and unemployed East Germans for the meager social resources locally available.

For the East German Jewish organizations, then, the rupture with
their past existence is, in many cases, almost total. The East Berlin
Jewish community—the largest in the GDR—was disbanded in January
1991, and its two hundred members were absorbed into what had been
the West Berlin Jewish community of seven thousand. The Jewish community of Schwerin was also dissolved, and in the remaining Jewish
communities the older members are dying and the younger members are
leaving. The new membership comes from the former Soviet Union.

The Jewish communities of eastern Germany now operate under
West German law. New Agreements with Bonn and the eastern states
regulate their property and financing, and the German police protect
them against their newly anti-Semitic neighbors. Another new agent in
the production of public representations of Jewish life in the East is the
Israeli government, which recently opened a consulate in Berlin. The
Israelis have become active in organizing Jewish cultural events and
teacher and student exchanges between eastern Germany and Israel.
The Jews of the former GDR are now Ossis (easterners) in the Federal
Republic; they are Jews in a population increasingly aware of its Germanness; and they have also become strangers in their own Jewish
communities.

---

26. For the details regarding all these issues, see *American Jewish Year Book 1992*,
373–82.

27. Since shortly after unification, the statistics on anti-Semitic crimes have been
reported on a national basis. They do not distinguish between the western states and the
former GDR.

Jews and Jewish Communities in the Eastern States of the "Berlin Republic": Everywhere and Nowhere

The years since the collapse of the GDR have also brought new segments of the East German population and new institutional forms to Jewish life in the "five new states." In East Berlin, two maverick Jewish institutions have opened. Both are recognized as corporate bodies by the now-unified city of Berlin, but they are seen as imposters by Berlin's established Jewish community and by the Central Council of Jews in Germany. Adass Jisroel, a neo-orthodox family enterprise, and the Jewish Cultural Association, a community service organization with a strictly kosher kitchen, provide Jewish religious, social, and cultural services—in German and Russian. Many members of the Jewish Cultural Association were not identified with Jewish life before the "Wende." In GDR times, they were active in the state prosecutor's office, the university, the media, and the foreign ministry. Now ultra-orthodox rabbis from Israel lead them in Friday night prayers; the women have to pray in a separate room.

Outside the now united Berlin, the eastern German Jewish communities still represent a miniminority—a population of 458 souls. Nonetheless, Jewish infrastructure has mushroomed under Jewish and non-Jewish auspices. A Moses Mendelssohn Center for European Jewish Studies has opened at the University of Potsdam. A klezmer group has been founded in Quedlinburg, a small town in the Harz Mountains with no Jewish inhabitants. In 1992, Rostock, which had neither Jewish inhabitants nor a Jewish community, boasted a German-Israeli Society, a Jewish Society of Mecklenburg, and a Meeting Place for Jewish History and Culture.[28] And in Dresden, which is also blessed with two Jewish cultural institutions in addition to its Jewish community of 196 members, an idealistic city official tried to reform a group of self-confessed neonazi juveniles by sending them on a trip to Israel at the taxpayers' expense.

Less publicized and less felicitous is the "de-Aryanization" and "desocialization" of property. In 1991, the Central Council of Jews in Germany filed claims to 1,270 formerly Jewish communal properties in eastern Berlin and the "five new states."[29] Property claims have exacer-

---

28. In 1993, Soviet Jewish immigrants were settled in and around Rostock. There is now interest in establishing a Jewish community for them.

29. These included 477 properties in eastern Berlin, 176 in Brandenburg, 109 in Mecklenburg-Vorpommern, 103 in Saxony-Anhalt, 293 in Saxony, and 112 in Thuringia. This step led to some unexpected consequences. For example, in December 1992, the

bated tensions within the Jewish population as well. Members of the Dresden Jewish community have expressed resentment over the handing over of all formerly Jewish properties in Dresden to the New York–based Jewish Claims Conference. The Dresden Jewish community—which had doubled in size—was facing considerable financial difficulties, which rental income from some of these properties could alleviate.

Beyond these uncomfortable regional manifestations, since unification Jews throughout the "Berlin Republic" have lost their unique status as the "victims" of German history. Since 1991, the dramatic increase in right-wing violence has been directed primarily against asylum seekers from the former Eastern bloc and the Third World in the eastern states and against the resident "foreign"—that is, Turkish—population in the former Federal Republic. Jews have been only secondary targets.

In this volume Bodemann describes how in the antiracist candlelight demonstrations of December 1992 Jews—and especially Jewish leaders—found themselves standing alongside Germans in condemning antiforeigner violence. The threat to German national consolidation posed by the invading masses from the south and the east was defused by the bureaucratic sealing of the German border in July 1993. Since then, the native handicapped, homeless, and homosexual populations have become the newest victims. Ignatz Bubis, the leader of unified Germany's Jewish communities since 1992, describes himself as a "German citizen of the Jewish faith," highlighting the ambiguous space that Jews now occupy between the "Germans" and the "foreigners" and other marginal groups.

And what has become of the East German Jewish intellectuals? Some of them can be found in the successor to the Socialist Unity party, the PDS. Others are involved in neighborhood actions to create community, to integrate Soviet Jews and other "foreigners" and refugees, and to resist the rent hikes and increasing unemployment that continue to threaten the eastern German life-style and standard of living. In other words, many of these people have returned to their political commitments of the 1960s. They articulate the anti-Fascist sensibility and develop a—now backward-looking—Socialist culture in eastern Germany.

Central Council protested the demolition of a former synagogue in the town of Malchow (in Mecklenburg-Vorpommern). The owner of the building had been given permission to demolish the structure, which he had designated as a storage shed, though it covered an area of three hundred square meters. The local authorities claimed they had no idea that the building was a former synagogue, despite the presence of papers filed by the Central Council to reclaim the structure.

Bibliography

Arndt, S., H. Eschwege, P. Honigmann, and L. Mertens. 1988. *Juden in der DDR: Geschichte—Probleme—Perspektiven.* Duisburg, Brill.

Bodemann, Y. Michal. 1991. "Die Endzeit der Märtyrer-Gründer: An einer Epochenwende jüdischer Existenz in Deutschland." *Babylon* 8: 12–13.

Botting, Douglas. 1985. *From the Ruins of the Reich: Germany, 1945–1949.* New York, Crown.

Burgauer, Erica. 1993. *Zwischen Erinnerungung und Verdrängung: Juden in Deutschland nach 1945.* Reinbek bei Hamburg, Rowohlt.

Eschwege, Helmut. 1991. *Fremd unter meinesgleichen: Erinnerungen eines dresdner Juden.* (East) Berlin, Ch. Links.

Gaus, Günter. 1983. *Wo Deutschland liegt: Eine Ortsbestimmung.* Hamburg, Hoffmann und Campe.

Groehler, Olaf. 1992. "Aber sie haben nicht gekämpft!" *Konkret* 5: 38–44.

———. 1993a. Juden erkennen wir nicht an." *Konkret* 3: 50–54.

———. 1993b. "Der Umgang mit dem Holocaust in der Sowjetischen Besatzungszone Deutschlands und in der Deutschen Demokratischen Republik." Paper presented at the Annual Conference of the German Studies Association, October 7–10, Washington, D.C.

Harman, Chris. 1983. *Class Struggles in Eastern Europe, 1945–83.* 2d ed. London and Sydney, Pluto.

Herzberg, Wolfgang. 1990. *Überleben heisst Erinnern: Lebensgeschichten deutscher Juden.* (East) Berlin, Aufbau.

Honigmann, Barbara. 1991. *Eine Liebe aus Nichts.* Berlin, Rowohlt.

Leo, Annette. 1991. *Briefe zwischen Kommen und Gehen.* (East) Berlin, Basisdruck.

Niethammer, Lutz. 1992. "The Structuring and Restructuring of the German Working Classes after 1945 and after 1990." Paper presented at McMaster University.

Noll, Chaim. 1992. *Nachtgedanken über Deutschland.* Reinbek bei Hamburg, Rowohlt.

Ostow, Robin. 1989a. "Das neue nationale Bewusstsein der Juden der DDR." In *Die DDR im vierzigsten Jahr: Geschichte, Situation, Perspektiven,* ed. Ilse Spittmann and Gisela Helwig. Köln, Verlag Wissenschaft und Politik.

———. 1989b. *Jews in Contemporary East Germany: The Children of Moses in the Land of Marx.* London, Macmillan.

———. 1991. "Helden und Antihelden: Zwei Typen jüdischer Identität in der DDR." *BIOS* 2/91: 191–204.

———. 1996. *Juden ausder DDR und die deutsche Wiedervereinigung.* Berlin: Wichern Verlag. Forthcoming.

Richarz, Monika. 1985. "Jews in Today's Germanies." In *Leo Baeck Institute Year Book.* London, Leo Baeck Institute.

Thompson, Jerry E. 1978. "Jews, Zionism, and Israel: The Story of the Jews in the German Democratic Republic since 1945." Ph.D. diss., Washington State University.

Jews and the Transition to a Post-Yalta Order: Germany, Austria, Eastern Europe, and the United States

Andrei S. Markovits

Introduction

This chapter starts with the assumption that the forty-odd years of the Yalta world were quite unique for the Jews everywhere in the world. Following the perennially incomprehensible horrors of the Shoah and liberal democracy's as well as communism's unconditional victory over fascism, the Jews were finally blessed with a period of unusual social respect, political acceptability, economic comfort, and even the exercise of state power *qua* Jews *and* citizens. The processes begun in the era of the Enlightenment and continued throughout the state- and nation-building epochs of the eighteenth and nineteenth centuries, and the extension of citizenship and bourgeois rights in the wake of the French and American revolutions, all seemed finally to come true for the Jews as well. Surely, prejudices and age-old patterns of anti-Semitism persisted everywhere. Ironically and sadly, in complete contradiction to Zionist hopes and strategies, Jews in the post-Shoah world seemed physically safe in most parts of the globe excepting the state of Israel, which was, in the Zionists' hopes and beliefs, to have provided the safest haven to a people ravaged by an unprecedented tragedy. Nevertheless, the state of Israel also lent the Jews immense pride and the unprecedented experience in the modern era of exercising political control and power in a state of their own. Jews in the United States and Canada became fully accepted members of their countries' respective middle classes where they prospered economically, attained social acceptance, and excelled in a number of areas crucial to the successful maintenance of hegemonic bourgeois culture such as the universities, the media, and the art world, both "high" and "low." There can be no doubt that the Jewish experience in North America must be labeled an unmitigated success story in the larger scope of Jewish history in general and in its twentieth-century variant in particular. This success, although clearly cemented in the pre-Shoah world and quite particular to North American—especially U.S.—history, truly unfolded in the forty years of the Yalta era. On the western half of the European continent, too, the traumatized and demeaned Jewish communities "enjoyed" a particularly tranquil time for a change, informed by the general populations' amnesia and exhaustion coupled with some sense of contrition and guilt, the area's unprecedented economic prosperity, and the loss of political power and complete sovereignty to the two respective superpowers, the United States and the Soviet Union. Only in the Communist world of Eastern Europe and the Soviet Union did the Jews continue to experience state-induced and state-encouraged anti-Semitism, which on rare occasions threatened them physically but typically just left them in a state of permanent tension. Even though anti-Semitism remained alive and well in the state-run societies of Eastern Europe and the Soviet Union, it was—as much else—an "organized" anti-Semitism, devoid of the laissez-faire character of its prewar existence. The state channeled anti-Semitism. In doing so, it opposed any "rivals" that it might encounter in civil society, thus giving the Jews a certain calculability and predictability regarding the calamities that were to befall them. This, in turn, translated into a sad but curiously transparent form of normalcy and order. These state-run systems altered the randomness and pogromlike expressions of prewar anti-Semitism into a well-ordered form of state-controled and state-guided definition of the "other."

The central argument proposed in this chapter revolves around the notion that in the past six years we have witnessed the dissolution of this Yalta world, which, in turn, has already proved to have major ramifications for the Jews as well. In no way do I want to argue that the next forty years will be filled with horrors and massively lethal experiences for the Jews of the world (North America, Europe, Israel) on anywhere near the order of magnitude experienced in the Shoah or even in the unorganized (and occasionally pogromlike) forms of anti-Semitism that informed the world of much of Europe's pre-Holocaust Jewry. However, I do submit that there will arise complications and difficulties for the Jews in this new post-Yalta arrangement that we thought had been happily resolved once and for all by the Yalta compact's triumph over global fascism. Things will not be the same for anybody, including the Jews. Let me assert as an important caveat that this cautious assessment of the Jews' existence in a world devoid of the Yalta order in no way stands for a neo-Stalinist defense of the old status quo in Eastern Europe and the Soviet Union, nor for an extolling of the allegedly "orderly" and "ordering" virtues of the Cold War, as has been fashionable in certain academic and intellectual circles. Indeed, despite the numerous setbacks and the horrors of the wars in the former Yugoslavia, I maintain my belief that the current events in Eastern Europe have proven without any doubt the complete bankruptcy of Leninism as a legitimate and effective form of political rule in advanced industrial societies. These events underline most emphatically, among others, the irresistible human urge for freedom, which is much better served by liberal democracy than by any kind of collectivist dictatorship. And, despite the tremendous difficulties confronting most countries in Eastern Europe, which are in the process of undergoing the unprecedented transition from Leninist command economies to those subject to the laws of capitalist production and the exigencies of the market, the new liberal democratic order has not collapsed in countries such as Poland, Hungary, Slovakia, the Czech Republic, Slovenia, and a number of other places. Liberal democracy is very much alive, if not altogether well, which was to be expected given the magnitude of the transition on the domestic front and internationally to this new and still ill-defined post-Yalta order.

Moreover, I also continue to rejoice about the increasing delegitimation of anticommunism and the Cold War as the most important axial principles of western—especially American—political dogma and strategic thinking. The demise of communism has also meant the death of anticommunism, which, in turn, has finally liberated the nondogmatic and nonorthodox Left in the West from the albatross of Leninism with which it had to contend willy nilly for over seventy years. As a whole, I welcome the demystification of all large projects with the various "isms" as their ubiquitous suffixes and find the growth of a healthy skepticism, a creative "Unübersichtlichkeit," and a secular "muddling through" intellectually refreshing and politically exciting. This demystifying process, which accompanies the immense transformation of the hitherto orderly Yalta world into what George Bush correctly called a "new world order," will, in addition to creating much excitement and change, also by definition exact much uncertainty. The overall changes will—I believe— constitute major improvements in the human condition as a whole, which is, of course, not to say that we will manage to stay clear of deteriorations in a number of specific areas when compared to the past. There already have been many losers, and there will be more. Uncertainty has affected the Jews and will undoubtedly continue to do so. Moreover, the demise of the Yalta world will not only increase the uncertainty for Jews in the most immediately affected areas of Eastern and Central Europe but in the United States and Israel as well. In the subsequent parts of this chapter, I would like to concretize this speculative argument empirically by analyzing noticeable shifts in Germany, Austria, Eastern Europe, and the United States. Although these areas constitute vastly different political settings and experiential "spaces" for Jews, I perceive some interesting commonalities that should give us food for thought. Following a brief discussion of each of these cases, I will conclude by spelling out some of these commonalities.

Germany: From Bundesrepublik to Deutschland

The old Bundesrepublik is dead. The changes wrought by the demise of the German Democratic Republic and the ensuing geographic expansion of the Federal Republic as well as its growth in population entail more than a mere change in quantity. The new Deutschland is also qualitatively a different entity from the old Bundesrepublik. The jury is still out (and will be for some time to come) on the question of whether this massive change is for the better or worse for all concerned. The fact is, however, that its enormity is already evident in every aspect of German and European politics.

Two important features that defined the old Bundesrepublik are currently subject to major discussion in Germany and Europe and will undoubtedly be redefined in the years to come. The first pertained to the Federal Republic's lack of an independent foreign policy; and the second (and related feature) centered on the Federal Republic's subordinate role as a military power. Both were manifestations of the Federal Republic's lack of total sovereignty and autonomy and a concomitant deference to and dependence on the political leadership of the United States in the global arena and France in the European theater. This structural arrangement formed the core of that quintessentially bundesrepublican trait aptly characterized by the adage "economic giant but political dwarf." This syndrome vanished on November 9, 1989. With Deutschland came full sovereignty. The only remaining question is how will the metamorphosis of the political dwarf into a regular person, a political adult, change things in Germany and Europe? Will this person necessarily become a giant? If so, will it be a gentle giant or a bully? Does it have to become a giant even against its will? Or could it manage its growing-up process so that it develops into a regular, "normal" person? The end of the Bundesrepublik and the beginning of Deutschland means nothing more than a process of normalization. But, given Germany's troubled history, this normalization process may be everything but normal. At the heart of this immensely complex transition period is the interaction of power and democracy in the new Deutschland. These two have not had a happy coexistence in German history. Indeed, one could argue that it was perhaps the Bundes-republik's greatest achievement to have institutionalized democracy to a degree hitherto never experienced on German soil. But, so the coun-terargument goes, this democracy was basically a fair-weather one, which was never put to the true test of the exigencies of power politics. To be democratic as a sheltered and privileged rump state under American tutelage benefiting from being on the front line of the Cold War is a different proposition from remaining democratic as a newly united sover-eign state embodying the unquestioned power house of the new Europe.

While the eventual results of this interaction between power and democracy are far from certain at this stage, one can discern the following three-pronged development. On an institutional, legal, and formal level the continuity between the old Bundesrepublik and the new Deutschland is quite remarkable. Short of the enlarged Bundestag and, more impor-tantly, the enhanced Bundesrat in which the voice of the five new Laender attain an otherwise unparalleled clarity, very few institutions have changed in any substantial way since the fall of the Berlin Wall on Novem-ber 9, 1989. In the areas of institutions such as parties, interest groups, and government agencies, the old Bundesrepublik continues more or less unabated. Unification amounted to little more than a takeover operation of the German Democratic Republic by the Bundesrepublik.

Curiously, however, this virtually seamless continuity on the formal institutional level seems a bit frayed on the level of policy. Be it in the areas of immigration and asylum or the extension of social benefits to the increasingly marginalized members of a crisis-ridden society, the new Deutschland has proven to be just a touch harsher than the old Bundes-republik. If one can point to certain domestic policies of the new Deutsch-land that have clearly impinged on the old Bundesrepublik's generous democratic arrangements (without, of course, annulling them in any way), one can equally discern policy changes in the new Germany's for-eign and European affairs, which bespeak an obvious change in power that the country wants to project. Be it Germany's disastrous foray into the Yugoslav tragedy or its occasional difficulties with France in maintain-ing the endangered relationship of the formerly vaunted Franco-German alliance, in which the Bundesrepublik clearly played a subordinate role, the new Deutschland's policies are increasingly subject to the logic of power and sovereignty rather than the former Bundesrepublik's logic of cooperation and coexistence.

But it is on the ephemeral, yet immensely tangible, level of atmo-sphere and political culture that one can discern the most noticeable change between the old Bundesrepublik and the new Deutschland. For fairness' sake it is important to point out that harbingers of this atmospheric shift had already appeared in the course of the 1980s in the old Bundesrepublik. One need only think of the Bitburg incident in the spring of 1985 and the "Historikerstreit" beginning in the summer of 1986 to point to instances in which the very essence of the old Bundesrepublik— especially its ties to the West, both in terms of power and culture, and its constitutional rather than national character— were subjects of acrimonious controversies. There can be no doubt that, atmospherically speaking, the new Deutschland is a different place from the old Bundesrepublik. One need only read the editorial pages of Germany's paper of record, the *Frankfurter Allgemeine Zeitung*, to witness this atmospheric change. What had once been a centrist newspaper with a deeply conservative streak became a rightist paper with a nationalist bent. The change from Bundesrepublik to Deutschland has been—to nobody's surprise— particularly marked on the right of the political spectrum. Here one needs to mention the radical or fringe right's newly won political and thematic, if not necessarily numeric, prominence. More alarming, however, is the established and salonfaehig right's precipitous movement into the nationalist camp away from its bundesrepublican tradition of a catch-all kind of centrist and constitutional conservatism. This is best characterized by the transition and generational shift in the Christian Democratic Union (CDU) from men like Helmut Kohl, who always anchored their conservatism in a deeply felt commitment to the Bundesrepublik's identity as a western entity in a supranational Europe and NATO, to men like Wolfgang Schaeuble, who do not even bother to conceal their primary allegiance to German nationalism pure and simple.

Obviously, the change from Bundesrepublik to Deutschland has also affected the Jews. Here, too, the tripartite division into institutions, policies, and atmosphere/culture yields similar results. Little has changed for the Jews on the levels of institutions and policy in the transition from Bundesrepublik to Deutschland. This, however, is certainly not the case in the area of atmosphere and culture. On the most obvious level, the Jews are in the process of losing their function of helping to legitimate the Bundesrepublik internationally, something they did more twenty-five years ago than recently but which never quite disappeared until now. Germans will become less guilt-ridden as well as responsible vis-à-vis Jews, meaning that the Jews, too, will become "normalized." One can already observe two dimensions to this normalization. The first manifests itself in a much more open and blithe expression of anti-Semitism on a quotidian basis. Thus, recount many Jews (including the head of the German-Jewish Community,

Ignaz Bubis), whereas in the past they typically received all their anti-Semitic hate mail anonymously, these unwelcome and threatening intrusions (including packages of human excrement) now arrive with the sender's name, return address, and fax number. In other words, expressing one's anti-Semitism has become much more open and accepted. Indeed, there has developed a certain caché to treating the Jews like everybody else, which surely also includes expressing one's hate for and dislike of them. In other words, the "Schonzeit"—the protective "no hunting season"—that characterized the Jews' status throughout much of the Bundesrepublik is definitely in the process of ending as a hegemonic ideology in the new Deutschland. Whereas sentiments of this sort of "normalization" were obviously present in the old Bundesrepublik—after all, the expression itself hails from a Frankfurt theater director who defended the production of Rainer Werner Fassbinder's openly anti-Semitic *Garbage, the City and Death* in the fall of 1985—they will become much more acceptable in the public discourse of the new Deutschland. The second dimension of normalization entails an even greater abstraction and "museumization" of Jews than had been the case in the old Bundesrepublik. There will be even more synagogues without congregants, just as one can expect a proliferation of museums and exhibits without the context of real existing and current experiences. Thus, as long as most Germans still refer to Jews as "jüdische *Mit*bürger" instead of "jüdische Bürger," the current craze for klezmer music among a certain segment of the educated intelligentsia may indeed widen this group's musical erudition and enjoyment; it will, however, remain ephemeral to the larger issue of the Germans' understanding of the Jews and their predicament in Germany and Europe, past and present. This decontextualization of Jews means that the Germans will never be able to come to terms with the Holocaust no matter how good their intentions have been or might still be. This is because coming to terms with any past—let alone with one burdened by the heinous magnitude of the Shoah—necessitates the real, material, physical, concrete presence of the victim on a scale a good deal larger than the circa forty thousand Jews currently living in Germany. Coming to terms with one's past cannot be thought and abstracted. It has to be experienced on a daily basis. For that there are simply not enough Jews in contemporary Germany. And, regardless of the welcome success of the film *Schindler's List* among the German public, not even Stephen Spielberg's genius is capable of creating a world in which Jews can once again be properly contextualized in the new Deutschland. Given the tragedy of the Shoah this might not be a bad thing.

Austria

The negative comparisons with the Federal Republic's already meager attempts at a "Vergangenheitsbewaeltigung" are much too well known to be repeated here. Austria's easy way out via the Moscow Declaration of 1943, which exonerated Austria from any complicity with the Nazi Reich, instead making the Austrians the Germans' "first victim" of the war, needs no further elaboration. The fact is that the myth of the German rape helped exonerate and exculpate Austria in the eyes of the global public. This myth also helped Austria attain its vaunted neutrality in 1955, which meant that the country was spared many problems of the Cold War, most notably that of physical division, which we know so well from the German case. It also resolved the issue of sovereignty much sooner and with less pain than in the German situation. Indeed, we now know with the benefit of hindsight that the Austrian second republic's sovereignty has become inextricably tied to the country's neutrality. Neutrality developed into a potent state *and*—miracle of miracles— nation builder. The fact that nearly 90 percent of Austrians routinely believe today that there is such a thing as an Austrian nation, while barely a third did in the early 1950s, attests to the success of the second republic's abilities to create a distinctly political (as opposed to regional and cultural) Austrian identity. Most important, however, the myth about the Austrians being Nazi Germany's first victim absolved the Austrian people from a sense of collective responsibility for its actions during the Third Reich. It provided an "exit option" that the Germans— particularly those in the Bundesrepublik as opposed to those in GDR who used their communism as a convenient exit, at least from this predicament—simply did not have. Two significant developments of recent vintage in Austrian politics deserve brief commentary in the context of this paper. The first concerns the Waldheim affair and the second the rise of Jörg Haider and Haiderism as significant expressions of a new Austrian populism that—as is always the case—has many parallels in other European countries but is also sui generis.

As to the Waldheim affair, I would analyze its immediate effects and short-term legacy as very positive for the development of democracy and the voices of compassion in Austria. The affair demasked taboos and opened hitherto forbidden debates. It highlighted more than any other event the continued existence of a conservative "Schmäh" and "Schickeria" anti-Semitism of the centrist Catholic "Lager" represented by the Austrian People's party (ÖVP) for the last fifty years. Although a good deal less rabid and less explicitly racist than its "grossdeutsch" counterpart, which—due to its direct linkages to national socialism—has always been better known in the world, this form of anti-Semitism has, if anything, played an even more pernicious role in the institutionalization of anti-Semitism as a regular part of politically accepted discourse in Austria and even beyond. Precisely as a consequence of its "Salonfaehigkeit" and its social acceptability, this anti-Semitism has been perceived by the world as much more harmless—perhaps even good-humored—than its "völkisch" counterpart. The Waldheim case clearly conveyed the links and overlaps between these two forms of anti-Semitism and demonstrated the symbiotic relationship of the two in the very person of Kurt Waldheim. The affair also brought the Austrian situation squarely before the eyes of the world. Suddenly, this Alpine paradise of "Gemütlichkeit," waltzes, and Mozart confronted a radically different, entirely negative public image that it had conveniently avoided for forty years. Largely as a consequence of this exogenous shift, there developed a serious endogenous debate the likes of which had never occurred in post-1945 Austria. While nowhere nearly as sustained and involved as the one in the Federal Republic of Germany, definite attempts were made in Austria to uncover events that had hitherto merely served as consensual symbols in the perpetuation of the myth regarding Austria's victimization by the Germans. Thus, had it not been for the Waldheim affair, it is very doubtful whether the fiftieth anniversary of the Anschluss would have led to such interesting and revealing confrontations inside Austria with the country's own past. The Waldheim affair and the overwhelmingly negative global echo that it created were largely responsible for the fact that the observances of the Anschluss in 1988 did not degenerate into the previously routinized collective "Gejammer" about having been raped by the wicked "Piefkes" in 1938. This, most certainly, demonstrated respectable progress. Particularly telling was the tireless engagement of a considerable segment of the Austrian intelligentsia against Waldheim. Bespeaking a certain secularization (also pluralization or westernization) of Austrian politics, this opposition on the part of the intelligentsia was not only confined to the usual "red" subculture of the country but also included a growing coalition of free floaters of indeterminate coloration even though it still lacked "blacks" (Catholic-conservatives) and "browns" (völkisch-nationalists) for obvious reasons. The Waldheim affair spawned a soul searching and a historical introspection that had no precedent in Austrian history. It thereby contributed to a widening of the country's democratic debate. But, as we know, democratic debate also entails the introduction and legitimation of the less tolerant qualities of human life such as prejudice, hatred, and exclusion. These also emerged—or attained invigorated voices—in the wake of the Waldheim affair.

Most important, the affair made anti-Semitism completely acceptable in public discourse once again. The affair rendered manifest anti-
Semitism "salonfaehig" in Austrian political campaigns. Frequently deployed in a latent manner, anti-Semitism as a campaign tool was rarely
used in such a manifest fashion as it was in the election campaign of 1970
when the ÖVP's candidate, Josef Klaus, portrayed himself as a "wahrer
Oesterreicher" in juxtaposition to the SPÖ's (Austrian Socialist party's)
Bruno Kreisky, who, presumably by virtue of being Jewish, was clearly
portrayed as not being a "true Austrian." Such obviously anti-Semitic
tendencies became quite the norm in the ÖVP's campaign for Kurt
Waldheim's presidency. All the standard clichés about the Jews—their
supposed control of the American press, their allegedly conspiratorial
linkages across the globe, their supposed shiftiness, their reputed thirst
for revenge—were deployed in one form or another by the pro-Waldheim
forces during the campaign: indeed, quite successfully, judging from the
results.

The Waldheim affair reinforced and reaffirmed—if it did not
create—the phenomenon of Joerg Haider who has since arguably become Austria's most popular (certainly most populist) politician. It
should be added that Joerg Haider in many ways also embodies at least
an indirect creation of Bruno Kreisky's strategy, which was predicated
on an intensive courting of the Freiheitliche Partei Oesterreichs (FPÖ)
in order to destroy the ÖVP as the main political rival of the SPÖ,
thereby replicating the Swedish model in Austria where social democracy would also have enjoyed a hegemonic position of power vis-à-vis its
bourgeois challengers. Although the Kreisky strategy met with eventual
failure in that it did not lead to a substantial weakening of the ÖVP—at
least not in Kreisky's time—it most certainly provided the FPÖ with a
legitimacy in Austrian politics that it had never previously enjoyed.
While the Kreisky boost first helped the party's "liberal" wing, led by
Norbert Steger, it was its more dominant and traditionally more prominent "national" wing, under Joerg Haider, that had carried the day by
the mid 1980s. Armed with a charismatic new leader and a populist zing,
this party benefitted immensely from the atmospheric changes wrought
by the Waldheim affair, which paved the way in legitimating and popular-
izing the FPÖ's increasingly neorightist, xenophobic, and anti-Semitic
positions in Austrian politics.

While Haider represents in one sense the FPÖ's and the Austrian
right's traditional völkisch nationalism, which harkens back to the
world of this movement's founder, Georg Freiherr von Schoenerer,
Haiderism also expresses something quintessentially "second republican" in that it embodies an aspect of a new Austrian right that is very

much a creation of the post-1945/post-1955 neutral and independent second Austrian republic of the Yalta world. Indeed, Haiderism represents the first indigenous and sovereign Austrian right that is neither völkisch and pan-German, as had been the FPÖ's tradition, nor Catholic and "ständisch," as had been the ÖVP's legacy as embodied by Waldheim. Haiderism is a curious mélange of populism laced with a heavy dose of xenophobia, anticapitalism, antiwestern attitudes, and anti-Americanism. It is obviously contemptuous of social democracy and most aspects of the traditional and new Lefts, though its overt interest in ecological issues does lend it a vaguely greenish hue. Unlike the two traditional Austrian Rights, Haiderism is most definitely young and modern. Like its leader it appeals to the young, service-sector, professional-managerial class and has also proven to be quite successful in wooing skilled workers, who have hitherto always embodied the most loyal supporters of social democracy. Thus, it was this mixture of a modern Right—a self-consciously New Right—which made the FPÖ the second-strongest party in Vienna, relegating the ÖVP to a distant third place and inflicting heavy wounds on the Socialists, who for nearly a century had seemed to be all but invincible in their "red" bastion. Above all, Haiderism—in notable contrast to all previous FPÖ positions—is not particularly pro-German. It does not advocate any Anschlusslike arrangements with the new Deutschland and was in fact quite subdued during Germany's unification. Indeed, Haider's localized and particularistic brand of a New Austrian Right made him a vocal critic of Austria's joining the European Union and—thus indirectly—the Federal Republic. In other words, the Austrian Right has undergone a mutation during the last twenty years of which Haiderism is a powerful expression. Just like the country as a whole, the Right, too, does not define itself by its Germanness and its relationship vis-à-vis the big brother to the north. Haiderism has rendered the Austrian Right completely sovereign. As such, it is quite similar to other comparable phenomena in the rest of Europe, both East and West.

Lastly, the Waldheim affair brought to the fore a consistently present but formerly dormant "antiwesternism" in Austrian public discourse. Much more than in the old Bundesrepublik, Austria's "Westbindung" has been tenuous at best. After all, this country never knew any ties to such powerful western integrators as NATO or the European (Economic) Community. Indeed, Austria's neutrality mitigated against the country having any kind of explicit ties with the West comparable to the Bundesrepublik's. With neutrality becoming a meaningless political category in a Europe without any blocs, Austria could finally take the step to join the

European Union, though with much reluctance and apprehension. Precisely at a time when Austria was finally ready (and permitted) to become a full-fledged member of the West, this entity, too, had metamorphosized into something quite different from what it meant in the Yalta world. The breakup of the Yalta compact rendered Austria's previous "homelessness" the European norm. In a sense, Austria had always remained part—if not the core—of Mitteleuropa. The Habsburg legacy, seemingly experiencing an immense revival and relevance as a consequence of the astounding developments altering the political landscape of the European continent, always informed the political reality of this small Alpine republic. In a way one could take Austria out of the Habsburgs but not the Habsburgs out of Austria. This, in turn, leads me to a brief discussion of the situation in Eastern Europe.

Eastern Europe

Lest there be *any* misunderstandings, I am of the firm opinion that the complete delegitimation of Leninism as a form of political rule and its eventual demise everywhere in Eastern Europe and the Soviet Union represents one of the key turning points in the political history of the modern world. Moreover, I am also convinced that this poses not only a most fundamental challenge to the progressive Left, in both Eastern and Western Europe, but that at the same time it also provides hitherto unprecedented opportunities for the Left's redefinition and revival.

Leninism's most debilitating legacy has been its utter failure to reform some of the most pernicious cleavages that led much of Eastern as well as Western Europe into the abyss of fascism and World War II. Whereas—conforming to Marx's observations—markets had an enlightening, internationalizing, and ultimately emancipating effect on Western Europe in that they by and large defanged and depoisoned the nationalist snake, the Leninist imposition from above failed to make any significant changes in the nationalist sentiments that East Europeans had harbored in the pre-1939 world. This is not to say that nationalist sentiments have disappeared in Europe's western part, nor that racism has miraculously abated. Regarding the latter, even the most cursory perusal of the political landscape of most West European societies during the 1980s and early 1990s would make it amply clear that racism is—if anything—on the rise and becoming politically acceptable and socially salonfaehig once again in most, if not all, West European countries. It is quite telling, however, that this West European racism has largely focused either on non-Europeans (Arabs, Africans, Moluccans, Kurds, Tamils, Pakistanis, Indians) or on Europeans from the continent's peripheries (mainly Turks but also Serbs and to a lesser extent Greeks, Spaniards, and Portuguese). With the possible exception of the Irish and the Basque situations, national attachments in West Europe and vis-à-vis other West Europeans have on the whole been transferred to the realm of cultural and linguistic attachments, *not* matters of particularistic exclusion accompanied by open hostilities and a clear wish to destroy the "other." Indeed, few Frenchmen like Germans, and the British rooted in large numbers for Argentina, with whom they had just fought a war, rather than for the Federal Republic when these two countries' soccer teams met in the World Cup final of 1986. As the fiftieth anniversary celebrations of D-Day have made amply clear once again, the legacy of World War II is very much alive in the political cultures of West European countries. But rooting against the Germans and fighting them are two very different propositions. West Europeans may not love each other, but their animosities, if indeed politically still relevant, are very distant from bellicosity. There simply do not exist any irredentist feelings in West Europe anymore. Border disputes are matters of the past and no country has any claims on its neighbors' territories. I am quite certain that even the most rabid Front Nationale enthusiast could not be enticed by any calls "à Berlin" to march much past her or his neighborhood. Similarly, no REP or NPD member would make much headway even within the most right-wing milieu in the new Deutschland by claiming Strassbourg for a "Grossdeutschland." Turks are definitely hated by much of the German population. They are also subject to right-wing terrorism, which, as in Moelln and Solingen, led to the murder of small Turkish children. With all the animosities that the Germans bring to bear against the Turks, it would still be unthinkable to have the Turks in Germany subjected to the blatant and often violent forms of conversion and/or expulsion as happened in Bulgaria in the late 1980s. Whereas these prewar sentiments have largely been contained, if not eliminated, by the Yalta world's successes in West Europe, thus attesting to perhaps the single most impressive achievement of the European integrative process, they have reemerged with a vengeance in Eastern Europe where Leninism concealed them for forty years without altering them in any way. National identities in Eastern Europe are still very much defined by the outside. Regardless of what an individual may think of herself or himself in terms of national identity, the person *is* Hungarian, Croat, Bulgarian, or Jewish because the outside world says so. National identity remains an objective fact rather than an individual's subjective choice. It still remains a nonnegotiable issue in which individual choice and volition matter very little, if at all. Put crudely, the Bosnian tragedy would simply be unthinkable in Europe's western half, while it embodies, to be sure, the most extreme expression of a structure and logic that are daily realities of politics in Eastern Europe.

The same pertains to anti-Semitism. While obviously present in West Europe and growing as part of the package of xenophobia and prejudice, it has not attained the virulence and openness that one experiences in the contemporary politics of Russia, Romania, Hungary, Slovakia, and even—to an alarming and surprising degree—in the Czech Republic. Anti-Semitism, never far from the surface in most of these countries and always part of the politics of their particularistic identities, has come in handy for a variety of groups on a number of occasions in the uncertainties of the post-Yalta world. It has obviously been used to attack Leninist orthodoxies and to denounce the "Left," just as it has been central in criticizing the new order of market economy and parliamentary democracy. The Jew embodies a two-pronged evil. He is the representative of the ancien Leninist regime. As such, he is identified with the Left and hated for his involvement with the Yalta order, which continues to be despised in most East European countries. However, the Jew also represents all the problems associated with the creation of a post-Yalta order. He is identified with the market's inequities (as well as its iniquities), the lack of political authority and legitimacy, and the inevitable turbulence and hardships associated with the historically singular transition from a party-run, command economy to a market-driven, pluralist society.

With the rapid introduction of the market as the allocator and regulator of much of public life in Eastern Europe, there also developed a marketplace for ideas and political programs. Some of these exhibit anti-Semitic tendencies in various forms and quantities. Freedom of opinion does allow the freedom to hate. This in no way means that Leninist state-dominated and regulated societies were devoid of anti-Semitism. Examples abound, from the "doctors' plot" anti-Semitism of the late Stalin years in the Soviet Union to the Moczar era of the late 1960s in Poland; virtually every East European regime used anti-Semitism for its purposes at one time or another. Nevertheless, market-mediated anti-Semitism has been differently transmitted and experienced than its state-mediated counterpart, which means that the Jews face a different set of circumstances in the current situation from the one they did during the presence of the Yalta order. On the one hand, there can be no doubt that this market-mediated anti-Semitism has been much more egregious, pernicious, and dangerous than its state-run predecessor precisely because it benefits from the freedoms inherent in the new order. Anti-Semitism in the current era has been raw, unmediated, and uncensored. It needs neither guises of anti-Zionism nor euphemisms of rootless cosmopolitanism. The Csurkas and Zhirinovskys of this world can say exactly what they want with no retributive consequences. On the other hand, however, one might also expect the freedom of the new post-Yalta order to work in favor of the Jews. Most important, of course, is the freedom of pursuing an exit option, which the Jews most certainly did not have in Leninist times. The fact that Jews can leave, and have indeed done so in large numbers, makes all the difference in the world. Yet, even for those Jews who opt to stay for reasons of "loyalty" or "voice," one can imagine an improved scenario, which, though optimistic, may not appear unduly unrealistic: the countervailing forces (which exist and are not negligible) could indeed mobilize against the current atmosphere of hatred and anti-Semitism, and defeat both in the marketplace of ideas as well as that of political forces, thereby relegating anti-Semitism to West European levels, meaning that it will continue to exist but with a substantially diminished public and political relevance. Were this scenario to occur, the victory of the "good guys" would be all the more decisive because it would have been wrought not by a dictatorial state "from above" but by forces indigenous to civil society "from below." That, of course, would mean the ultimate triumph of a viable pluralism in East Europe comparable to that of the liberal democracies that ruled West Europe during the forty years of the Yalta order and continue their unabated and unquestioned hegemony in that part of the continent despite the enormity of the changes that those countries, too, are currently experiencing. In the meantime, however, things will not be easy for the Jews of East Europe during this transition period.

The United States

Be it Arthur Herzberg or Seymour Martin Lipset, the late Ben Halpern or Marshall Sklare, and most of all the late Irving Howe, all experts trying to explain the experience of Jews in the United States via an explicit comparison to its counterpart in Europe come to one overarching conclusion: put succinctly, in the words of one of Ben Halpern's fine articles, "America is different." It would be well beyond the scope of this chapter to enumerate the many reasons for this profound difference. Suffice it to say that this difference hails from the absence of feudalism in the development of modern American society, which, in turn, meant that politics, the extension of citizenship, and the individual's relationship to state and society evolved quite differently in the New World compared to the old. Indeed, many of the crucial factors accounting for America's "exceptional" development vis-à-vis the rest of the industrialized world, that is, its not having a large, mass-based, working-class party espousing some sort of socialist or social democratic ideology (and the absence of soccer as a mass sport as well as culture), also seem instrumental in explaining "American exceptionalism" in Jewish history.

By being the first new nation, by having enjoyed the luxury of being born bourgeois without having to become so, and above all by being an immigrant society America developed a unique blend of identity, which allowed the continuation of old—that is, pre-American—particularisms in conjunction with the rapid acquisition of a new American universalism. Hyphenation as an expression of this composite identity, which has been so woefully absent in most of Europe, created a mechanism that allowed the coexistence of old and new identities in a more or less harmonious manner. Above all, true to its bourgeois nature, ethnic identity in America—in diametrical opposition to the situation in East Europe—developed into a matter of personal choice. With the notable—and tragic—exception of African-Americans, whose unique situation in American life begins with their having been brought forcibly to the New World rather than choosing to seek its promises, ethnic identities can either be totally forgotten in the United States after only a few generations or they can be remembered in folkloric fashion such as the annual Columbus Day, St. Patrick's Day, or Steuben Day parades. For Jews, America inevitably became the *goldene medinah*. While this term denoted this country's enormous wealth and material possibilities, it mainly described a sense of liberation and a semblance of opportunity, which—even if far from equal—permitted some dignity and absence of the subjugation so closely associated with all of Europe, including its western, "enlightened" part. Despite the continued existence of anti-Semitism in all walks of life, America has seemed to the Jews—and has been—incomparably better on all counts than Europe had ever been. Indeed, there is simply no contest as to where the Jews met with greater acceptance, security, even appreciation. "To find evidence of serious anti-Semitism in America for much of the time Jews have lived here, you need to put on knee pads, and go searching in the nooks and crannies of history," writes David Klinghoffer in the *New York Times Book Review* of April 17, 1994, in reviewing two recent books on anti-Semitism in America. Thus, even concerning the phenomenon of anti-Semitism, America—one of the most overtly religious and Christian of nations—represents a clear, and in this case much appreciated, exception.

Especially after World War II and the tragedy of the Shoah, American Jews prospered to a degree not expected even by the most inveterate optimist. Acceptance in virtually all parts of the American public had been attained by the Jews certainly by the late 1950s. Indeed, the American success story has been perhaps best exemplified by the Jews and their integration into and acceptance by American society. Jews reached prominent positions in the academy (not only as professors but even as presidents of Ivy League universities), the media (print and electronic), the arts, publishing, medicine, law, and even business, with the notable exception of the world of large banks and industrial companies such as General Motors, Ford, Exxon, and IBM (with DuPont, however, offering a compelling counterexample). Jews became an integral part of American politics on all levels (elected and appointed, local, state, and national). Partly as a consequence of their repressed and persecuted European legacy, Jews became disproportionately engaged on the Left-Liberal side of the American political spectrum. Without exception, Jews have remained far and away the most liberal nonblack ethnic group since the New Deal to this very day. This pertains as much to local, state, and national politics as to the entire gamut of issues. Be it on the "class" dimensions of distributive politics, on issues pertaining to economic equality and justice, or on "value" dimensions centered on freedom of speech, reproductive rights, patriotism, and the separation of state and church, Jews have consistently remained the most progressive nonblack ethnic group in the United States. This continued to be the case even during a period when prominent Jewish intellectuals, formerly from the Left-Liberal spectrum of American public life, assumed leading positions in an intellectual and political movement known as "neoconservatism."

Due in good part to this acceptance of Jews by the mainstream of American society, Auschwitz developed into the epitome of immorality and evil in the minds of Americans. Anything associated with the Shoah and Auschwitz immediately enters the realm of pure evil and is thus perceived as illegitimate by the vast majority of the American public. The power of this remains so overwhelming that no other consideration can even be raised in debating the validity of the issue. Thus, for example, in the case of Bitburg, as well as the Waldheim affair, very few, if any, arguments attained legitimacy with the public by emphasizing the primacy of American interests instead of moral convictions in the formulation of policy. Indeed, when Ronald Reagan tried to legitimize his visit to Bitburg in the name of current American interests, his popularity fell to an all-time low and his arguments were dismissed as illegitimate in the name of morality. Whenever matters center around anything vaguely related to Auschwitz, the politics of interest becomes completely subordinated to the politics of morality. Hence, it is interesting to note that in heated debates, such as the current conflict about abortion, each side is trying to delegitimize the other's stand by denouncing it as Holocaustlike. The invocation of the Shoah by both sides is a calculated strategy to land a knockout punch by pushing the opponent into the corner of absolute evil and thus changing the debate from the politics of interest to that of an absolute moral category.

The singularity of Jewish suffering has created an absolute evil that in fact has become universalized in contemporary America. As long as the issues are defined on what one could call the "morality-memory" axis, much of American public opinion will be completely congruent with Jewish feelings and preoccupations. However, as soon as the controversy leaves this "morality-memory" realm and enters the area of contemporary interest politics, this consensus becomes a lot less solid. Intra-Jewish cleavages, as well as those between the Jewish community on the one hand and other ethnic communities on the other, become pronounced, in certain cases even acerbic, as soon as the playing field shifts from morality to contemporary politics. Be it the case of Israel or black-Jewish relations, issues concerning religion or the economy, the protective mantle of the Shoah simply does not pertain in this area. Indeed, what makes the conflict between African-Americans and Jews particularly acerbic is their seemingly mutually exclusive contestation for a victimization that is of such magnitude (slavery vs. the Holocaust) that its universal acceptance by other Americans appears to depend on its singularity. Thus, it is particularly hurtful for Jews to hear black nationalists and separatists lace their anti-Semitism with the accusation that Jews played a leading role in the enslaving of blacks. With this argument blacks are not only robbing the Jews of Auschwitz but in essence are making them complicitous in the Auschwitz of African-Americans. The seriously strained relations between the Jewish and the African-American communities of the past twenty years ranks among the most serious political and social setbacks for the Jewish community in its American experience. The nadir of this relationship for the Jews was reached on a hot August night in 1991 when young blacks in a pogrom-style riot killed a Jew in the Crown Heights section of Brooklyn, thereby realizing their vile exhortation of "Kill the Jew." A commonplace in Europe, where Jews have been killed by the millions merely because they were Jewish, the Crown Heights pogrom assumed a rare, if not a unique, place in American history. (Thus, for example, a very similar incident to the one in Crown Heights occurred in Malden, Massachusetts, in 1911 when young Irish thugs beat up Jews in the streets, shouting "Kill the Jews.") Adding insult to injury, the public authorities have yet to find the Crown Heights culprit nearly five years after the traumatic event. Making matters worse between Jews and African-Americans has been a noticeable animosity—indeed, open hostility—against Jews on the part of many black progressives. Whereas affect and sympathy for, as well as solidarity with, the plight of African-Americans has always been—and continues to be—perhaps the single most important political tenet of progressive Jews in America, antagonism toward Jews bordering on outright anti-Semitism has, alas, become a commonplace among many, if not all, progressive African-Americans.

One of the dangers for the American Jewish community in having relied too much on the overwhelming moral power of the Shoah is that with the passage of time the Shoah's unique moral position might wane. And there could develop the following paradox: the more the Jewish community emphasizes—and insists upon—the singularity of the Holocaust, the more it actually might run the risk of excluding itself from the historical experience of the American mainstream. In a sense, this singularization of the Holocaust continues to "singularize" the Jews vis-à-vis all other ethnic communities in a multiethnic and multicultural country correctly priding itself on having created a singularly cohesive unity precisely—and solely—based on diversity and multiplicity. Yet, it is exactly this singularization of the Shoah that has successfully created and upheld a universalized moral consensus approved by virtually all parts of American society. Auschwitz as evil incarnate continues to remain as close to a moral icon as anything in American life, including the Constitution. Thus, it is not by accident that the most important Holocaust museum in the world stands in the midst of America's most cherished shrines in the nation's capital. Judging from the completely unexpected mass of daily visitors to the museum it is quite evident that the Shoah has—at least for the time being—been appropriated by the American public virtually as an American tragedy. Dialectically speaking it is therefore not surprising that while thousands of Americans flock to Washington to visit the museum and millions are moved by Steven Spielberg's sensational movie *Schindler's List*, 35 percent of the American public (according to one survey) doubts the Holocaust's existence, at least in some fashion, and the so-called Holocaust deniers are attaining unprecedented publicity on television talk shows such as "Donahue" as well as on news programs such as "Sixty Minutes."

With the universalization (or Americanization) of the Holocaust and the concomitant weakening of its singularization, Jews in a sense "risk" becoming like everyone else, which in essence means their assimilation. In this very process, however, the Jews will have lost some of the moral consensus that they shared with much of the American population precisely as a consequence of the singular nature of the tragedy informing their recent history.

Conclusion

As promised in the introduction, I would like to conclude by speculating on some commonalities that one can discern in all of the cases discussed in this chapter. It seems clear that the fundamental rearrangement of the global order will have an effect on the Jews, both as citizens of this world and as Jews. The Yalta world, both in its adequately functioning liberal democratic West and its miserably failing Leninist East, allowed a certain interbloc balance, which accounted for an uneasy—albeit existent—peace for over forty years, at least as far as the First World was concerned. Internally, both of these blocs pursued a certain measure of universalism, which held previously pernicious and undemocratic particularisms in check. Here, too, the West's record has proven to be superior to the East's. As discussed in this chapter, the West's universalism—strongly supported by its economic successes—has by and large transformed formerly explosive particularisms, which often led to wars, into cultural diversities for which wars have become basically unthinkable. Not so in the East. Old particularisms are alive and well there, in good part bespeaking the failure of the Leninist model. The tragedy of Bosnia is merely the most acute and heinous expression of a politics of identity that continues to be dangerously endemic in much of the post-Soviet world. The revival of these particularistic identities does not bode well for the Jews. Even in the West, certain "neoparticularisms" are in the process of being politically institutionalized in a politics of identity that perceives itself as a fundamental challenge to the universalist agenda that on the whole had proven to be the Jews' only friend in a history of many enemies. While certainly not endangering the Jews physically or existentially, the policies exacted by the adherents of identity politics and the advocates of the new particularisms may be at crosspurposes with the kind of policies and politics that served the Jews quite well in the Yalta world.

To be sure, nothing conveys the victimized nature of Jewish history better than a constant self-preoccupation of which the perennial question "will it be good for the Jews" is a telling marker. Clearly, the momentous changes currently engulfing all of Europe and transforming the Yalta world into an unknown future, has in and of itself *nothing* to do with the Jews. Yet, by living in this world as human beings and by participating in its political arrangements as citizens, Jews will inevitably be affected by the outcome of the changes that are presently redefining the European and global order. Behooving the uncertainty of the form and content of the post-Yalta era, the score card for the Jews, too, remains unclear at this juncture. Some things have improved for them while others have rapidly deteriorated. Given the vicissitudes of Jewish history, this uncertainty alone must enhance the negative tally of the ledger for the Jews.

Germany, the Jews, and Europe: History and Memory and the Recent Upheaval

Dan Diner

Now, at their political as much as their nominal end, the past hundred years manifest themselves as a German century. It is only now, with the reintegration of the political community of the Germans, with the end of the ideological antinomy between East and West, between liberalist freedom and the ideal of literal freedom, with the end of the worldwide civil war of values, which lasted from 1917 until 1989, that the contours of the century appear clearly. Beginning with the foundation of the German nation-state in 1871, which prompted the breakdown of the traditional balance of power in Europe, via the First World War— indeed, a German war—which took the United States from its oceanic isolation onto the old continent, and on to the Second World War, all crucial historical developments were to be occasioned by the behavior of the realm in the center of Europe. This is as true of the presence of the Soviet Union at the Elbe River as it is of the confrontation between East and West, which came about not least because of the presence of the Allies in Germany. So it is no accident that the end of the Cold War, with its polarized values, and the return of Germany are connected historically as well as logically.

To be sure, the return of Germany is no singular event in the context of the upheavals in Europe, but until now it is clearly the prominent feature of the end of the East-West conflict. When one looks at the return of Germany, it becomes apparent that, apart from the social upheavals that are tied in with the end of the ideological era, one can see also a distinctly national dimension. In fact, this seems to be its lasting result.

Translated by Harold Ohlendorf.

Throughout all of Europe, in fact, one can notice that the way people perceive themselves and others has increasingly national connotations. Such a return of national views and interpretations of political reality, something believed to have been left far behind, need not lead to an immediate revival of the roaring nationalism of the period between the wars. It appears rather that the use of national terms analogous to the past is merely an attempt to shed light on the new opacities. The debits and credits of the historic upheaval in Europe are weighed, as it were, with the conflicting scales of the nation-states that everyone believed had long since been buried and that are known to be outmoded. Not all in the West with its commonality of values ought to rejoice over the defeat of its eastern opponent in light of these background noises from the past. The United States and Germany—above all Germany— gained much more from the decades-long conflict between East and West than, say, England or France, for whom sharing the success has a certain bitter taste. The reasons for such despondency are very clear: the end of the Cold War meant for both England and France a considerable loss of political influence compared to that of Germany. The United States participated in the conflict solely on the basis of contrasting values—freedom versus uniformity—whereas Germany, split territorially and at risk of civil war, was engaged not only in a struggle over ideological values but also over national unity. This made the German question during the phase of the Cold War indeed into a singular problem. England and France had, of course, also a dual interest in the conflict, a national and an ideological one, but toward opposite ends. Both powers participated in the ideological Cold War but were also intent on countering any increase in power of a national Germany and its potential rapprochement with Russia as the main successor of the Soviet Union. The French in particular looked in the traditional manner—if such characterization be permitted—to square the circle of the classical European balance of power. If possible, Germany should be weaker than France but at the same time stronger than Russia. Viewed from the perspective of the nation-state, the return of a unified Germany—born out of the ideological struggle between East and' West—translates for England and France into some loss of power.

Whether such internal differentiation of the West will assume real political significance or whether it is only a matter of residual mentalities from a past long since laid to rest remains to be seen, even though cracks seemed to open up between Germany and France on the Yugoslav problem, albeit in attitude only. And yet such things appear as traces recalling the traditions of the interwar period. For the time being, however, looking to old European patterns of perception has meaning only as a tool for the interpretation of the new reality. The new phenomena are to be located somewhere between a new reality and a simulation of the past. For these purposes, the interwar period functions as a storehouse of historical memory that one is tempted to conjure up. This is true also of the European phenomenon of anti-Semitism, which returned to the stage like a symbolic core of identity of the old times. Its sudden rearing up throughout all of Western Europe following the vandalism of the graves in Carpentras triggered in France a wave of republican self-reassurance by the democratic forces. It was something like a political ritualistic act reminiscent of the mobilization of the Left, the centrist republicans, and the democrats on the occasion of the Dreyfus Affair. It was as if, now that the ideological conflict was over and Germany had returned, the French had to assure themselves of the values and certainties that in the past had shaped their identity. All protestations to the contrary notwithstanding, the changes in Europe had significantly unsettled the political class in France. As the birthplace of human rights the French republic was after all firmly on the side of the victors in the Cold War, but, as La Grande Nation, France will have to content herself with a subordinate role in Europe, a role that was assigned to her with the unification of Germany in 1870–71.

The real meaning of the anti-Semitism after the Carpentras incident and of the demonstrative anti-Semitism in France can hardly be determined conclusively at present. We shall not know whether the meaning of that ritualized appeal to the past is a return of the old or a mere simulation of collective consciousness. A plainer picture, albeit no less complex, presents itself in the formerly politically homogenous Eastern Europe with the reemergence of the old and only too familiar features of nationalism and anti-Semitism. They are the phenomena that inform culture and identity in a newly differentiated political, historical, and ethnographic relief. There the new is marked far more prominently by the stains of the past than in the West. The concepts of nation and religion had been the cornerstones of an interpretation of the world that Marxism-Leninism had forced the general consciousness to repudiate. Now they have reappeared almost as if there were no alternatives and are moving into the ruins of consciousness left behind by the system. They will fill almost as a matter of course the holes slashed into individual and collective lives.

The spheres of religion and nation overlapped in Eastern Europe during the interwar period and before. They were traditionally not disentangled. By and large only a relatively small number of the intelligentsia, as they were called, worked toward full secularization. They were joined in their efforts by the minorities, by Jews above all, that were excluded from those totalities. Similar configurations emerged in the wake of moves toward modernizations organized from above. The industrialization of the Russian empire, especially the more recent push around the turn of the century, exhibited a classic contrast: western modernism versus the largely Slavophile opposition. The Jews again were the primary symbol of modernization and secularization. It was not surprising, therefore, that some of them found themselves among the Bolsheviks, although enlightened Jews to the extent that they were Socialists felt far more attracted to the Mensheviks. And yet, reactionaries of all stripes then and now identify the Jews exclusively with the revolution and name them even as those responsible for the crimes of Stalinism.

The return of religion and nation, the rising tide of nationalism—it appears—might yet again spill onto the Jews as if nothing had changed. On the other hand, it may be wise to consider whether the anti-Semitic occurrences in Russia might not be expressions of simulations of the past at a time of disorientation—rather like the events in France in 1990 but with a greater probability for a new outbreak. At any rate, it should be noted with interest that, in France as well as in Russia—these classic countries of anti-Semitic convulsions at the end of the nineteenth century, France with its Dreyfus Affair and Russia with its pogroms and the Protocols of the Elders of Zion—hostility toward Jews is on the rise. And this is happening in a historically remarkable contrast to a Germany that is also once again facing itself in terms of being a nation. It was in Germany after all that practical as well as "scientific" anti-Semitism, after a temporary decline during the 1890s, was lashed onto the political culture, belatedly but all the more portentously, by the National Socialists. At the turn of the century, the differences among the anti-Semitic traditions were well understood. They were differences that distinguished Germany positively from the anti-Semitic culture in Eastern and Eastern Central Europe. Perhaps that explains the profound shock, the utter disbelief, among the Jews that it was Germany of all places where civilization was so rigorously cast aside.

Today, Germany has returned as a nation-state, has returned as a national community and as a place where the historical memory evokes multifaceted skepticism and fears. Whether they are in fact justified may indeed be doubtful. But since the Nazi regime had such a horrific impact the whole history of the German nation will remain tainted forever by these unending twelve years. There have also been revisionist consequences for public awareness: an example is the assessment of the First World War. The imperial prehistory of the war and the war itself may well weigh German guilt and responsibility quite differently than Hitler's unchecked drive toward world domination. And yet, for the universal memory the latter will affect the former. Looking back at the history of the German nation, it always will be interpreted—no matter how inappropriate this may be in individual instances—mindful of the fact that the National Socialist regime grew out of it. Germany as a nation-state, whether newly constituted or "reunified," will trigger concerns and doubts especially on the part of those whose fate was so negatively tied in with the culmination of the German power state.

Let me repeat, a repetition of the past, a new edition of the peculiarities of German national history, is hardly indicated. The prospect is rather for a future colored by paradox—something that will be particularly true for the Jewish memory. Thus, it is by all means thinkable, given the tendencies of present events and keeping in mind the cleansing effect of the Nazi past and the high standards of social development and culture, that Germany could once again be very attractive to Jews from Eastern Europe. If historical references and analogies should have any merit, Jews may look at Germany perhaps as they did during the last years of the Kaiser until the enumeration of Jews in 1916 or in the heyday of the Weimar Republic. Given the turmoil and upheavals that in all likelihood will characterize the changes in Eastern Europe for some time to come, there is reason to fear that especially a nonterritorial and therefore unprotected minority such as the Jews in the disintegrated Soviet Union will have their security and lives threatened. Protection and support, on the other hand, could be expected primarily from the stable and enlightened center of Europe with a strong Germany at its core.

Germany as protector of Jews in the East? Perhaps a rather macabre irony of history, yet it is still within the realm of the imagination in a world that just recently witnessed the nigh impossible. A closer look will reveal this scenario as not at all far-fetched. The return of Germany and the collapse of socialism in Eastern Europe, accompanied as they are by an increasing number of national and religious particularisms, suggest in fact the analogy to Europe at the turn of the century as a useful tool in understanding present-day events.

But what about the Jewish state of Israel as an alternative? What perspectives offer themselves in light of the dramatic changes in Europe? Paradoxical as it may sound, faced with the huge flood of immigrants from Russia it will be impossible for Israel to maintain in the long run its Zionist claim of being the refuge of suffering Jews. The lack of economic resources as much as the social fabric that has emerged pose quasi-natural barriers. In spite of its Zionist raison d'être, Israel has in the meantime lost its socio-ideological character as a land for immigrants. The ethos of social equality, which was a condition of the mass immigration and integration of the late forties and especially the fifties, has given way to a social reality that furthers egotistical self-realization. Here again is a tendency that strikes one as supremely paradoxical: whether the state of Israel will remain a state for the Jews of the world or whether the Israelization of Israel will do away with it appears to be more a function of the near impossibility of integrating the flood of immigrants than was the lack of immigration during past decades.

But it is not just the mass of immigrants, which Israeli society can scarcely accommodate, that points to a deep change. The end of the Cold War also has consequences for Israel. The Jewish state is losing the role it has held for the past forty years—even if it was only a small one—as a strategic partner of the West in the East-West conflict. This became evident during the Gulf War when the United States and its allies planned to prevent Israeli involvement at all cost and succeeded. Since then it has become clear that the United States wants to bring a peace settlement to the Near East as a region. With the end of the Cold War, Israel's privileged status has reached its structural boundaries.

This change, by the way, reveals an interesting context that leads us back to Europe. During those forty years of worldwide civil war, the incomplete state of the West German Federal Republic and Israel shared some significant features. To begin with, there is the symbolic proximity of the years of their foundation: 1948 and 1949, respectively. The historical time frame they share contains some rather evident elements but also some things that may be less obvious. Both political entities were the product of the profound upheavals that were the consequences of the Second World War. But, more importantly, both their existence and their stabilization are tied in with the beginning of the Cold War and not least with the first hot military confrontation between East and West—the war in Korea. Both states were connected with the United States in a triangle of interests. The young Federal Republic had included positive relations with the Jews, and that meant also with Israel, as part of its raison d'état in the hope that it would create good will for itself in American public opinion, which in turn would be useful for expanding and firming up what it had gained in sovereignty from the West. Israel made use of the needs and aspirations of the FRG to obtain financial help for the integration of the mass of immigrants. As for the United States, Israel played a much more important role in the internal politics of the country than in its global strategy. At the same time, Israel played the effective public role of the moral litmus test for the relationship between the United States and the western part of Germany. The recent changes in Europe will lead to a gradual retreat of the United States from the old continent. The return of Germany and the positive self-image of the Germans, which goes along with it, will entail the gradual demise of the constellation of values surrounding their foundation in the late forties. The future will yet reveal dubious consequences of these developments.

Whatever the effects of the return of Germany may be on the political reality of the Jews, this Germany—whose western portion underwent thorough Americanization and westernization during the last forty years and shed many a negative characteristic—is with its expansion now running the risk of becoming more national, more eastern, and more Protestant. Germany will shift from the institutional state of the Federal Republic toward a strengthened sense of a national self in spite of its integration into Europe or perhaps because of it. These shifts and Germany's location at the borders between East and West will have the effect that the memories of events that have given a bitter taste to the concept of nation will gradually fade. In this respect, the consequences of unification will indeed be those of reunification. As regards memories, history will continue to present Germans and Jews in conflict: the more the Germans move positively toward becoming a nation, the more today's community will fit into the continuities of the national history, and the more the memory of national socialism and its crimes will shrink.

There is hardly another case known in which nation and regime were so intensely intertwined as they were in National Socialist Germany. The regime represented and monopolized the nation in a quasi-negative apotheosis. It is no accident that the "twentieth of July," which commemorates the attempt of conservative officers, who wanted to preserve national values, to overthrow the National Socialists, can only be celebrated as a day of failure. The relationship between regime and population in the Soviet Union, to make the standard comparison, was quite different. There the population was victimized by the Stalinist regime. The line that separated those who belonged from those who were excluded and became victims ran through the Russian population just as it did through the people of the other Soviet republics. What is more, the Stalinist lust for power and its paranoia could almost randomly turn the perpetrators of today into the victims of tomorrow. Stalinism was blind rule in the literal meaning of the word. The terror could strike at anyone. In fact, it was fear that grew from the randomness that was designed to strengthen the system. By contrast, the National Socialist regime found its victims essentially outside of the community or excluded them by reason of their birth. Using pseudoscientific criteria the Nazis neatly split their world into biologically defined fellow countrymen and ethnic foreign enemies of the Reich.

All of this raises questions for each of the respective collective memories with regard to the present and the future. As for Stalinism, it is essentially a problem to be dealt with internally. National socialism, on the other hand, touches above all on the relationship of the Germans to others. That is the main reason why the history of the regime is also intertwined with the history of the nation. The return of the nation and the elevation of the concept into the sphere of raison d'état makes it rather difficult to maintain an active collective memory of the Nazi horrors notwithstanding all the ritualistic cultivation of that memory. Just as the National Socialist regime and the German nation became one during those eternal twelve years, it will be only possible to resurrect the idea of the nation at the price of the memory of the regime and its crimes.

The process of forgetting is accelerated by the oppressive evidence of past Stalinist crimes, which has only recently come to light in East Germany. There is increasing acceptance for the view that national socialism and Stalinism are the destructive dioscuri that characterize our era. This view has far-reaching consequences for the consciousness of our age. It seems as if East and West have come to an almost historic agreement on the nature of the two regimes. If so, it would give a fundamental importance to the theory of totalitarianism in interpreting the intellectual history of the century. Such a shift in the framework of values by the overreaching West was in fact brought about by the Communist party and its historical interpretation of National Socialism as fascism. Indeed, all other oppositional interpretive schemata can be traced back to it. The antifascist simplification has mutated to an historical lie. Communist antifascism monopolised the memory of the Nazi crimes and reduced them to their purported class character. Communism has collapsed and with it the ideological distortion of reality, which had been a part of the raison d'état especially in the GDR. Disappearing with it is the memory of those victims of National Socialism that truly characterised it, that is those who were victimised irrespective of their social status.

The return of the German nation affects the self perception of the Jews living in the western part of the state quite differently. Until now it was in tidy harmony with the self-perception of the FRG: both saw their status as provisional. The arrangement, in which and with which the Jews existed in the FRG, was relatively unproblematic in spite of the occasional coy protestations to the contrary. The reasons were that the FRG was tied into the Atlantic defense alliance and into the European institutions, and above all because of its proclaimed provisional nature—the national question was unanswered—which paradoxically kept the FRG at a distance from the nation. The FRG was a constitutional state, was a political entity whose self-perception was linked to the goal to establish an economic and a social order. It had also taken a clear position in the world wide civil conflagration of the Cold War. It may have been indeed any number of things, but one thing it was not: a nation state.

The Jews in the West were to a much greater extent citizens of the Federal Republic because of their self evident distance to the nation than were the ethnic Germans. The history of those Jews, however, who remigrated to the GDR and who in contrast to the majority of Jews in the West thus made an existential choice, is indeed tragic. They were the stereotypes of the ideal citizens of the GDR no matter how much they felt a distance to the communist regime because the state boasted about itself as "the other Germany." Now that there is an all German political entity again, the conflicting self-perceptions of the Jews in the former partial states are at issue once more. It is highly doubtful that the Jews can join in a new German sense of self that has a national foundation. After all, everything that relates to a national "Germany" is closely tied to National Socialism. Looking to the past the Jews do not make up some fictional trauma. They experienced it, it was their reality.

The interconnection of regime and nation in National Socialist Germany, exemplified for instance by the links between the SS and the military, continued as a deeply rooted notion in post-war consciousness. From this perspective, the partition of Germany was perceived psychologically as a just and justified punishment for the crimes of the Nazis. This does not reflect the reality, however. Only the presence of the allied troops on the territory of the former German empire was a direct consequence of the war the Nazis had started. The partition itself was the result of the disagreement among the allies over the fate of Germany, which in turn was already a sign of the impending Cold War. But these insights do not undo any causal linkages in peoples' minds.

These interconnections bore of course also some significance for the majority of ethnic Germans. They too saw the partition, the border, and above all the Wall as a contemporary reminder of the National Socialist past, indeed as punishment. The fall of the Wall and overcoming the partition must in a way appear as a kind of collective amnesty, as the release at long last of the National from the jaws of the Nazi-infected memory. Amnesia of the crimes may follow right behind.

The return of Germany as a reconstituted nation in the center of Europe entails a rather paradoxical feature: it is obvious already that Germany could again be of central importance for the fate of Europe's Jews. As the eastern power of the West, this country could have a similar allure to the Jews of the East as it did around the turn of the century. We will have to reconcile ourselves to the notion that Germany will be the leader in an increasingly integrated Europe. In that capacity it will be called upon, indeed may feel called upon, to be the protector of endangered Jewish minorities in Eastern Europe, especially in Russia where the political turmoil will not be settled for years, perhaps not even for decades to come. Thus, real history faces off against the history of the constitutive elements of collective memory. The price for the restitution of positive national continuities in Germany will at best come in the form of ritualized remembrances of those everlasting twelve years, forms of remembering that might better be called forms of forgetting.

A Comment: The End of the Postwar Era and the Reemergence of the Past

Moishe Postone

The opening of the Berlin Wall on November 9, 1989, dramatically marked the end of the postwar era; it also signaled the reemergence of the past, however refracted its form. That the symbolic unification of the two Germanys was enacted on the anniversary of the Nazi pogrom of 1938 (Kristallnacht) manifests the continuing, complex, partially sub-terranean workings of Germany's National Socialist past on its present. What had been the day the Federal Republic officially commemorated the Jewish victims of nazism now became the day Germany symboli-cally overcame its defeat in the Second World War and regained full sovereignty. This displacement raises the question of how a newly sover-eign Germany will negotiate its relation to its past. The character of such a process of negotiation will be crucial in determining Germany's political culture and, hence, the course of future German (and Euro-pean) development. It will also have very important consequences for Jews and Jewish self-understanding, for the reemergence of the past in Europe has been such that the trauma of the Holocaust has also begun to reemerge.

During the 1980s, Jews, Germans, and Austrians had already be-gun renegotiating the past in very different ways. The various shifts in sensibilities that occurred, and the concomitant changes in the relation of history and memory, were early indications that the postwar period was drawing to a close. These processes entailed the articulation of Jewish and German (and Austrian) identities that tended to develop in opposite directions. Martin Löw-Beer has indicated that, unlike their parents, many young Jews in Germany and Austria in this period no longer considered their situation provisional. They began to develop and express a new self-conception as Jews in Germany and Austria; they neither considered themselves German or Austrian Jews in the classical pre-Nazi sense nor Jews who ultimately belong elsewhere, for example, in Israel (as had been the general attitude in the postwar period). These younger Jews became more willing, consequently, to engage themselves in the social, cultural, and political problems of the countries in which they live; they did so, however, as members of a distinct cultural group. In particular, they became far more willing than members of the previous generation to take public stands on issues like anti-Semitism and the relation of postwar Germany and Austria to their National Socialist pasts.

This new self-understanding, first articulated by younger Jews and expressed by new journals such as *Babylon,* is becoming more general among Jews in Germany today and has important implications for the nature of German self-understanding as well. The notion that members of an ethnically culturally distinctive group are at home in Germany, are German citizens, but are not "Germans," necessarily points in the direction of a multicultural and multiethnic society. And, indeed, Ignaz Bubis, the head of the Central Council of Jews in Germany, has explicitly articulated the broader implications of this newer form of Jewish self-understanding and has emerged in the public sphere recently as one of the most outspoken voices against racism and for tolerance and multiculturalism in Germany today. In breaking with the traditional postwar self-understanding of Jewish leaders, Bubis has implicitly indicated that this new Jewish self-conception in Germany not only differs from that of the decades following 1945 but also requires public intervention in debates that will influence the character and development of German political culture.

Just as the implications of this new Jewish self-conception extend beyond the confines of Jewish communities, its viability depends on a number of more general social, cultural, and political conditions. For example, it depends on the extent to which Germans and Austrians are willing to openly deal with the Holocaust and other crimes against humanity in an ongoing and serious manner and to regard Nazism as a national shame. It also depends on the degree to which Germany and Austria will develop in the direction of multicultural and multiethnic societies in which the notion of "citizen" would become separated from that of membership in the German *ethnos.*

This latter issue has become central to German political and cultural life since 1989. It is far from certain, however, whether such a development toward multiculturalism is a real possibility, given the recent strong nationalist and racist responses to the structural problems of

German society. Relatedly, even the first condition has been called into question by this resurgence of German national sentiment, a resurgence that has been fed by attempts to reformulate the relation of the present to the Nazi past in a way that more positively incorporates that past. Such attempts to establish a greater degree of continuity with elements of the German past that had since been discredited have been at the heart of a concerted campaign by the conservative government and by conservative intellectuals since 1983 to reverse many political-cultural developments that had occurred in the Federal Republic since the mid-1960s. This campaign included such well-known events as the Kohl-Reagan visit to Bitburg in 1985 and the Historikerstreit in 1986. This right-wing nationalist campaign gained momentum after 1989, when wide-spread feelings of national vindication were accompanied by a government campaign against asylum seekers and by attempts on the part of conservative cultural critics to disqualify much postwar German thought and literature as expressions of the "colonization" of Germany by the victorious Allies.

These public campaigns have not only found their echo in the growth of neo-Nazi violence; they have also been paralleled by a more general turn to nationalism on the part of many intellectuals. In this situation, the political groupings one might have expected to constitute an oppositional force to the resurgence of German nationalism—such as the SPD or the Greens—seem to have become, at best, very ineffectual in this regard.

The grounds for these troubling developments are very complex. Whatever their causes, they can, on one level, be understood in terms of a strong desire on the part of Germans to "normalize" their relation to the past. The nature of that normalization is diametrically opposed to the sort of normalization attempted by the new generation of Jews in Germany and Austria; it is predicated upon a fundamentally different attitude toward the past. The sort of recovery of the past that is related to the recent growth of national feelings in Germany, negates, or at least marginalizes, Jewish collective memory and is at odds with the newer self-conception recently articulated by younger Jews in Germany and Austria.

The difficulties in bringing together the collective memories articulated by Germans and by Jews are not only the obvious ones made evident by the polarization between newer forms of Jewish self-understanding and resurgent German nationalism. More subtle difficulties can also be seen in recent attempts by German scholars and artists to appropriate their past in new ways by means of local history and the history of everyday life (Alltagsgeschichte). These local histories have included a new wave of local histories of Jews in Germany; the character of these histories, however, is frequently quite ambivalent. On the one hand, they express a greater awareness of the degree to which many Germans were implicated in the crimes of national socialism. They also can be interpreted as indicating the beginnings of a pluralistic redefinition of Germany. Nevertheless, such works can and have also served to shift attention from the perpetrators to the victims. They thereby deflect attention away from further investigation of everyday national socialism and contribute to the continued exoticization of the Jews. Indeed, as Monika Richarz, among others, has pointed out, some recent local histories of the Jews have even adopted—if not consciously—anti-Semitic clichés.

The recent turn to local history and the history of everyday life in Germany is also problematic on a more general level. In attempting to get at the micrological aspects of social life, such approaches frequently dissolve the terrible specificity of national socialism and of the Holocaust. They are reminiscent of Michelangelo Antonioni's film, *Blow-Up,* in which a photographer attempts to reconstruct a crime by successively enlarging a photograph. His efforts end up dissolving the object they were intended to elucidate: they result in a huge screen full of dots that lack any meaningful pattern. Similarly, micrological approaches to social life, regardless of their content, can, through their very form, contribute to the dissolution of nazism and exterminatory anti-Semitism as historical objects. In this way they can contribute to the process of "normalization" discussed above.

These problems raise the question of whether it is at all possible to develop a conceptual framework that could encompass the strongly diverging and opposed experiences and memories of Jews and Germans. Such a framework would have to allow both Jews and Germans to consider that past in a manner that might enable them to move into the future, rather than remaining fixated on the past, or attempting to move into the future by repressing the past (which, of course, does not allow for a qualitatively different future). An additional problem for any contemporary critical theory attempting to construct such a framework is that it must necessarily consider whether it is possible to do justice to Auschwitz and still formulate a theory of the historical possibilities of human emancipation. Such an approach would have to break radically with any notion of historical development as linear historical progress, while retaining a conception of possible emancipatory historical transformations.

The difficulties of constructing a historical framework that could encompass both perpetrators and victims would have been great under any circumstances. This task has been rendered even more difficult by the revolutionary political changes taking place in Europe today. These changes are the culmination of subterranean historical processes which have led to global shifts in economic and political power. Those shifts began to be perceptible around 1973, after the collapse of Bretton-Woods, when the United States began to lose its clearly hegemonic role in the world market system and the Soviet Union entered a long period of economic decline. What has now emerged out of the relative decline of the two superpowers can, on one level, be seen as a partial reversal of the outcome of the Second World War. Germany and Japan have re-emerged as the primary capitalist competitors of American world power and Germany has once again become the dominant power in Central and Eastern Europe, where the dissolution of Communist hegemony has been accompanied by the reemergence of structures and movements apparently similar to those that characterized those areas between the wars.

There is, however, one major exception to this "return" of the past in Central and Eastern Europe: there no longer are Jews there (with the partial exception of Budapest and parts of the former Soviet Union). This aspect of the Second World War is irreversible. The Jews and Jewish life have been eradicated.

This aspect of the current "re-Europeanization" of Europe will have a great effect on the few Jews left in Central Europe and, perhaps more generally, on Jews everywhere. What is crucially important in this regard is not so much the reemergence of overt anti-Semitism (although that has been the case in much of Eastern Europe and the former Soviet Union). Rather, it is a potentially more traumatic reemergence: the character of the postwar period cushioned many Jews from the full effects of the Holocaust. Nazi Germany had been defeated by powers that strongly rejected its racist and anti-Semitic ideology. (The different ideological effects of the struggle against nazism on the United States and the Soviet Union is an important problem that can only be alluded to here.) Both emerging superpowers, moreover, supported the establishment of the state of Israel in 1947–48, which, for many Jews, signified a sort of redemption, a vindication of life in the face of the death and immense suffering that had preceded it. As traumatic and terrible as the Holocaust was, it seemed to be an event of the past.

Today, that period with its protective character has ended. The victorious powers of the Second World War are in relative decline, Germany has reemerged as a great power, and there is growing uncertainty among many Jews whether Zionism successfully addresses the question of how Jewish life can be viable in the modern world. As the tide of the postwar period has ebbed, the Holocaust has also reemerged from beneath the surface of history. Suddenly it seems that the trauma of being history's victims may not have been resolved historically. This can give rise to a very strong sense of isolation, helplessness, and vulnerability among Jews.

Whether this will be the case will depend to a large extent on the character of the newly sovereign Germany and its attitude toward its Nazi past. At issue is not whether Germany's reemergence as a great power means that some form of national socialism and exterminatory anti-Semitism will necessarily reemerge as hegemonic. Clearly, very important positive political and cultural changes have occurred in the Federal Republic of Germany since 1945, especially in the late 1960s. Nevertheless, there is no reason to assume that the more democratic, tolerant, and socially progressive forms that were developed in the Federal Republic will simply continue to develop linearly. Indeed, events of the last decade have shown that the rise of German power has been tied to a very perceptible rise in German national consciousness. The real question, then, is what the effects of increased German power will be on the nature of German political culture. The extent to which the trauma of the Holocaust will, once again, become actual will also depend on how that political culture will develop.

The practical issue for Jews in Germany today is whether they can actively contribute to the development of that political culture. Some sort of active Jewish response to the new situation is necessary, one that would try to help maintain democratic consciousness in Germany and help modify German political self-understanding. It thereby would indirectly also induce citizens of other Central and Eastern European countries to begin dealing with the Holocaust.

Such a task is very difficult. Apart from the many objective difficulties involved, such a response would require, subjectively, the further spread and development of the new form of Jewish self-identification in Germany outlined above. This identity would not be religious in any traditional sense. Although there is a resurgence of synagogue life and of Jewish schools in Germany today, Jewish religious identity is not very strong. Traditional Jewish religious forms there are less a possible vital source of identity than expressions of a tension between the destroyed character of Jewish life and a desire to hold onto some form of Jewish identity. The new form of identity that has begun to develop in Germany is that of an ethnic group with distinctive, historically rooted, religious-culture traditions.

Such an identity could serve as the basis for an active Jewish response to the new situation. Recent developments have indicated that some such response has become necessary; they have dramatically shown that, now more than ever, normalization for Jews in Germany is not possible in the absence of fundamental changes in German consciousness of the past and in the nature of German identity. The question is whether Jews can contribute at all to such a process of transformation or whether they will be steamrollered by the resurgence of German history.

One thing seems clear. The reemergence of Germany as a power means the end of the postwar form of Jewish existence in Germany. That existence, with all its distortions and problems, was rendered possible by the fact that each of the Germanys officially adopted the values of its patron superpower and neither was very powerful; in a sense, neither was fully German. This period has ended.

Jews must now find a voice that is tied to a new form of life in Germany. If German self-consciousness and awareness continue to become increasingly nationalist, however, present historical developments will acquire the following, very unsettling significance for many Jews: not only had Jews been radically victimized, their murderers gone largely unpunished, and most Germans' reckoning with the past been utterly inadequate—but Germany ultimately did not lose the war. The situation is at a critical juncture. If, as a consequence of its resurgent power, Germany continues to become more emphatically German-nationalist, a very basic self-understanding developed by Jews since 1945 will be shaken, and the prospects of Jewish life in Germany will become very bleak.

Contributors

Y. Michal Bodemann is Professor of Sociology at the University of Toronto and a past visiting professor at Humboldt University in Berlin. He has published widely on issues concerning postwar German Jewry and is currently conducting research on the East German nomenklatura after 1989. His book, *Gedächtristheater. Die Jüdische Gemeinschaft und ihre deutsche Erfindung* (Theater of Memory: The Jewish Community and its German Invention) will appear later this year with Rotbuch Verlag, Hamburg.

John Borneman, Assistant Professor of Anthropology at Cornell University, has also taught at Harvard, the University of California, San Diego, and as visiting professor at Humboldt University in Berlin, Stockholm University in Sweden, and Bergen University in Norway. His previous work has focused on German nation-building processes. He is currently completing a project on criminalization and the position of victims in the united Germany.

Michael Brenner is Assistant Professor of Modern Jewish History at Brandeis University. His books include *Nach dem Holocaust: Jüdisches Leben in Deutschland, 1945–1950* (Munich: C. H. Beck, 1995) and *The Renaissance of Jewish Culture in Weimar Germany,* to be published later this year by Yale University Press. His contribution to the four-volume *German-Jewish History in Modern Times* (Columbia University Press, 1996) covers the nineteenth century.

Micha Brumlik is Professor of Education at the University of Heidelberg and has published widely on issues related to Jewish Theology and Contemporary German Jewry. He has conducted research on theories of deviant behavior, theories of social works, and on the philosophy of education, especially related to questions of ethics. He is coeditor of *Babylon,* a Jewish periodical published in Frankfurt, and of *Jüdisches Leben in Deutschland seit 1945,* a collection of essays on postwar German Jewry, published in 1986.

Dan Diner is Professor of Modern History at the University of Essen and is the Director of the Institute of German History at the University of

Tel Aviv. He recently published *Kreisläufe: Nationalsozialismus und Gedächtnis,* a collection of essays.

Cilly Kugelmann is curator at the Jewish Museum in Frankfurt. She has written extensively about postwar German Jewry and is an editor of *Babylon.*

Martin Löw-Beer teaches Philosophy at the Free University, Berlin, and is a coeditor of *Babylon,* a Jewish journal published in Frankfurt. His book, *Selbsttäuschung* (self-deception) was published in 1990.

Andrei S. Markovits is professor in and chair of the Board of Studies in Politics at the University of California, Santa Cruz. He continues his affiliation and active involvement with the Center for European Studies at Harvard University. Markovits has published widely on many aspects of German and European politics, including German-Jewish relations.

Robin Ostow is a Resident Fellow at the Centre for Russian and East European Studies at the University of Toronto. She has written extensively on East and West German Jewry. Her book, *Jews in Contemporary East Germany: The Children of Moses in the Land of Marx,* appeared in 1989.

Moishe Postone is Associate Professor of Sociology and in the College at The University of Chicago. He has written extensively on National Socialism and antisemitism and the relations of Germans and Jews in the postwar period, as well as on critical social theory. His recent books include *Time, Labor and Social Domination: A Reinterpretation of Marx's Critical Theory,* (New York and Cambridge: Cambridge University Press, 1993), and *Bourdieu: Critical Perspectives,* coedited with C. Calhoun and E. LiPuma (Chicago and Cambridge: University of Chicago Press and Polity Press, 1993).

Frank Stern teaches Modern European and German History at Tel Aviv University with focus on German culture and film, and problems of German-Jewish relations. In 1995 he was visiting professor at Columbia University in New York. He has published widely on related issues and is currently working on images of Jews in German film and literature from 1945 to 1995. Among his recent publications are *The Whitewashing of the Yellow Badge: Antisemitism and Philosemitism in Postwar Germany* (Oxford: Pergamon Press, 1992); *Jews in the Mind of Germans* (Bloomington: Jewish Studies Program, 1993); coauthor of *Sprachen der Vergangenheiten: Öffentliches Erinnern in Österreich und Deutschland* (Frankfurt am Main: Suhrkamp Verlag, 1994).

Jack Zipes is Professor of German at the University of Minnesota and has previously held professorships at New York University, the University of Munich, the University of Wisconsin-Milwaukee, and the University of Florida. He has published numerous articles on twentieth-century German literature and has focused specifically on the relations between Germans and Jews in *Germans and Jews since the Holocaust* (1986), edited with Anson Rabinbach, and in *The Operated Jew: Two Tales of Anti-Semitism* (1991). One of the editors of *New German Critique,* Zipes is currently writing a book on German-Jewish cultural relations since 1945.

Index

DATE DUE

DEC 2 0 1996		
INTERLIBRARY LOAN NOV 1 2004		
JUN 0 1 1997		
DEC 01 1997		
		DEC 1 5 2008
DEC 1999		
DEC 2000		
MAY 0 5 2001		
		Printed in USA

HIGHSMITH #45230